Punks in Peoria

MUSIC IN AMERICAN LIFE

A list of books in the series appears at the end of this book.

Punks in Peoria

Making a Scene in the American Heartland

JONATHAN WRIGHT

AND

DAWSON BARRETT

UNIVERSITY OF ILLINOIS PRESS
Urbana, Chicago, and Springfield

Library of Congress Cataloging-in-Publication Data
Names: Wright, Jon (Jonathan David) author. | Barrett, Dawson,
    author.
Title: Punks in Peoria: making a scene in the American heartland
    / Jonathan Wright and Dawson Barrett.
Description: Urbana: University of Illinois Press, 2021. | Series:
    Music in American life | Includes bibliographical references
    and index.
Identifiers: LCCN 2020053056 (print) | LCCN 2020053057 (ebook)
    | ISBN 9780252043802 (cloth) | ISBN 9780252085796
    (paperback) | ISBN 9780252052705 (ebook)
Subjects: LCSH: Punk rock music—Illinois—Peoria—History and
    criticism.
Classification: LCC ML3534.3 .W75 2021 (print) | LCC ML3534.3
    (ebook) | DDC 781.6609773/52—dc23
LC record available at https://lccn.loc.gov/2020053056
LC ebook record available at https://lccn.loc.gov/2020053057

It was about dreams of flying to spite a falling sky . . .

Contents

Acknowledgments

DIY punk is a subject near and dear to our hearts. As young people, our involvement in the Peoria scene pushed us to be just a little more daring than we might have been otherwise. Both of us have played in bands, released our own records, and booked and promoted shows. Each of us also left central Illinois as young adults—Jon for Denver, Dawson for Portland—seeking to blaze our own trails, right alongside our Peoria friends.

While this book engages a history far beyond our own experiences, our proximity to it was an invaluable advantage—but a hazard, as well. Much like the story it tells, this project has been both heartwarming and heartbreaking. At times, it offered us the joy of learning new things about our hometown, revisiting fond memories, and interacting with friends old and new. But it also haunted us with the occasional nostalgia for youth and longing for those we have lost.

Examining these stories with decades of hindsight has been illuminating—a reflection on the limitations of youth countercultures but also an important reminder about why we found punk rock so exciting and necessary at the time. In short, this book has given us an opportunity to visit the past, but we are glad not to be living in it.

These pages reflect countless hours of interviewing, writing, reading, editing, and e-mailing. Any errors are our own, but like the community it documents, this book reflects the contributions of a vast range of people. To that end, we would like to express our deep gratitude to those who shared their photographs, flyer collections, music, and memories with us, including Dustin Addis, Amber, Jeremy Ross Armstrong, Todd Arnold, Jon Beattie, Tim Beck, Tim Beeney, Chris Bennett, Sharon Berardino, Tim Boniger, Joe Borsberry, Julie Bozman, Jeanette Brickner, Jarrod Briggs, Steve Byrne, Ed Carper, Kyle Christians, Bart Todd Clifton, Mark Coats, Chuck Coffey, Chris Cowgill, Colin Coyle, Sam Dantone, Dan Dirst, Jen Boniger Dixon, Kevin Dixon, Stacey Donovan, Kate Dusenbery, Patrick Dwyer, Jeff Eagan, Charlie Eberle, Erica, Josh Finnell, Charles French, Geoff Frost, Brett Fugate, Paul Gentile, Brian Geurin, Jon Ginoli, Jay Goldberg, Chris Golwitzer, Bob Gordon, Brian Gould, Jared Grabb, Jeff Gregory, Jered Gummere, Josh Haller, Justin Hartman, Chris Hauk, Jason Heller, Bob Herington, Joel Hess, Stephen Howeler, Bill Hudnall, Todd Hueser, Jeff Hyde, Mike Isenberg, Greg Jaeger, James, Dave Johnson, Lawrence Keach, Jeremy Kerner, Kelly Kilpatrick, Eric Kingsbury, Bill Knight, John Koch-Northrup, Brad Krohn, Jeremiah Lambert, Blair Landon, Tom Lane, Kami Tripp LaVallier, Rob Lawrence, Ben Leitch, Sean Lervaag, Samantha Lester, Nick Lippert, Doug Love, Kimberly "Sparky" Luft, Brody Maag, Julie Maag, Jared Madigan, Joel Madigan, Mike Malin, Rocky Maple, Chasity Marini, Tyson Markley, Beth Martin, Ryan Martin, Douglas McCombs, Drew McDowell, Sam McIntyre, Tim Mead, Melissa, Bloody Mess, Dave Moe, Craig Moore, Guthrie Moore, Jim Moran, Briggs Mushrush, Matt Nieukirk, Tom Nieukirk, Gared O'Donnell, Mike "C. P." O'Russa, Brandon Ousley, Teresa Ozuna, Erin Page, Judy Page, Jason Pellegrino, Mike "Rugg" Perveiler, Greg Peters, Eric Peterson, Bryan Polk, Sean Pope, Chris Rice, Molly Miller Rice, Mike Ricketts, Chris Riley, Nick Roseman, Ben Ruddell, Sandy, John San Juan, Marsha Satterfield, Tom Satterfield, Mac Scarle, Brent Schlosser, Josh Shane, Matt Shane, Jimmy Singleton, Becky Slane, Cliff Stanton, Barry Stepe, Chopper Stepe, Jon Sterling, Joshua Stonewall, Rob Streibich, James Strevels, Frankie Sturm, Amee Snyder Suydam, Leanna Sweetland, Bruce Swigart, Jason Teegarden-Downs, Mike Theobald, Gary Thomas, Melissa Uselton, David Harshada Wagner, Graham Walker, Jeff Warren, Kyle Waters, Tracey Bettermann Wetzstein, Brian White, Adam Widener, John Williams, Eric "Suit and Tie Guy" Williamson, Jeff Wilson, Andrew Wisecarver, Marty Wombacher, Stan Wood, and Ed Young. Given this project's duration, it is inevitable that we forgot to thank someone—we apologize and thank you now.

Doug Hoepker, Mae Gilliland Wright, and Zack Furness were among those who read and critiqued early drafts of this project. The book changed radically in its scope and content over the last five years and benefited greatly from their thoughtful comments.

We also want to express our appreciation to Laurie Matheson, Ellie Hinton, Julie Bush, and everyone at the University of Illinois Press for sharing our vision and preparing our words for print. Special thanks to Chris Farris at Peoria Public Library for research assistance, to Chris Gilbert at Alona's Dream Records for expanding the scope of possibilities, to the Cretin for permission to use his lyrics, and to Joe Biel at Microcosm Publishing for being an early believer in this book's potential.

* * *

Dawson: I do not have the words to adequately express my appreciation for Jon's willingness to embark on this adventure with me. Working on this project with him has been an absolute pleasure. In addition to my deep gratitude to Beth, Genora, and Henry for keeping me happily grounded in the present, I would also like to thank my mom and dad for letting me, at age thirteen, go see the Jesus Lizard show that Jon put on. It changed my life—and led me to some of my oldest friends, favorite bands, and most cherished memories.

* * *

Jonathan: When I agreed to coauthor this book, I had no concept of the time and energy it would entail. To that end, I owe an eternal debt of gratitude to my love and life partner, Mae, for her patience and understanding as I spent many evenings and weekends alone at the keyboard. I could not have asked for a better collaborator than Dawson, who talked me off the ledge more than once and kindly extended free rein to my editorial micromanaging. Finally, I'm forever grateful for the lifelong friends I've made through music. This project has been significant in ways I cannot quite define, and I hope others find meaning in it as well. Onward!

Punks in Peoria

Introduction

Since its founding in postwar Peoria, Illinois, Exposition Gardens has been a trailing indicator of conventional popular culture. With its outdoor arena and pavilion, a 14,000-square-foot exhibit hall and quaintly charming "Opera House," half a dozen livestock barns and parking for miles, the complex sprawls across eighty acres and hosts a wide range of community events: gun shows, flea markets, concerts, fundraisers, cat competitions, beer festivals . . . and the list goes on.

Built to house the Heart of Illinois Fair, it opened in 1950—a proud, nine-county agricultural showcase of the fruits of Illinois's rich black soil. Back then, before urban sprawl pushed Peoria's boundaries northward, Expo Gardens was in a rural part of town. The fair was timed to coincide with the Caterpillar Tractor Company's two-week summer shutdown, and hundreds of thousands of Illinoisans flooded its gates every July for a nine-day extravaganza of carnival rides, fried foods, tractor pulls, demolition derbies, and live music. During the off-season, the facility's various buildings were available for the public to rent. With its traditional and innocuous fare, Expo Gardens encapsulates Peoria's midwestern identity in aggregate—a microcosm within a microcosm.

As much as any other city, Peoria can credibly claim the title of "Anywhere, USA," the prototypical midsized industrial town, nestled in the heart of the nation's breadbasket. With a population of 115,000 (as of the 2010 census) and more than triple that number in the larger metro area, it is the largest city on the Illinois River, centrally located within a day's drive of half the country. To quote one former resident, Peoria is "three hours from everywhere"—or about that far from Chicago, St. Louis, and Indianapolis, anyway.[1]

In the early twentieth century, Peoria was a prominent stop on the vaudeville circuit, a proving ground for national performing acts. It was commonly believed that if a show "played in Peoria," it could play anywhere. Whether intended as praise or disparagement, the phrase has endured. Popularized by Groucho Marx and adopted by politicians and pollsters, it remains perhaps the best evidence for Peoria's quintessentially mainstream nature. For similar reasons, the city was frequently used as a consumer test market, measuring public sentiment on products ranging from Kleenex to Pampers to the McRib. Even in recent years, Peoria has been described in the national media as "ground zero for old-fashioned American values."[2]

If the various activities at Expo Gardens exemplify an atmosphere of normalcy, they may also reflect an underlying conservatism—a worldview rooted in midwestern pragmatism, a blue-collar work ethic, evangelical Christianity, and various combinations thereof. Even the outlier events at Expo seem to bear this out.

In 1973, Christ Is the Answer—a group of ragtag evangelicals born of the post-hippie "Jesus People" movement—held a nearly monthlong big-tent revival at the fairgrounds. During the group's residency, twenty-five members were arrested for trespassing while preaching the gospel at multiple Peoria shopping centers. Three years later, Alabama governor George Wallace, among the most notorious segregationists in US history, addressed an Expo Gardens audience of 1,500. According to newspaper accounts, he received a four-minute standing ovation, and his speech was "interrupted numerous times by the jubilant crowd."[3]

And one night in 1995, Expo Gardens hosted a legendary post-punk band from the opposite end of the country—and the political spectrum. With its high-energy live act and thoughtful stances against consumerism, racism, violence, and misogyny, Washington, DC's Fugazi offered a temporary antidote to Peoria's doldrums, at least for the 900 mostly young people who paid five dollars apiece for the experience. From an outsider's perspective, the juxtaposition of band and venue might seem odd, but such contradictions were the norm for Peoria punk rock.

Several months earlier, the Jesus Lizard—loud, sweaty, playful, and occasionally overexposed—came down from Chicago to play another unconventional venue: downtown Peoria's American Legion Post 2. In the years to come, Nebraska band Cursive would perform on the concrete floor of a tiny clubhouse across the river, while Against Me!, from Florida, would headline a church basement in Peoria. These long-running indie/punk bands—well-loved and critically acclaimed, if not commercial hitmakers—arrived in Peoria under the radar, their presence unappreciated by most of the townsfolk.

Among the young people who attended these shows, there was little knowledge about the local punk scene of several years earlier. Few knew that hardcore legends 7 Seconds (from Reno, Nevada) once played a Peoria ice rink, or that scum-punk provocateur GG Allin once . . . performed, so to speak . . . at a VFW hall in the nearby village of Creve Coeur.

In the pre-iPhone era, documentation of the local music scene was sparse by nature. As one "generation" of youth replaced another, each left behind only thin threads of continuity—slightly older punks whose oral recollections and stash of flyers sufficed for institutional memory. But they held something else in common: they all made meaningful attempts to rip away the fabric of test-market normalcy to discover something new, different, and exciting inside of "Anywhere, USA."[4]

*   *   *

Peoria has long embraced its reputation as a national measuring stick for the cautious and conservative. For nearly a century, Illinois's Eighteenth Congressional District has exclusively sent Republicans to Washington; in recent presidential elections, area voters have habitually supported conservative candidates. While Peoria County went for Democrats in 2016 and 2020, the surrounding counties voted overwhelmingly for their opponent, some by two-to-one margins.[5]

And yet: a 2017 Fourth of July parade in West Peoria found space for a float featuring a naked President Donald Trump seated upon a golden toilet, tweeting from his cell phone. Though a public outcry forced an apology from city leaders, its presence afforded a glimpse at the subtle political dualities that have long existed in central Illinois.[6]

Three years earlier, a parody Twitter account mocking Peoria's Republican mayor prompted law enforcement to raid the home of its creator, leading to a lawsuit from the ACLU and national ridicule on *The Daily Show*. Yet the same mayor who directed this ill-advised police raid could also be seen at a 2016 rally in support of the Black Lives Matter movement. If this dichotomy raised eyebrows in Peoria, the reaction went relatively undocumented.[7]

For several decades, punk rock provided young people a vehicle for rebelling against what they perceived as their city's quaint, Rockwellian image. But Peoria's boosters and its critics alike tended to present oversimplified takes on their city and its past. The modern facade of conservatism masks a much more complicated history of rebellion, vice, and turmoil—a Peoria that was a bit more sinister (a one-time stomping ground for Charles Manson) and occasionally a little radical (the hometown of feminist Betty Friedan and Black Panther Mark Clark).[8]

In 1885, the newspaper of a neighboring town reported that "Ungodly Peoria" was "reeking with immorality and brazen-faced criminals," noting that 612 young men were seen entering saloons (in one hour) on a Saturday night, while just 302 were counted at church the next morning. To be sure, Peoria's many breweries and distilleries were producing ungodly amounts of beer, bourbon, and rye whiskey at the time—quite literally more than anywhere else on earth. Peoria was widely known as the "Whiskey Capital of the World," and its Great Western Distillery, built in 1881, was the world's largest distillery.[9]

Nearly seventy-five whiskey distilleries existed in some form or another across central Illinois between 1837 and 1919. Sixteen of them, including the Great Western, stood along a mile-long stretch of Peoria's riverfront dubbed "Whiskey Row." More than one million gallons of spirits flowed from this property daily, producing vast wealth for the city's so-called whiskey barons, who in turn funded the creation of Peoria's grandest homes, parks, theaters, colleges, hospitals, hotels, and other civic structures.

At its peak, Peoria's whiskey industry was an indispensable resource for the US government; before the income tax was established in 1913, revenue from Peoria-made whiskey accounted for an outsized portion of the overall federal budget. When Prohibition went into effect seven years later, most of Peoria's bars and saloons became "soft drink parlors" overnight. Under the watchful eye of Mayor Edward Nelson Woodruff, Peoria remained a "wide open town"—a hub for drinking, gambling, prostitution, and other unseemly behaviors. When Prohibition ended in 1933, those soft drink parlors quickly became bars and saloons again, while Hiram Walker wasted no time bringing the world's largest distillery back online.[10]

During the same broad time period, the Peoria area experienced labor strikes by the likes of coal miners, coopers, corn product workers, streetcar operators, railroad switchmen, constables, and newspaper workers—protests that were often met with violence and force. Despite labor's deep roots in central Illinois, its strength was consistently put to the test.[11]

Only in the wake of World War II—after a reform movement scrubbed the city clean—did Peoria firmly establish the Cold War–era conservative bona fides that would lead Richard Nixon aide John Ehrlichman to assure the president he could ignore his liberal critics because his policies would "play in Peoria."[12] The construction of Expo Gardens—that modern beacon of heartland normalcy—coincided with this movement.

As heavy industry overtook distilleries as the city's chief economic driver, Caterpillar hit the jackpot with government contracts for World War II and the postwar Marshall Plan. Periodic strikes by the United Auto Workers compelled the company to share some of those gains, effectively establishing the city's middle class, if only for a generation. But even this labor unrest was steeped in conservative politics. Caterpillar's workforce did not reflect the city's racial demographics, while union contracts almost exclusively benefited white residents. At times, both management and the UAW resorted to red-baiting and race-baiting in attempts to increase their bargaining power.[13]

In 1940 the pioneering comedian and social critic Richard Pryor was born in segregated Peoria; he later quipped in his memoir that his hometown was considered a "model city" because it so perfectly modeled white supremacy, keeping its Black population "under control." The city had snubbed him for decades, skirting around his contentious legacy even as he rose to the top of his field. It was only in 2015—a full decade after his death—that Peoria finally acquiesced to Pryor's formidable worldwide impact, erecting a bronze statue of the legendary entertainer in the city's Warehouse District.[14]

In 1947, following the "Red Scare" lead of the House Un-American Activities Committee, the Peoria City Council banned African American singer Paul Robeson from performing in the city, even sending police to intercept him at the train station. A nationally known civil rights activist, Robeson accused the local government of fascist behavior and performed there anyway—at the home of a supporter. This may have been Peoria's first house show.[15]

In 1950, American Legion Post 2 pressured the Peoria Public Library to censor its film collection, objecting to cinematic portrayals of racial equality and the United Nations as insufficiently "American." One can only imagine what those Legionnaires would have thought of hosting the Jesus Lizard on their stage nearly half a century later.[16]

During the tumultuous sixties, Peoria, like many US cities, was rocked by civil rights protests targeting employment discrimination, housing practices, and inequality in its public schools. These issues, left inadequately addressed, ensured the continuation of strikes, sit-ins, and marches into the next decade as well. Peoria was a majority-white city, and its politics, industries, and cultural institutions reflected as much. That Alabama governor George Wallace played in Peoria in 1976 was not a political aberration.

Within this context, and with this baggage, the city's economic bottom fell out. Amid recession and companies relocating their factories in search of ever-cheaper labor, manufacturing employment in Illinois, Indiana, and Michigan declined 23 percent between 1978 and 1983. The United States as a whole lost 2.1 million industrial jobs between 1979 and 1982. It was the beginning of the end for the industrial middle class, leaving many to grasp at straws—including a presidential candidate whose 1980 campaign slogan was "Let's Make America Great Again."[17]

In Peoria in 1982 and 1983, deindustrialization meant tens of thousands of layoffs and a contentious 205-day strike at Caterpillar, while the Pabst brewery closed altogether. Soon retirement pensions, bargaining rights, and even job security itself—middle-class norms for decades—would seem radical and utopian.

As it happens, this was also the moment when hardcore punk was spreading across the United States, city by unsuspecting city. And like so many other trends, it arrived in Peoria a few years behind the curve.

* * *

The same factors that made Peoria a four-time "All-America City" and a useful test market also facilitated a stifling environment for freethinking misfits of all kinds. The thousands of acres of surrounding cornfields were akin to "cornstalk prison bars," to quote one local punk band, ensuring some degree of cultural isolation, especially in the pre-internet era. But if boredom foments creativity as well as despair, Peoria was an ideal place for punk rock, in its broadest sense, to develop among outcast youth. In the words of numerous Peoria punks: "We had to entertain ourselves."

As the "do it yourself" punk movement grew in the 1980s and flourished in the post-Nirvana '90s, Peoria was ripe for something different. Like earlier incarnations of youthful rebellion—the greasers, hippies, and garage rockers— punk rock offered a sense of belonging, a community in opposition to "the system." To do it yourself was to seize control of your own destiny, if only for a fleeting moment.

Unlike New York, San Francisco, or Chicago, however, Peoria was never able to sustain a proper punk venue. As a result, its underground music scene learned to be DIY in a very active and unorthodox way. Promoters, bands, and their friends were constantly hunting for venues they could repurpose for an evening—a revolving hodgepodge of banquet halls, houses, church basements, and after-hours businesses, both in Peoria proper and within a dozen or more surrounding towns.[18]

When various complaints drove these provisional venues to close their doors to the punk scene, new and increasingly unconventional spaces had to be found. Peoria's music underground relied on word of mouth, flyers at local record stores, and later the "Peoria Shows" website to direct interested parties toward bands and shows. Through this process, the scene connected youth from different towns and high schools who would not have otherwise met, building a community of outcasts, if an imperfect one.

There is no obvious place for Peoria in the punk rock pantheon. It is not a valued national treasure. But in many ways, the story of its underground music scene in the late twentieth century is fundamentally American. It was a time when the area's major employer, Caterpillar, relocated its production and repeatedly clashed with its labor union. Many of this book's characters were the children of Cat's workers.

Much of this story takes place among the remains of bygone generations' social organizations (many of whose members had been Cat employees as well): the Itoo Hall and Optimist Club, the German American Hall and Italian American Hall, the VFWs and American Legions, to name a few. With membership dwindling, these clubs were desperate to keep from joining the industrial ruins of boarded-up warehouses and abandoned factories—so desperate they would consider renting their halls to teenage punks. Many have since disappeared.

Like these once-formidable institutions, Expo Gardens, too, grapples with the fate of decline. In some ways, diminishing attendance at the Heart of Illinois Fair—now a five-day event rather than nine—mirrors the outcome of last century's industrial economy. And like Expo Gardens, Peoria at large feels the pain. In 2017, Caterpillar uprooted its world headquarters in favor of a Chicago suburb. While Cat remains Peoria's largest employer, the move left this self-proclaimed "company town" without its company.[19]

And yet, Peoria soldiers on. Restaurants, breweries, and art galleries have injected new life into old riverfront warehouses, while the city finds hope in a growing medical community and the innovations of its artists, entrepreneurs, and creatives.

The history of Peoria punk rock, despite being so openly oppositional, more or less runs parallel to that of its namesake. It may even provide a model of sorts, as generations of youth refused to accept the status quo, rolled up their sleeves, and built something new on top of the old. For them, the 1980s, the 1990s, and the decade that opened the twenty-first century were a fresh beginning—not just the miserable end of a supposedly great era.

*　*　*

This is a book about love/hate relationships with one's hometown, about hope and possibility, and about frustration with potential unfulfilled. "Peoria came close to greatness on more than one occasion, only to settle for less, time and again," declare Greg Wahl and Charles Bobbitt in their 2009 book, *It Didn't Play in Peoria*, flipping the famous vaudeville phrase on its head for an entire volume of "missed chances, lost causes and plain bad luck."[20] Building on that lineage, this history, too, contains failures as well as triumphs. For all their successes, Peoria punks routinely burned the bridges that they built, while their scene reflected many of the social dynamics of the city they so openly criticized.

The story arc is straightforward. It begins in the early 1980s as Peoria punk was born, piecing together the remnants of a modest rock and roll past. It then follows the growth, in fits and starts, of a sporadically vibrant music scene and culminates at the turn of the twenty-first century, when several area bands achieved national and international recognition.

But this narrative is a bit deceiving. Historical peaks and valleys are often a matter of perspective, especially so within countercultures. Rather than building to a crescendo, the Peoria scene experienced a series of highs and lows. No one person witnessed this entire period up-close; most know the fits and starts only of their own era. Understandably, many might think their own moment was the most important or consequential—or the most authentically "punk."

Punk generations turn over quickly, and as punk-author George Hurchalla notes, the evolution is not so much the passing of a torch as "a series of less than pretty *coup d'états*, each one overthrowing the previous generation's approach."[21] In Peoria's case, punks were generally unaware of those who had come before them and thus doomed to continually reinvent the wheel. Rather than telling a single story, this book cobbles together dozens of overlapping histories—of bands that quickly burned out and of young people who lived and breathed punk for a few short years before moving on.

Above all, what follows is a story about making the most out of very little. Peoria's DIY punk scene featured dynamic, haphazard, and (sometimes) surprisingly well-attended all-ages shows in a place with few other countercultural offerings. Hardcore, pop-punk, indie rock, ska, and death metal bands habitually shared bills; the fans of each were too few in number to sustain their own scenes. (And we ask forgiveness for referring to Peoria's "skids," "cornchips," "megs," and other cultural misfits collectively as "punks.")

This is their story—or at least one version of it. It is as accurate as possible, though some fragments may be as much folklore as fact. Flyers were discovered for shows that almost certainly never happened and for others that may or may not have. Sometimes eyewitness accounts were in direct contradiction. Memories can be deceiving, after all.

In any case, this is the past as we have come to understand it. Peoria's DIY punk scene was (and is) the collective product of hundreds of people's actions across multiple decades. This book is a tribute to that work—a recognition that it was important and that it was not easy.

We hope to have captured some of this spirit, though we admit that we could not include every band or individual worth mentioning. In the DIY tradition, if it doesn't reflect *your* history, we encourage you to write it!

PART I

The Rise of Peoria Punk Rock: 1956–1986

As a midsized city in the rural, conservative Midwest, Peoria was an unlikely setting for a countercultural arts scene. Its proximity to Chicago and St. Louis, however, had long made it a convenient add-on date for entertainers of various stripes—a low-stakes proving ground for new material. During the 1960s and '70s, Peoria was a regular stop for musical acts who needed dates in smaller cities to sustain their tours between bigger gigs. It was well steeped in rock and roll but mostly missed the punk rock wave of the late 1970s. Peoria's connection to bands like the Ramones, the Clash, and the Sex Pistols was largely limited to a minute selection of albums at local record stores.

When a real punk scene finally emerged in Peoria in the mid-1980s, it was guided not by the comparatively listenable music of that earlier period but rather by hardcore—a new iteration of punk rock that was both more aggressive and more bluntly political. Just as DIY torchbearers like Minor Threat, Black Flag, and the Dead Kennedys flatly rejected corporate attempts to monetize punk, hardcore fans made their own magazines ("zines"), and bands put out records on their own labels and booked their own tours.[1]

Paralleling the rise of hip-hop during this period, hardcore bands also lashed out against the reactionary politics embodied by President Ronald

Reagan. Flyers for early hardcore shows routinely featured anti-Reagan images, and in cities like San Francisco (home of the Dead Kennedys), Washington, DC (Minor Threat and the Bad Brains), and Los Angeles (Black Flag and the Circle Jerks), bands offered a broader political critique. In central Illinois, however, Reaganism was the well-accepted norm. Not only did the area vote overwhelmingly for the Reagan-Bush ticket, but "The Gipper" was an Illinois native and graduate of nearby Eureka College, just a twenty-minute drive from downtown Peoria.[2]

Peoria's early punks were united less by politics—or even specific musical tastes—than by a broader disdain for mainstream culture. The Reagan Revolution, after all, represented much more than public policy. To the young people of the 1980s, it reflected the uptight conservatism of their grandparents' generation—a throwback to the conformity, sexual repression, and unquestioning patriotism of the 1950s.

Peoria's early punk scene was also far from monolithic, drawing influence from both the anti-drug, "straight-edge" Minor Threat and the shock rock of heavy metal pioneers like Black Sabbath and Alice Cooper. It began as just a handful of aspiring musicians and skateboarders. But within a few short years, Peoria's punk rebellion was a veritable youth counterculture with its own social spaces and even its own unique slang terms.

CHAPTER 1

Heebie Mesolithic Eon Drizzle

> Midwesterners were distinguished by their lack of distinguish-
> ing characteristics. Anything but flamboyant, they supposedly
> had no discernible accent or clothing or customs. Their culture,
> like their history and their landscape, was linear and straight-
> forward, without major drama, without peaks or valleys.
>
> —Richard Sisson, Christian Zacher, and Andre Cayton,
> *The American Midwest: An Interpretive Encyclopedia*

> We all know that Illinois ain't such hot shit, right? . . . In fact, about
> all the Land of Lincoln does have going for it is its all-star dirt,
> squoozed out of the bedrock by some heebie Mesolithic eon drizzle and
> laying there a few million years waiting for the first soybean seed.
>
> —*Rick Johnson Reader*

It's a working-class river town built on manufacturing and agriculture—the now-former home of Caterpillar's world headquarters, an ancestral hub of midwestern vaudeville, and perpetual purveyor of the old phrase "Will it play in Peoria?" Musically speaking, Peoria, Illinois, may be best known as the hometown of soft-rock singer-songwriter Dan Fogelberg or REO Speedwagon guitarist Gary Richrath (of East Peoria, across the Illinois River). At times Peoria has seemed stuck in the past, depressingly static as a steady stream of bar bands served up watered-down imitations of Ted Nugent or Cheap Trick, rock and roll covers with a side of the blues. Artists whose work was not middle-of-the-road—the city's most talented native son, comedian Richard Pryor, for example—tended to be studiously ignored, if not ardently reproached. Such was the consequence of a deeply rooted heartland conservatism, a widespread lack of stomach for anything remotely "edgy," and, in Pryor's case at least, a formidable mountain of institutional racism.

Ever lagging behind the times, the self-described "Heart of Illinois" was certainly an unlikely incubator for the punk rock revolution slowly making its way inland in the 1980s. But rewind a few decades to the supposed peak years of the city's cultural homogeny—to the early days of rock and roll—and the Peoria region had a lively and active music scene . . .

*   *   *

On February 7, 1957, the *Peoria Journal Star* made the announcement with deft alliteration: "Professional Presleyans Put On Peoria Premiere." Despite the fears of parents across the nation, rock and roll had landed in middle America. A series of "shindigs"—Peoria's "first public rock 'n' roll dances"—were held at the Itoo Hall on South Adams Street, a gathering place for the city's sizable Lebanese immigrant population. Admission to local impresario Bill Reardon's "Teen-Age Frolics" (featuring "2 sensational rock-n-roll singers" and "a red hot 7 piece band") was just ninety cents.[1] Advertisements in the newspaper touted the unique events:

> Dancing—entertainment country style . . .
> Everyone invited!
> No age limit
> No intox. allowed.
> Police protection.
> Dancing starts 8 p.m.
> Snack bar open.[2]

Elvis mania had arrived one year earlier. By the fall of 1956, following the performer's dazzling first appearance on *The Ed Sullivan Show*, hundreds of enthusiastic teenage admirers lined the block outside Peoria's downtown Rialto Theater for a special matinee showing of Presley's film debut, *Love Me Tender*. In a typical headline, the local newspaper questioned this new development: "Rock n' Roll: Is It a Menace or Harmless Teen-Age Fun?" The same would be asked of subsequent generations—and their own musical innovations—in the years to come.[3]

In 1959, the Rockin' R's from the nearby village of Metamora, Illinois, took their swingin' rockabilly rhythms all the way to Dick Clark's *American Bandstand* on ABC-TV. The band's hit instrumental, "The Beat," spent eight weeks on the national charts and earned them gigs opening for their idols, Jerry Lee Lewis and Gene Vincent. They were eventually inducted into the Rockabilly Hall of Fame.[4]

The following year, another early pioneer of rock and roll settled in Peoria. Byron "Wild Child" Gipson was the lone African American in one of America's first integrated rock bands, Freddie Tieken and the Rockers, from Quincy, Illinois. Prior to that, he had been a sideman and road manager for Little Richard. Wild Child was well acquainted with Peoria, having played many gigs at Harold's Club, where an up-and-coming Richard Pryor polished his stand-up act in between sets. Gipson tore up Peoria stages throughout the sixties and would be a fixture on the local jazz and blues scene for decades.[5]

Though overshadowed by its proximity to Chicago, one of the world's premier blues cities, Peoria was plentiful with blues talent of its own. Most prominently, Luther Allison enjoyed a decades-long musical career and was renowned for his soulful guitar work, even as he plugged away at day jobs in Peoria, working for Caterpillar and Keystone Steel and Wire. Both Eddie King and Emmett "Maestro" Sanders played guitar for Chicago's "Queen of the Blues," Koko Taylor, and both died relatively unheralded, overdue legacies buried amid their hometown's underappreciated blues scene.

In the mid-sixties, teenage rock and roll bands like the Coachmen, the Wombats, and the Shags started popping up in Peoria-area garages, playing school dances, and battling it out in high school gymnasiums—just like everywhere else in the country. As the British Invasion gave way to the psychedelic era, local groups like Suburban 9 to 5, Abaddon, and Zimmo's Thanatopsis began taking cues from Hendrix, Cream, and the Jefferson Airplane. Shaggy-haired teenagers were pushing the boundaries and remaking American culture for a new age.

The Kinks, the Hollies, the Yardbirds, and the Who were among the wave of prominent Brits who found their way across the Atlantic to play in Peoria. All four bands took the stage at Exposition Gardens, home of the Heart of Illinois Fair—that prototypical celebration of livestock competitions, amusement rides, and motor contests. With multiple buildings available for rent to the public, it was one of the area's top concert venues, though the conservative Midwest was not an especially welcoming place for the emerging sixties counterculture.

The Kinks' 1965 visit to Peoria, for example, was shaped by widespread aversion to the "long-haired British invaders," including one frightening encounter with "a redneck punk who [drove] the band around for the promoter, brandishing a gun in the process."[6] The incident left such an impression on Kinks singer

Ray Davies that he recounted the anecdote in both his 1995 autobiography and his subsequent stage show.

Three years later, the Strawberry Alarm Clock found their Expo Gardens concert canceled following a midnight-hour raid on their East Peoria hotel room. All five members of the California band were arrested, and two were charged with drug possession. In Peoria, the scandal was front-page news. But when a prominent San Francisco attorney flew into town to advocate for the musicians—claiming they were framed by local authorities hostile to their long hair and hippie attire—the charges were dropped.[7]

In September 1967, the Doors managed to avoid arrest when they played a high school gymnasium in the small town of Canton, about thirty miles southwest of Peoria, just four days before their notorious *Ed Sullivan* debut. While "Light My Fire" hit the top of the charts that summer, the band "came and went with almost no fanfare, noticed mostly for their long hair in a conservative burg still struggling with widespread cultural change."[8]

When the Who took the stage at Expo Gardens on March 10, 1968, a BBC crew was on hand filming a documentary about popular music that examined the revolutionary possibilities of rock and roll at a time when cultural revolution was very much in the air. To this day, footage of Pete Townsend and bandmates trashing their gear after a particularly scorching rendering of "My Generation" remains a touchstone of Peoria musical lore. But the Who's three-hour late arrival angered promoter Hank Skinner, who refused to pay the remainder of their $1,500 guarantee—and the band was not happy about it. "They wanted their $750!" exclaims Craig Moore, frontman of Iowa garage-rock legends GONN, Ilmo Smokehouse, and a string of other bands, who moved to Peoria in the mid-seventies and became an agent for Skinner's Peoria Musical Enterprises. "[Hank] told them . . . to pack up their shit and get out."[9] The promoter allegedly swiped Pete Townsend's white Beatle boots before running the band out of town—notwithstanding Townsend's threats of legal action, which ultimately proved hollow.

Incidentally, two of the local acts that opened for the Who at Expo Gardens—Suburban 9 to 5 and the Coachmen—counted among their ranks Gary Richrath and Dan Fogelberg, respectively. Three years later, when Black Sabbath played the same room, it was Richrath's REO Speedwagon that opened the show—the hometown boy making good.[10]

Across town in the pre–rock and roll era, a large horse stable on the northern outskirts of Peoria hosted big bands and traveling orchestras, country troubadours

Figure 1. Among the acts to play in pre-punk Peoria were high-powered Detroit rockers MC5, shock-rock pioneer Alice Cooper, and renowned heavy metal band Black Sabbath, who performed at Expo Gardens in August 1971. Jack W. Davis, "Black Sabbath at Exposition Gardens" promotional poster, Jack W. Davis Papers, Sousa Archives and Center for American Music, University of Illinois at Urbana-Champaign.

like Webb Pierce and Red Sovine, rodeos, and other popular entertainment of the day. In the early sixties, it was known as Baty's Barn—a regular stop for emerging R&B acts on the "chitlin circuit," including James Brown and Ike and Tina Turner.[11] When Booker T and the MG's failed to show up for a December 1962 gig, the ensuing unrest made national headlines. "The crowd went berserk and began ripping up plumbing fixtures and breaking windows," went the account in *Jet* magazine—a familiar scenario to Peoria's punk scene some three decades on.[12]

Several years later, as the sixties dissolved into the seventies, Baty's Barn, then known simply as "the Barn," hosted performances by a flood of up-and-coming rock bands and solo artists, including the Allman Brothers Band, Alice Cooper, Bob Seger, Uriah Heep, Fleetwood Mac, and King Crimson (whose song "Peoria," from the 1972 live album *Earthbound*, was actually recorded there). The Barn also played host to a Detroit band whose anti-establishment panache would serve as a blueprint for the punk movement to come. The MC5 took the electric energy of the Who to new and exciting heights, but as one concertgoer recalls, the band's Peoria show started rather sluggishly: "When they played [Peoria] they were not on their game. About five songs into their set, people actually started going outside. The lead singer got upset and screamed out, '*OK, you motherfuckers, it's time to kick out the jams!*' And with that song, they pretty much turned it around."[13]

Among those promoting shows at the Barn, Bill Love and Jay Goldberg established their own record stores in the area. As the ambitious young partners brought bigger and bigger acts to Peoria, the shows and their shops went hand in hand. The stores were "our base for not only selling tickets, but also to gauge the market and see what artists the people were buying to determine whom they would want to see in concert," Goldberg explains.[14] He went on to become Peoria's most successful concert promoter, while Co-Op Tapes and Records (as Love and Goldberg's merged outfit was eventually known) would serve as ground zero for bringing the local punk scene together.

* * *

Across the river and ten miles south of Peoria, the hometown of Bill Love and Jay Goldberg was an unlikely hotbed of musical activity. Despite having a population less than a third the size of its sister city, Pekin had its own record stores, head shops, coffeehouses, folk singers, and rock bands, signaling the inroads of the sixties counterculture in a stronghold of conservativism. An outsized number of area musicians found their roots in Pekin, from the early days of rock and roll to the punk era and beyond. During the 1970s, Pekin hosted performances by the likes of Kiss, Blue Oyster Cult, the Runaways, Rush, and Journey (with a then-unknown Tom Petty opening). Perhaps more significantly, Pekin was home to the Golden Voice Recording Company—the finest recording studio in Illinois outside of Chicago.

Surrounded by cornfields on the south end of town, Golden Voice is best known for helping Dan Fogelberg and REO Speedwagon get their start in the music industry. Styx and Head East recorded there, and one of the music industry's most successful engineers launched his career at the studio. "The reason Nirvana's album *Nevermind* sounds the way it does is in part due to Golden Voice's influence on Andy Wallace," notes Chris Gilbert, a Pekin native responsible for reissuing scores of nearly forgotten Golden Voice recordings on his own Alona's Dream Records. "Teenagers will still be listening to Nirvana in twenty years, maybe longer, and Golden Voice played a role in that."[15]

During the 1960s and '70s, Golden Voice presented a unique opportunity to musicians from central Illinois and beyond: high-quality, professional recordings at affordable prices. Just about every Peoria-area band of note recorded there. Among them was Pekin's answer to the Beatles and one of the Midwest's most successful regional acts of the seventies: the Jets. Riding a wave of hype fostered by a local radio station, the band drew throngs of screaming fans to their early Peoria and Pekin shows, not unlike what the Beatles themselves had done a decade earlier, albeit on a smaller scale. Though stylistically more power-pop than proto-punk, the group may rightly be considered provincial forerunners of the punk mindset and attitude in central Illinois.

In early 1974, the Jets broke up over some members' obsession with David Bowie; out of the ashes came the Peoria area's first glam band: the Jetz. For singer-guitarist Graham Walker, Bowie represented the next logical extension of rock and roll in the post-Beatles era, both musically and culturally—and hinted at the shape of punk to come: "We'd all gone to Chicago and gotten glitter/glam clothes. I dyed my hair orange and shaved my eyebrows off [as Bowie had famously done]. We were just teenagers, running around Peoria and Pekin. . . . To walk down Main Street in Peoria with no eyebrows, hair dyed bright orange, and a glitter shirt on in the seventies . . . *people wanted to kill us!* You couldn't be any further out. No one understood what we were doing—it was like we were from outer space."[16]

On Friday, May 24, 1974, Walker and his Jets/Jetz bandmate Gregg Clemons drove to Co-Op Records to pick up Bowie's brand-new *Diamond Dogs* LP. "We bought the record at noon, and by 12:30 it was on our turntable," he recalls. "We had our guitars with us and were playing along. The song that stood out was 'Rebel Rebel.' By 2:00 or 2:30, we were having our first run-through with it." The band played it out that very night—a seminal moment Walker later described as "Peoria's introduction to punk."[17]

The Jetz, however, lasted less than a year. Toward the end of the decade, a revived power-pop incarnation of the Jets (including Walker) released a single

19

on Minneapolis's Twin/Tone Records, a key independent label of the burgeoning post-punk underground. The band even had a number-one hit in Minneapolis (where a young Prince Rogers Nelson reportedly attended the record release party) and once opened for the Ramones, further tying the group to the emergence of punk rock.

For sixteen-year-old Douglas McCombs, who grew up in Peoria and Pekin, the crucial "aha" moment arrived with Devo's 1978 performance on *Saturday Night Live*. "Before that I was barely interested in music," recalls the cofounder of the experimental rock band Tortoise. "The next two years were occupied with trying to find a context for how Devo even existed, connecting dots and filling in gaps":

> I had been obsessed with skateboarding since around '72, but had not made any connection to rock n' roll. . . . When I discovered Devo, I started to notice that [skateboarders] Jay Adams and Tony Alva were no longer wearing Ted Nugent t-shirts in the magazines and their hair was shorter. Interesting development.
>
> I was able to eventually figure out that there were a couple of other people in my town who were interested in the same things I was. . . . We would scour the cutout bins at Co-Op Records in Pekin and Peoria for anything that looked weird, and without any information at all we discovered Television, Pere Ubu, Wire, X, the Cramps, the Stranglers, the Buzzcocks, etc. We got some dud records, too.
>
> We would go to this gay bar in Peoria . . . because they never carded us and they played good records. I learned about Iggy Pop and Lou Reed from there (didn't know anything about the Stooges or Velvets until later) as well as Wax Trax in Chicago. We would go on buying trips to Chicago for records and skateboard parts.[18]

For sixteen-year-old Jon Ginoli, punk was something exotic and intangible, existing only within the pages of magazines like *Circus, Hit Parader*, and *Creem*. "We'd heard about punk rock . . . but we had no idea what it sounded like!" explains the former Peorian. "It was all very secondhand—none of that was on the radio here."[19]

"In Peoria, it seemed like the world was happening somewhere else," he adds. "There really wasn't much to do except buy records." So when the Ramones' debut album hit Ginoli's ears in the spring of 1976, it arrived as a revelation—as did "Anarchy in the U.K.," the Sex Pistols' debut single, later that fall. "I managed to order a copy from a record store in New York," he explains. "I remember listening to it once, going 'Hmmm . . .'; listening to it twice, going 'Interesting

. . .'; and then the third listen . . . I was like, 'Oh my god, this is the greatest thing I've ever heard!'"[20]

The mark the Ramones left on Ginoli proved indelible. Fifteen years later and a world away in San Francisco, he would stake his claim as the founder and frontman of Pansy Division—"the first all-gay rock band that any of us had ever known of." Pansy Division's in-your-face approach to queer sexuality, quite radical for its time, could scarcely have been envisioned by Ginoli's younger self, an alienated teen growing up on the culturally repressive Illinois prairie. It was forged there nonetheless via punk rock: a ticket for him to embrace his outsiderness. "I wasn't out yet and I was really uncertain of my sexuality," Ginoli explains. "I was very frustrated. And punk rock is very good for channeling those frustrations."[21]

But beyond a few LPs in the racks at Co-Op, punk rock might well have not existed in Peoria. Aside from that lone MC5 show, the Bowie-isms of the Jetz, and a 1979 visit from British pub rockers Eddie and the Hot Rods, there is little trace of anything remotely "punk" playing Peoria in the seventies. All-ages shows, a staple of the DIY punk scene, were unheard of.

"If you wanted to see a rock show you went to a bar, and I certainly wasn't able to do that," Ginoli notes. But he was able to buy records—and that wasn't the only aspect of the punk movement that inspired him. "I read that people were putting out zines . . . and I was able to mail-order some of them. So I thought, '*I'll* do a zine.'"[22]

In 1977, during his junior year at Richwoods High School, Ginoli created *Hoopla,* Peoria's first punk rock fanzine, its sixteen xeroxed pages crammed full of typewritten missives of punk culture. Yet few Peorians knew or cared; it was distributed almost entirely through mail order. "*Trouser Press* had a section where you could place short ads, so I would put ads for *Hoopla* in there and people would mail-order it," Ginoli explains. "It was sort of like having pen pals. Because apart from a couple of people, I really couldn't find people in Peoria who related to it."[23]

*   *   *

As Peoria hardly offered a supportive backdrop for musicians who wanted to make it, leaving in search of better opportunities would become a recurring theme for the city's music scene. Douglas McCombs moved to Chicago right after high school, just in time to take part in that city's early punk scene. He has

Figure 2. *Hoopla* was Peoria's original punk rock zine, first published by Richwoods High School student (and future Pansy Division frontman) Jon Ginoli in 1977. From the collection of Bob Gordon.

since remained an integral member of Chicago's indie rock community, playing in seminal bands like Tortoise, Eleventh Dream Day, and Brokeback.

Graham Walker and Jon Ginoli both left Peoria for the University of Illinois, ninety miles down the interstate in Champaign-Urbana: a "real" university town. Ginoli formed the Outnumbered—who released three records and toured the country with the Replacements, Violent Femmes, and Soul Asylum—before heading west to San Francisco, where he started Pansy Division in 1991. As for Walker, when the Jets broke up for good in 1980, he joined forces with another Pekin-to-Champaign transplant, forming a band that would see great success in the Reagan era.

Like Walker, Brad Steakley was a Pekin native with youthful dreams of rock and roll stardom. He'd played with Walker in the short-lived Jetz lineup, and when that group folded, he and a few other musicians carried on as Jet—a new band mixing glam-inspired originals with covers of Bowie, Queen, the New York Dolls, and such. Jet soon morphed into Star (named for the song from *The Rise and Fall of Ziggy Stardust and the Spiders from Mars*, the mythmaking fantasy that immortalized Bowie as the world's greatest rock star), and the band built a modest local following. But to take things to the next level, Steakley believed that he and his bandmates, too, had to leave their hometown.

Star became Screams upon moving to Champaign-Urbana, and as their punk-tinged edges were refined into a crunchy new-wave pop, they seemed on the cusp of bigger things. Screams' debut LP was released on Infinity/MCA Records in 1979; they spent three months on tour with Van Halen and headlined a UK tour of their own that fall. Then the bottom fell out.

The Infinity label was suddenly dropped by MCA, the result of ruthless cost-cutting amid a worldwide record-industry recession. Screams were collateral damage, fizzling away with the excess of the seventies (and replaced by the excess of a new decade). Brad Steakley soon found kindred spirits in Rob Newhouse and fellow Pekinite Graham Walker (the latter having joined Screams in its final months), and the trio took on new names: Brad Elvis, Rob Elvis, and Graham Elvis. In the year of MTV's launch, the Elvis Brothers from Champaign, Illinois, were there to ensure that rockabilly-dusted power-pop found an audience in the synth-driven age of the New Romantics.

Back in Peoria, the city's once-thriving rock and roll scene had almost completely dried up. When the state increased the drinking age to twenty-one, its bars and nightclubs suffered greatly. Many closed for good. As feminist activist and Peoria native Betty Friedan described a visit to her hometown in 1980, "Main Street is deserted, shadowed by massive layoffs . . . at the big Caterpillar tractor plant."[24]

Times were tough, and then they got worse. By 1982, the Pabst brewery and Hiram Walker distillery—two of the "Whiskey City's" largest employers—had closed for good, throwing tens of thousands out of work. At the same time, a seven-month strike at Caterpillar culminated in mass layoffs, another ominous chapter in the slow-motion decline of American labor. Businesses went belly-up, the housing market collapsed, and by 1985 the Peoria area had lost 30,000 jobs. With unemployment nearing 18 percent, a popular bumper sticker expressed a common view of the day: "Would the last person to leave Peoria please turn out the lights?"

The toll of deindustrialization, as anthropologist Kathryn Dudley warned, was "not limited to lost jobs, sagging tax revenues, boarded-up shops, and vacant lots." The economic restructuring of the post-1960s period amplified not only poverty but fear, hopelessness, and anger. "Not knowing what the next day's news will bring," Dudley argues, created intense political and social divisions— "a cultural problem that confronts every American, not just those in the rust belt industries."[25] The United States was in crisis, and cities throughout the heartland appeared to be on the cusp of failing.

Meanwhile, in Los Angeles, San Francisco, Detroit, and Washington, DC, a new generation of teenage rebels were hopping into vans and touring the country, starting up record labels, and building a brand-new underground culture. Punk rock's DIY ethos of self-reliance and fierce independence—codified by Black Flag and later perfected by Fugazi—attracted thousands of youthful adherents. A loose network of independent bands, promoters, record labels, and distributors rose up to proclaim a gospel completely outside of the mainstream—but one that eventually spread to every town in America.

Black Flag *almost* played in Peoria. Fugazi eventually did. And Peoria itself— part Rust Belt, part Bible Belt—offered up its own idiosyncratic brand of punk rock.

CHAPTER 2

Creating the Peoria Scene

Livin' in Peoria, it sure will bore ya / No punx or Oi boys, just plenty of
farm boys.

—Electric Cool-Aid/Chips Patroll, "Livin' in Peoria"

Growing up in Peoria was boring, but music saved my pathetic soul! I
helped create the first punk rock scene in Peoria back in the early '80s
and it wasn't so boring after that!

—Bloody F. Mess

Midwesterners tend to take for granted that they're a year or two (or more . . .)
behind the coasts. With punk rock, it was no different. If Chicago was punk's
"redheaded stepchild," lagging behind Los Angeles, San Francisco, New York,
and Washington, DC (as the 2009 documentary *You Weren't There* suggests),
Peoria was the Second City's own downstate black sheep. *You Weren't There*
chronicles the early punk scene in Chicago from 1977 ("the year of punk") to
1984. But in that Orwellian year, even as the Chicago scene was fracturing, the
scene in Peoria was only just getting started.[1]

Like so many music scenes, it started at a record store. And in the way that
Chicago had Wax Trax, Peoria had Co-Op.

"I went into Co-Op and there was a flyer up: 'Want to start a hardcore band,'"
recalls Bob Gordon, who later worked at Co-Op before opening Acme Comics
in the early nineties. "I asked [the clerk] Russell, 'Who are these guys?' He's like,
'They're these kids; they came in on skateboards. . . . They're crazy. They're from
Chicago.'"[2]

No one realized it at the time, but that flyer essentially launched Peoria punk
rock.

Naturally it was the Caterpillar Tractor Company, as the Fortune 100 firm was then known, that brought those "crazy kids" 150 miles down from the Chicago suburbs to the corn and soybean fields of central Illinois. Their father, a Caterpillar engineer, was about to be transferred—it was either Brazil or Peoria, as Barry Stepe recalls. "It turned out to be Peoria."[3]

All music scenes need catalysts: dedicated soldiers to do the footwork, true believers to spread the word. In Peoria, they arrived in the form of four skateboarding brothers from Willow Springs, Illinois, fresh from the task of introducing hardcore to Chicago's western suburbs.

*   *   *

Between 1978 and 1987 alone, the Stepe brothers—Steve (b. 1963), Barry (b. 1965), Todd aka "Chopper" (b. 1968), and Kyle (b. 1971)—are credited with having formed more than 100 "bands" (or rather, 100 different names for various combinations of Stepes) and recording dozens of demo tapes. First came the Schteppies in 1978, with Steve on bass and Barry on drums and vocals. Among the highlights of their *Rubber Chicken* cassette was the song "Punk Rock Janitor,"

Figure 3. Steve, Chopper, and Barry Stepe (*left to right*) in Willow Springs, Illinois, before their family's move to East Peoria, early 1980s. Courtesy of Barry Stepe.

which detailed their misadventures mopping the floor at a Mr. Donut franchise. But the Stepes' first band of significance was Negative Element, featuring Barry on guitar and Chopper on bass.[4]

With nods to British Oi!, Black Flag, and the Circle Jerks, Negative Element embodied the aggressive hardcore sound that was beginning to crystallize across the country. "The Brothers Stepe (that's S-T-E-P-E) along with [drummer] Keith Lyons and [vocalist] Tom Faulkner were among the first true hardcore (as opposed to punk) bands to emerge in the Chicago area," asserts the Reckless Records review of *Shouts of Rebellion,* a 2017 reissue of the band's discography. "[They] helped define the underage scene, as well as fathering the western suburban punk scene that followed in their wake."[5]

Their music was fast, chaotic, and quirky: adolescent posturing tinged with wry humor, rapid-fire skate rock propelled by teenage hormones. Along with punk-rock compatriots Rights of the Accused, Negative Element was largely responsible for incubating Chicago's all-ages scene as punk turned to hardcore. "It was a totally different atmosphere," Barry notes. "A lot more aggressive."[6]

Chopper Stepe was barely a teenager when Negative Element (then called the New Anarchists) debuted at a Willow Springs health club where the Stepes' mom worked. It was Halloween of 1981, the same night LA punk band Fear played *Saturday Night Live* and a crew of slam-dancing punks—including *SNL*'s own John Belushi, Ian MacKaye of Minor Threat, and members of the Meatmen, the Cro-Mags, and Negative Approach—caused a near-riot (and $20,000 in damages) on national television. That very evening in the Chicago suburbs, Negative Element was churning out covers of the Germs, the Dead Kennedys, Cockney Rejects, and Richard Hell, "plus a few originals to a bunch of joggers while trying to drown out the Pac-Man machine," Barry recalls.[7]

"We were messy and snotty, and we were still just little kids," Chopper adds. "We played sloppy, and we didn't give a shit."[8]

As Chopper and Barry cut their punk rock teeth in Negative Element, the eldest Stepe, Steve, played bass for Rights of the Accused, another group of adolescents unknowingly shaping the contours of American hardcore. It was that band's 1983 show with Naked Raygun at the Cubby Bear in Chicago that famously turned a thirteen-year-old Dave Grohl on to punk rock. "That night changed everything I knew about music," said the former Nirvana drummer and Foo Fighters frontman. "It just turned my world upside down."[9] And it was at Wax Trax, naturally, where Steve Stepe came across the ad that brought him into the band.

The Stepes' parents graciously indulged their children's wayward pursuits, allowing them to venture into the big city on their own at an early age. "We would spend the weekend going to punk shows, record stores, and making fanzines," Barry explains. "We saw great bands like Black Flag, Misfits, Social Distortion, and Bad Brains and skated around as much as possible."[10]

Wired with inspiration, Negative Element began to make a name for itself with animated live performances. "I think we brought a lot of youthful, crazy energy into the Chicago scene," Barry says. "We met most of the bands at local shows and developed friendships with some of them. We used to go see Six Feet Under, Trial by Fire, DV8, the Effigies, and Naked Raygun, to name a few. Rights of the Accused were already friends with Naked Raygun and most of the other bands, and we all got along great."[11]

Articles of Faith was one of the great enduring bands of that early Chicago hardcore scene. Like Naked Raygun, they befriended their slightly younger brethren and supported their efforts to open up the scene to all ages. In April 1983, they invited Negative Element to join them on a road trip to Minneapolis to open for the Replacements. Unfortunately the Stepes had to turn down the offer: it was a school night, after all.

Negative Element's early, boom-box-recorded demos landed the group a slot on Version Sound's now-legendary *Meathouse* compilation, alongside Rights of the Accused, Battalion of Saints, JFA, and the Minutemen. That in turn led to the band's debut: the eight-song *Yes, We Have No Bananas* EP. Its title nodded to 1920s vaudeville (foretelling the brothers' soon-to-be home in Peoria), and today it's considered a classic of early hardcore. None other than Steve Albini—Chicago punk pioneer and in-demand sound engineer—raved about *Bananas*: "This 45 is just brimming with *real* enthusiasm, joy, intelligence, wit and well-directed anger. Better than some of the early DC records at capturing the essence of being a teenager who's too smart to play the game. Includes the two funniest thrash songs in North America, 'Whatever Happened to Elmer Fudd' and 'Anti-Pac Man,' as well as some blistering anti-religious and anti-police songs. Worth the trip."[12]

Three additional Negative Element tracks appeared on *Starving Dogs*, a cassette compilation released by Steve Stepe on his own Little Farmer Music imprint. His intent was to document the hardcore scene that he and his brothers were helping to foment—the same task Barry Stepe took on with *Primitive Noise*, the fanzine he published from 1982 to 1985. Throughout the eighties, all four Stepe brothers were involved in publishing punk and/or skate zines, employing the low-budget, cut-and-paste aesthetic of the day.

Despite plans for a follow-up release, Negative Element was forced to call it quits when Caterpillar came calling. "We were playing a lot of shows, opening for the Dead Kennedys, JFA, Minor Threat, Big Boys and others," Barry says. "It was hard to leave all that. But, my father got transferred to Peoria."[13]

It was 1983. Upon moving to "a farm town far removed from any sort of punk rock scene," as one review later summarized, the Stepes brought hardcore punk with them—and Chicago's loss became Peoria's gain.[14] "The Stepe brothers brought the tablets down from the mountain," declares Jeff Gregory, who would later help do the same for another generation of Peoria kids.[15]

*   *   *

Newly relocated from Chicagoland to central Illinois, the Stepe brothers embodied punk's DIY ethic: playing in bands, running labels, booking shows, publishing zines, and skateboarding. But in Peoria, "there were no punks, no skaters, no scene," says Chopper. "It sucked."[16] It was up to them to take what they'd learned and build a scene from scratch.

"We were disappointed when we moved to Peoria and didn't see any kind of a punk scene happening, like we were used to in Chicago. So we started our own!" Barry explains. "We made Co-Op Records on Main Street our main hangout. We met some skaters there and started skating downtown as much as possible. And we started to form bands."[17]

In those pre-internet days, record stores were much more than retail outlets; they were bastions of community—hubs for weirdos and outcasts to find one another and connect. Founded in the early seventies (as Budget Tapes and Records) by concert promoters Bill Love and Jay Goldberg, Co-Op Tapes and Records was a regional chain headquartered in Peoria, with more than two dozen stores dotting small towns across Illinois, Iowa, and Wisconsin. From 1977 to 1984, Love also operated *The Prairie Sun*, which essentially served as Co-Op's in-house alt-weekly, showcasing the latest releases and concerts alongside record reviews, comics, classifieds, and articles about music, pop culture, and current events. It was the Midwest's own *Rolling Stone*, serving up regular doses of record-store culture at the height of its significance.

Amid copious displays of smoking paraphernalia, the stacks at Co-Op Records trafficked almost exclusively in rock and roll, with little in the way of classical, jazz, country, or R&B. In Peoria, it was the only place where one *might* find a record by the Saints or the Damned or anything far removed from the Top 40 or remotely underground. "The guys who worked there knew that stuff," explains Bob Gordon. "Russell Hopkins, Charlie Eberle, Kevin Hein, Sheldon Eater . . . they were the hookups."[18]

Despite the staff's esoteric knowledge, however, Co-Op's music selection remained limited; it was still Peoria, after all. "All four of them [the staff] were buying early Cramps records [and] all this weird stuff . . . but there'd only be one or two copies, and Russell or Charlie would get 'em," Gordon laughs. "So I used to go to Bloomington, Champaign, and Chicago . . . because Co-Op didn't carry much of it."[19] Nevertheless, the shop was a welcoming home for Peoria's social misfits—and ground zero for its embryonic punk scene.

Across central Illinois, the punk community reached outward by necessity. "Since there wasn't much happening in Peoria, we started hanging out with this amazing skate crew in [nearby] Springfield," Barry recalls. "We would go down there on weekends, skate and play basement shows once in a while. They had a small but tight little scene happening. That's where we met Steve McDaniel, the original singer of Electric Cool-Aid."[20]

Electric Cool-Aid can probably claim the title as the Peoria area's first punk band. With McDaniel joining three Stepe brothers—Barry on guitar, Steve on bass, and Chopper on drums—their music was raw and primitive, retaining the adolescent humor of Negative Element. In songs like "Cow Tippin'," with its faux barnyard-animal sounds, and "Livin' in Peoria," an anti-anthem with the Stepes role-playing as hick farmers, they mocked their new hometown relentlessly, railing against the backwoods nature of the slow-moving, agrarian Midwest.

These tracks, recorded in the Stepes' smoke-filled East Peoria basement (dubbed "Rubberneck Studios"), somehow ended up on *Empty Skulls*, a forty-three-song cassette released on the California-based Fartblossom Enterprises label in 1984. The compilation featured cover art from the underground artist Pushead—soon to be famous for his Metallica and Misfits artwork—and tracks from Septic Death, Corrosion of Conformity, and Rights of the Accused (including the latter's "Mean People Suck"—often cited as the original source of the popular catchphrase, later to be stamped on buttons, bumper stickers, and T-shirts).[21]

But with the departure of Electric Cool-Aid's lead singer, Peoria's first punk band was short-lived. Although Barry filled in on vocals for a time, he and his brothers knew they needed a real frontman. "We soon put up flyers at Co-Op trying to find someone," Barry explains.[22]

They received a single response: "from a guy who called himself Bloody F. Mess," says Chopper. "He was an odd character, to say the least, but a great frontman."[23]

To be sure, there is no stronger personality in the annals of Peoria punk history than Bloody F. Mess. In a few short years, his antics would be the talk of the town, but at this point he was just "a burned-out, pot-smoking dude" and "mile-a-minute talker" with eyes on fronting a band.[24] At age fourteen, he took a page from his punk rock heroes, assuming a new name to match the larger-than-life persona he was just beginning to cultivate.

Figure 4. Chips Patroll, ca. 1984: Steve, Chopper, and Barry Stepe with frontman Bloody Mess (*left to right*), the yin and yang of Peoria's early punk scene. Chips Patroll changed its name to the Unaccepted soon after its formation. Courtesy of Bloody Mess.

"A buddy of mine said, 'You have to have a [stage] name, like Darby Crash or Sid Vicious,'" he explains. "We got drunk one night, and the song 'Bodies' played by the Sex Pistols, where it says 'fucking bloody mess!' He goes, 'That's it! Your name is going to be: Fucking Bloody Mess.' I arranged it to be Bloody Fucking Mess. Then later I shortened it, so it's more like a name: Bloody F. Mess. And finally, just Bloody Mess."[25]

Bloody and the Stepes weren't an obvious pairing. "I was this drug addict, alcoholic, non-skateboarding kind of metal/punk guy, and these guys were complete punk rockers, straight-edge skateboarders," Bloody recounts. "And we started a band called Chips Patroll."[26]

"It was a weird mix," agrees Bob Gordon. "But there were so few people into [punk], you'd welcome anybody."[27]

With Bloody F. Mess on board "screaming the blues," as he later called it, the Stepes had found a real frontman.[28]

CHAPTER 3

Punks Live on Straight Edge

A lot of middle Americans consider these guys weird. Curses from strangers bother them, the band members say, but not enough to sacrifice their individuality.

—Bill Knight

Don't take the Stepe bros and their antics too seriously . . . I know that we never did. All we did was participate in a hardcore/skate microcosm that was happening across the country and is still germinating throughout the world today.

—Barry Stepe

It was the summer of 1984—Ronald Reagan's "Morning in America"—and Peoria's economy was in a tailspin. "Pabst was gone, Hiram Walker was gone, all these factories were gone," recalls Bob Gordon of Co-Op Records. Then Co-Op went under, too. "[Drug] paraphernalia law had changed. Reagan was doing the 'Just Say No' thing. That's when the state really started cracking down."[1]

In those days, few record stores carried much in the way of T-shirts or band merchandise, aside from records and cassettes; bong sales helped keep the lights on. But amid Reagan's War on Drugs and the country's growing conservatism, record stores and head shops were easy targets for hostile municipalities and state legislatures. In 1982 the US Supreme Court upheld an ordinance imposing strict licensing requirements on paraphernalia sales at a record store in the Chicago suburbs (*Village of Hoffman Estates v. Flipside*). This decision was the final nail in the coffin for many small shops. Co-Op Records in Peoria was one of the casualties.[2]

"The bank took it over—all the records were half off," Gordon recalls. "[Co-Op clerk] Charlie Eberle moved to Florida, and they had a big going-away party at his house. Chips Patroll played. It was the Stepes and Bloody [Mess], a handful of their friends [and] Co-Op people . . . fifty people, maybe."[3] It was the fledgling punk band's second show. One month earlier, in May 1984, Chips Patroll debuted at another house party—and this appears to have been Peoria's first DIY punk show. Brent Schlosser recalls hosting it in his backyard:

> I met [the Stepes] at the [Co-Op] record store on Main Street and watched some of their rehearsals in East Peoria. My friends and I had a crappy band—we didn't really know how to play, but we threw a lot of parties. I told these guys . . . who were new to town [that] they could play at my house since I knew a lot of people. So it was on.
>
> It got a little wild and people were slam dancing. . . . At one point Bloody threw a kid over the fence into an old lady's roses. Then the cops came. My mom flipped out. But all bands got to play.[4]

There weren't many options for punk bands to play in Peoria; no legitimate venue would have them. Instead, there was band practice (often an open invitation for friends to show up), and there were house parties—intimate gatherings in someone's garage, backyard, or basement. Slowly but surely, a local scene was beginning to coalesce. Bloody Mess and the Stepe brothers were the yin and yang at its center.

Anxious to break out of their central Illinois confines, the boys of Chips Patroll went on the road, playing shows in Chicago, Wisconsin, and around the Midwest; opening for acclaimed punk bands like Necros and MIA; and at some point morphing into Unaccepted (same band, different name). The alliance between Bloody and the Stepes worked to a point, but their partnership was always uneasy.

"They would kind of make fun of me," Bloody recalls. "They called me a 'skid,' which was a nickname in Chicago for a metal dude. I was just happy to be in a band. They didn't like the fact that I did drugs or drank, and I was just like, whatever, you guys are straight-edge and I'm not. And I didn't skate. So we didn't hang out that much. But, they told me straight-up: 'We love your vocals; we love your lyrics; we love your energy. You're perfect for hardcore punk rock—*but we don't want to hang out with you*,'" he laughs. "That's kind of how it was."[5]

By this time, Washington, DC hardcore pioneer Minor Threat had broken up, but the anti-drug, straight-edge movement the band founded (despite quickly disavowing its more aggressive trappings) was a defining element of the genre.[6] For many of its youthful adherents, "straight edge" was less a deeply held philosophy and more a matter of circumstance. "Most of our friends in the Chicago scene in the early '80s were straight-edge, so we just carried that over to our band," says Barry Stepe. "We ran on pure adrenaline and hardcore punk. We were having too much fun to need anything else."[7]

"We were busy skating and hanging out—there was no time for booze. Most of the skateboard punk scene was straight-edge, almost from a practicality angle," adds Mike "C. P." O'Russa, whose lifelong friendship with the Stepes was also initiated at Co-Op Records. "I walked in and there was Chopper and Steve, standing there with skateboards. I freaked out, as I thought the skaters in Peoria consisted of me and a couple of friends. So I walked up and introduced myself. They were just as freaked out. We talked for a bit, and then they invited me over to their house in East Peoria. . . . I was probably at their house two or three days a week for all of high school."[8]

In addition to Co-Op, the friends made Fulton Plaza their central hangout, rechristening it the "Bum Box." "It was just a small, brick park in downtown Peoria," Barry explains. "The brick really sucked to skate on, but there were a lot of ledges to jump off. No one really hung out there in the old days, so we would spend the night talking with some really strange characters who told us the most messed-up stories, hence the new name. . . . We would bring music with us to skate to, and soon, more and more like-minded individuals started hanging out."[9]

"A big skater night would be twelve or fifteen of us; usually it was half a dozen," adds O'Russa. "The whole downtown area was deserted at night, and we had the place to ourselves. We would cruise the streets, ride off loading docks, and go down parking garages."[10]

"Skateboarding back then was a completely underground phenomenon," notes Brad Krohn, who met the Stepes around the same time. "You had to be shown skateboarding by someone cooler than you—that was the only way to discover it. In the Midwest, the only way to get an actual skateboard was to mail-order one from California out of the back of *Thrasher* magazine—and no one [in Peoria] even had a copy of *Thrasher*, except the Stepe brothers!"[11]

*   *   *

With youthful freedom a shared tenet, hardcore and skateboarding were a seamless pair. And with a half-pipe erected in their backyard (the Stepes' parents, ever supportive, had agreed to build one to atone for the family's move to Peoria), the Stepes hosted "heavy skate sessions on the weekends, blasting Verbal Abuse and DRI," Barry says.[12] When a mod-inspired Massachusetts punk band came through Illinois on tour, it even became a makeshift venue.

"The Not called me a day or two before and wanted to set up a show," Barry recalls. "At the last minute, we decided to have them play on our half-pipe.... Maybe twenty to twenty-five people showed up, but it was the beginnings of a punk rock scene in Peoria."[13]

O'Russa documented the affair in his fanzine, *Skate and Spurs*: "Even though it was a quick-notice show . . . news of it hit the town like Paul Revere's ride from the phone call efforts of Steve, Barry and Leo and the flyers which were put out at the local mall by . . . Bloody Mess."[14] For the Stepes, this was no ordinary gig. "It was a celebration of the last time they had to play with Bloody. For some reason, Bloody just wasn't the role-model lead singer Chips Patroll had in mind."[15]

"They kicked me out of the band—kind of behind my back," Bloody says. "I was really pissed off."[16] The show went on that day nonetheless.

"The police were called numerous times," Chopper recalls, "but upon arriving, [they] saw that we were well-behaved and under my parents' supervision. So they would take my mother aside and say, 'Okay, just *pretend* that I'm yelling at you. We need to put on a show for the complaining neighbors.'"[17]

"We were slam dancing around the ramp," Barry adds. "I remember the PA catching fire during the Not's set. They were very cool guys—we went skating downtown with them afterwards. [But] that was it for punk rock on our ramp."[18]

Also playing the Stepes' half-pipe that day was Unclaimed Luggage, better known as Constant Vomit—another of Peoria's earliest punk bands. "We changed it in an attempt to have a less-abrasive name," explains C. P., who started the band with Joe Borsberry (aka "Mr. Vomit") in the summer of 1983. "I think it lasted a couple months before we changed it back."[19]

"I'd known C. P. (short for 'Country Punk') since sixth grade," Borsberry recalls. "He had a bunch of instruments lying around his basement. . . . I played the drums to start with. I was awful, but I was good at writing lyrics. I'd hand him some lyrics, and he'd pick up the guitar and write a song."[20] Tongue firmly in cheek, they denied they were a punk band, instead describing their music as "puke rock." "The band name was based on a gross poem I wrote a girl in high school to try to convince her I was insane," Borsberry adds. "Mission accomplished."[21]

36

Meanwhile, after parting ways with Bloody Mess, the Stepes continued to form bands: Inspector Gadget, Baldy Sour, the Angry Skinz, and on and on. "We had a lot of different names . . . but basically it was all the Stepe brothers with different singers," Barry explains. "In Peoria, there were very few other punk bands at the time. We formed a number of bands [just] so we could have more bands to play with at shows, and tried to create a real punk 'scene.'"[22]

"When Bloody left, we got Matt [Ralph] and Matt [Rousey] to sing for us . . . one of the first hardcore singing duos!" he adds. "Matt [Ralph] also played synthesizer, which added a unique element to our punk songs. . . . Matt [Rousey] later sang for the Outbreaks, which my brothers Chopper and Kyle played in. We also formed some other offshoot bands, like the River City Blues Breakers, a total blues instrumental band, and the Wildtones, a pop-punk band with C. P. singing. It was a very creative and prolific time for us. I can't believe all the songs we wrote, places we skated, and zines we made in just a few years."[23]

*   *   *

But of all the Stepes' bands, it was Caustic Defiance, formed in 1985, that would make the most enduring impression on Peoria's punk scene. With Barry on guitar, Chopper on drums, Doug "Happy" Chasteen on bass, and a new frontman in Brad Krohn of Pekin, the band played "simple, stupid, unabashed hardcore, the way God intended it," Chopper notes.[24]

"We met Brad and Doug through skating," adds Barry. "We had a good energy. . . . We were very positive and had a good sense of humor."[25]

By 1985, however, the hardcore formula had grown stale. Local scenes across the nation were fragmenting. In Washington, DC, the "Revolution Summer" movement symbolized a progressive awakening: a reaction against the tough-guy machismo that had infiltrated and poisoned a positive youth subculture. Moving beyond benefit shows, DC punks began using flyers and performances to organize actual political action, including a series of loud "punk percussion protests" outside the South African embassy in opposition to apartheid. Musically, bands were slowing the tempo, experimenting with melody, and growing more complex. This was the cauldron in which "emo" and "post-hardcore" brewed (and a band known as Fugazi incubated). But in Peoria, straight-edge hardcore was still novel, and Caustic Defiance was its creative expression.[26]

"The hardcore thing was changing," recalls Jim Moran, one of the Stepes' good friends. "Some bands were going metal; some were going more artsy. But Caustic Defiance . . . that was their whole purpose: keeping the flame alive."[27]

A seventeen-song demo tape titled *Enough Talk* soon emerged from the depths of the Stepes' basement. "[It] was basically dubbed off two tape players, with a photocopied cover and lyric sheet," says Barry. "We made about thirty or so, and sent out a bunch for reviews to fanzines like *Maximum RocknRoll*. We sold a few to our friends and at some of the shows. But it was never mass-produced."[28] (In 2014, it finally saw official release on 7" vinyl by Kangaroo/Way Back When Records.) *Enough Talk* was a Peoria milestone: the first "official" release of original recordings by a local punk band—and it made a profound impact on the small circle who heard it. David "Flea" Wagner explains:

> I was a pretty miserable kid. . . . I was different, but had no clue what that meant. When I got to high school, my best friends John Mulgrew and Shawn Walsh had both been living in Texas, where they got turned onto hardcore. We were walking to Godfather's Pizza from the Richwoods football game . . . and Shawn had a boombox and a Caustic Defiance tape. They told me these guys were from East Peoria, of all places. I had been getting into punk music like the Sex Pistols and Dead Kennedys . . . but to hear that music that night—*my first hit of real hardcore!* It was full of feedback and hormonal angst. "Ignorance is Bliss" was the track I remember. By the time I got to Godfather's, I knew who I was: that I was not alone in this world. It was like my first awakening.[29]

Eventually the local press began to pick up on what the Stepes and their friends were doing. On July 30, 1985, the Caustic Defiance foursome found themselves on the front page of the *Peoria Journal Star*—a large photograph of the band (and their skateboards) atop the Stepes' half-pipe sprawling over the headline "Punks Live on 'Straight Edge.'"

"Homemade xeroxed 'stickers' abound: 'Battalion of Saints,' 'America's Hardcore' and the obvious Suicidal [Tendencies] and [Circle] Jerks bootleg jobs," observes Brad Krohn of the iconic image. "Indys and Converse everywhere, t-shirt sleeves as wristbands, and Chop's jeans read both 'Straight and Alert' and 'RKL' (Rich Kids on LSD)."[30] The ironies were real.

"That's when punk rock really blew open in Peoria: when the Stepe brothers show up on the front page of the *Journal Star* with their straight-edge thing," says Joe Borsberry. "It drew attention to them and their skateboarding."[31]

"We never thought it would make the front page," adds Barry. "We got a lot of phone calls because of it, and it was all very positive."[32]

The public's goodwill was short-lived, however. The very next day, GG Allin came to town.

CHAPTER 4

The Underground Goes Aboveground

> Peoria used to be used to test-market things. Then the economy col-
> lapsed. Peoria turned so conservative that Ozzy [Osbourne] was almost
> banned from playing here. An underground scene started who knows
> when with a few scattered small shows with mostly local bands. The
> underground went aboveground in late July 1985 with front-page
> newspaper coverage and GG Allin's feces. The rest is history . . .
>
> —*Livin' in Peoria* compilation cassette

His story is so extreme, it's hard to believe it's real. The name on his birth certificate was, literally, Jesus Christ: apparently his father believed his newborn son would be some sort of messiah. His older brother, Merle, pronounced it "Jee-Jee," hence the name he would propel into infamy. In his personal essay "The First Ten Years," GG Allin writes of growing up in a log cabin in the woods, under the thumb of an unhinged, abusive religious fanatic: "We lived in darkness. Father hated light. Air was suffocated in eerie tensions, filled with violence, despair and endless destruction. We were more like prisoners than a family. . . . [Father] always had planned to kill my brother and I, then commit suicide with mother. This was brought to our attention on many a blistering occasion."[1]

Story after story lays out a horrific upbringing—an unsettling foundation for the violence, crime, misogyny, drug abuse, and sexual deviance that would become GG Allin's calling card, as a performer and in life. Declaring himself "the last true rock and roller," he set out to reclaim rock as a subversive art form, and an army of "scum-rock" devotees would argue he did just that. To almost everyone else, however, he was a degenerate whose despicable behavior deserved the loathing it engendered—a state of affairs GG appeared to savor.

It was Barry Stepe who introduced Bloody Mess to GG Allin, by way of a single he had received in the mail for review in his *Primitive Noise* zine. "He hated it, but I loved it," Bloody recalls. "And so I wrote [GG] and we became buddies."[2]

"The Stepes didn't care about GG, but Bloody connected with the wild boundary-pushing right away," adds Mike "C. P." O'Russa. "The next thing I remember, he started talking about how GG was going to come to Peoria."[3]

After parting ways with the Stepes, Bloody Mess had joined Emerald, a heavy metal band that mixed originals with Metallica and Motörhead covers—"almost like the Misfits but a little harder," he explains.[4] It was the height of the hair band era, but Bloody's stint as a metal frontman proved brief, and he quickly returned to punk rock. Still upset over his firing from Chips Patroll/Unaccepted, he resolved never to let it happen again. "From then on, I always put my name in front of everything. I started a band called Bloody Mess and Hate. Our inspiration was the band Fear—we'd just get drunk and have fun. That was another whole crazy era."[5]

And so it was that on Wednesday, July 31, 1985—one day after Caustic Defiance landed on the front page of Peoria's newspaper proclaiming the virtues of straight edge—a mostly unknown GG Allin kicked off his first US tour at a VFW hall in the small village of Creve Coeur, across the river from Peoria. It was the local punk scene's first "hall show"—but that is not how it would be remembered in the years to come.

At this point, Peoria's embryonic punk scene could be split into two camps: the skateboarding, straight-edge high school kids, led by the Stepes and Caustic Defiance, and the sex-drugs-and-rock-and-roll nihilism of Bloody Mess and Hate. These dual and seemingly opposing energies would serve as the two opening acts for GG Allin's infamous performance, as well as a rough demarcation of the audience. (And similar splits would characterize the Peoria scene for decades.)

"The show was set up almost like a wedding," laughs Jim Moran. "There was the straight-edge side . . . and then there was Bloody and all his druggie friends on the other side."[6]

"GG was walking around with a jockstrap on," Bloody nods. "I was the first kid in Peoria with a big rooster Mohawk. And we had a drag queen and a few other weird people in our group. But there were more of them than us."[7]

With Hate's lineup in continuous flux, Bloody was the only constant member. Ironically, the version of Hate that opened for GG Allin included none other than Steve, Chopper, and Barry Stepe. That the latter two also played in Caustic

Defiance the very same night was proof that the straight-edge-vs.-druggie dichotomy was at best a loose and ambiguous distinction. "We'd kind of reconciled a little bit," Bloody recalls of playing with the Stepes again. "I'm not the kind of guy who holds grudges very long. But we never spoke about it. It was such a small scene at that time."[8]

With GG Allin only beginning to explore the nauseating depths to which he would sink for shock value, that night's public defecation—quite famously, his first ever onstage—was premeditated and by design. "I was with him when he bought the Ex-Lax," Bloody recounts. "Unfortunately, he ate it hours before the show, so he constantly had to hold it in or he would've shit before he got onstage."[9]

"Soundcheck involved him walking around the hall with the mic in his pants, broadcasting his farts," describes Caustic Defiance frontman Brad Krohn. "Everyone else was cracking up . . . but I was tripping out that I had to use that mic later for our set. In desperation, I found an old gardening glove behind the VFW and tried to sing with it over the mic, but it didn't work. I finally said 'fuck it,' barebacked the mic, and somehow didn't die of VD."[10]

Caustic Defiance opened the show with a characteristic set of blazing hardcore, while GG cut a provocative figure stalking the crowd in his satin bathrobe and trademark jockstrap—the words "EAT ME" scrawled in black on its waistband. Bloody Mess and Hate played next, mixing punk covers of the Feederz, Flipper, and Fear with originals like "Who Needs Jesus" and what would become their de facto theme song, the participatory "Spit on My Face."

"It was supposed to be over-the-top obnoxious," Chopper explains. "My brothers and I—with our shared warped sense of Stepe Brother humor—played it tongue in cheek, while I think Bloody was really in his element and took it a bit more seriously."[11]

After Hate's set, most of the crowd retreated to the parking lot; they were wise to what was coming. GG's set featured no backing band—just a cheap boom box, that nasty mic, and a cassette tape of instrumentals. His punk rock karaoke act lasted all of two songs. In a colorful 2013 blog post, Bob Gordon summed up the scene:

About 20 to 25 people were left in the building when GG started playing. Someone called me outside, and when I was just about to step out my buddy C. P. [Mike O'Russa] grabbed me by the arm and yelled, "*Bob, get in here! He's shitting on stage! Oh my God, he's really shitting!*" . . .

41

I ducked back in and the pungent whiff of punk rock poo blasted my nostrils. I mean, crap was everywhere! Floor, GG, chairs, microphone. What fans were left ran for the door holding their noses. Well, craggy and tumble-worn VFW guys don't take too kindly to a half-naked punk rocker shitting on their property. They came flying out of the kitchen and behind the bar ready to kick his ass. The only problem was, nobody wanted to touch his ass! The police were called and GG was shooed out the door like a muddy dog.

In the parking lot, the straight-edge kids were completely freaked out and fled instantly. I remember just standing there thinking: "This is one of the most disgusting things I've ever seen!" A grown-ass man lip synching in a jock strap covered in shit—but it was still more entertaining than a local Van Halen cover band.[12]

After the show, GG took off for Texas and ended up in the hospital with blood poisoning, while Bloody landed in jail on unrelated drug charges. But the two remained close. In 1986, Bloody hit the road with GG on his first "Hated in the Nation" tour, "doing drunken spoken word ramblings," and he brought Hate along for GG's second national excursion.[13] The road, in this case, was a sordid whirlwind of extreme alcohol and drug abuse, bodily fluids and public sex acts, trashed gear and smashed chairs, blood-covered bottles and broken glass, late-night visits to porn shops and seedy bars—and a host of canceled shows. The word had spread that GG Allin was nothing but trouble.

Bloody Mess and Hate's nine-song demo tape—allegedly "produced" by GG Allin in 1986—"was intended to be Peoria's first 7" punk record and my very first record," Bloody says, "but it just never happened." Instead, the recordings were circulated on cassette—the more economical option.[14]

Meanwhile, GG Allin would return to Peoria more than once over the years—including a November 1986 basement show that found him punched in the face—before a heroin overdose in 1993 sealed his fate. He remains a uniquely reviled and inexplicable figure in punk history, and his show in Creve Coeur remains widely discussed even today. (GG's tainted microphone, sealed in a plastic bag, ended up on eBay years later—Bloody sold it to a private collector.) But his performance, however memorable, was less than inspirational to Peoria's nascent punk scene.

*　*　*

In sharp contrast to GG Allin was the positive hardcore movement adopted by the Stepes and their circle of friends. "We were pretty sincere with the whole straight-edge thing and this idea of community," notes Mike "C. P." O'Russa. "We were totally into Youth Brigade, Minor Threat, 7 Seconds and these bands focused on positive change."[15]

The Better Youth Organization (BYO), created in Los Angeles by Shawn and Mark Stern of Youth Brigade, was in part an effort to counter the sensationalistic (and generally negative) accounts of punk rock in the news media. More than a record label or promotional vehicle—though it was both—BYO was a sincere and constructive illustration of alternative youth culture in the age of Reagan. Its ethos was inscribed in the liner notes of Youth Brigade's debut LP: "that 'youth' is an attitude, not an age, and that every generation has the responsibility to change what they feel is wrong in the world."[16]

It was a resonant message, inspiring the creation of local chapters across the country. "We formed the [Peoria Area] BYO to give us a little more cred in putting on shows," says Barry Stepe. "We had the opportunity to get 7 Seconds from Reno, Nevada, to headline a gig. . . . We formed a loose group who worked together to create flyers, get equipment, find the hall and promote the show. Everyone did their part for the scene."[17]

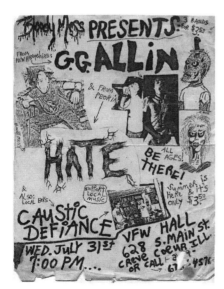 

Figure 5. Flyers for GG Allin's VFW hall show in Creve Coeur and the 7 Seconds show at Owens Center in Peoria, 1985. Bloody Mess organized GG Allin's notorious visit, while the Stepes and their circle of friends promoted the 7 Seconds show as the Peoria Area BYO (Better Youth Organization). Courtesy of Bloody Mess and Barry Stepe.

Formed in 1980, 7 Seconds were one of the first US punk bands to self-identify as "hardcore." Their debut album on BYO Records, *The Crew*, had been out for about a year when the band pulled their van up to an indoor ice skating complex in Peoria, towing their equipment behind in a trailer. It was August 19, 1985, and the Peoria Park District, which managed the facility, was unwittingly about to host its first punk rock show. Fortunately, word of the GG Allin debacle in Creve Coeur three weeks earlier had not yet seeped into the public consciousness.

Shows at Owens Center took place not on the ice rink itself but in a large adjacent room available for public rental—drab and unremarkable but for the neighboring assemblage of youth hockey players and their cheering parents, unaware of the rabble-rousing going on next door. There was no stage. Bands played on the floor beneath fluorescent lights and a generic drop ceiling, attempting to reimagine the austere setting as Peoria's first punk club.

Caustic Defiance opened that first show at Owens Center. And despite the main act's late arrival, 7 Seconds were enthusiastically received by a crowd of teens emulating the slam dancing they'd witnessed in the documentary *The Decline of Western Civilization.* "It was a great show!" Barry exclaims. "We had maybe 100 people show up, but that was a big deal at the time."[18]

In 7 Seconds frontman Kevin Seconds, Peoria's punks had found a kindred spirit; he later described his Nevada hometown in terms they often applied to their own. Reno, he says, was "very conservative, and there wasn't much going on. We decided that this was the perfect setting to start a punk rock band [in], so that's what we did."[19]

After the Owens Center show, the two bands crashed at C. P.'s house, where they watched skateboarding videos and talked into the early morning. "Kevin Seconds sat patiently through a 2:00 a.m. viewing of *The Bones Brigade Video Show* and made occasional comments on [how] we had 'kidnapped' him," recalls Brad Krohn. "He literally stayed up all night answering our questions about hardcore."[20]

"My mom used to talk about it all the time," C. P. adds. "Waking up with half a dozen punk guys sleeping in various rooms and a tour van with a trailer in the driveway. Super-nice guys. . . . But Kevin Seconds just wanted to watch Madonna and Bono on Live Aid, which I had just marathon-taped."[21] (His U2 fixation was revealing of 7 Seconds' future direction, as 1987's *New Wind* would embrace a more accessible sound.)

Although GG Allin's Creve Coeur fiasco was more renowned, the 7 Seconds show was a much more powerful catalyst for Peoria's punk community. "I always thought [it] was the show that really turned the corner, from kids hanging out, to kids organizing *real* shows—no longer just house parties," explains Doug Love, who found inspiration in the DIY ethos that was beginning to gain a foothold in Peoria.[22]

"The scene definitely began to grow more quickly after that gig, and we met a lot of new people who got involved," adds Barry. "It really seemed to bring everyone together."[23]

From late summer 1985 to the early spring of '86, Owens Center was a sporadic if unlikely venue for Peoria punk shows. In addition to local bands (such as Bloody Mess and Hate, Caustic Defiance, Concilatory [*sic*] Resentment, Unclaimed Luggage/Constant Vomit), midwestern hardcore legends Toxic Reasons (originally from Dayton, Ohio) played there, and Glenn Danzig's post-Misfits act "Samhain was actually booked there," Bloody notes, "but I couldn't put the money up, so they canceled." Owens Center was no CBGB, but it offered an alternative to house shows. "It was such a sterile environment, but it allowed for a lot of really good slam dancing and pits to go down, which was fun."[24]

As with most DIY punk venues, however, the shows at Owens were not built to last. Eventually the volatile mix of youth hockey and teenage punks proved untenable. At one show, when park district staff shut off the power during Bloody Mess and Hate, the crowd staged a "sit-in" in protest. "There was a pit going, and there was also hockey practice going on," recalls Bob Gordon. "Some parent came out with their kids . . . saw all these kids moshing, freaked out and called the cops."[25]

"Nobody left," Gordon adds.[26] Instead, they all sat down. By the time the police showed up, the self-styled protest had run its course, and the show was moved to a barn in rural Metamora, a twenty-minute drive, where the Kenosha, Wisconsin punk band 10–96 "played in the freezing cold to a small but fun crowd."[27] That, however, was the end of punk shows at Owens Center. The incident was news enough to make the *Peoria Journal Star* under the headline "Language, Spitting Close Concert Early":

> Peoria Park District police stopped a punk rock concert at about 8:45 p.m. Saturday after a band and an audience of about 150 young people at Owens Center allegedly began using excessively foul language and spitting on each other.

Lyrics sung by the band "Hate" were also instrumental in the decision. . . . The loudness of the music also interfered with play at a nearby youth hockey game.[28]

Peoria's underground had surfaced once again, even as punk's primal edge was beaten back by the more conventional outlet of youth sports. It was sanctioned versus unsanctioned—a pair of aggressive activities vying for public space. And hockey won.

That the primitive battle cry of Bloody Mess would attract willing participants ("We hate the human race / Come on everybody / Spit on my face") might seem a dubious distinction. But it contains another narrative as well: as a symbol of the collective self-loathing that can chip away at dignity in a hard-luck town, even as the young and naive attempt to wrestle free of such a fate. In Peoria's punk scene—whether Bloody's yin or the BYO's yang—this was a mission that could be agreed upon.[29]

CHAPTER 5

I Was a Mutant Cornchip . . .

How about the nicknames? Bloody, Chopper, Happy, Flea, Butthead,
Sparky, Jez, Little Ted, Flaming Ed, Big Hair Tim . . .

—Teresa Ozuna

"The Peoria-based chain Co-Op Tapes & Records, once 28 units strong, officially went under on June 30, 1984. Yet the Co-Op name continues as the chain rebuilds under franchise owner Dan Burich, fighting a depressed regional economy and competition from national retailers."[1] Thus began the account of Co-Op's comeback in *Billboard* magazine on December 21, 1985.

Burich owned a trio of Co-Ops in the Quad Cities—one each in Davenport, Iowa, and Rock Island and Moline, Illinois. These were independent franchise stores, unaffected by the chain's bankruptcy. The Peoria location, however, had no such luck. When it closed, Burich purchased what remained of its inventory and hauled it up to Rock Island, where twenty-three-year-old Bob Herington spent much of his summer in the store's basement sorting through it all.

Fourteen months later, when Burich decided to resurrect the Co-Op name in Peoria, Herington was tapped to launch the store. "The guy who was going to run it backed out at the last minute," Herington recalls. "They were like, 'Hey, you want to run a store?'"[2] So he moved to Peoria.

The new Main Street Co-Op Tapes and Records opened its doors late in the summer of 1985, just one block from the original flagship store. Peoria's cultural misfits once again had a public gathering place. "That era when Co-Op reopened, it was like: 'Oh my god, I don't have to go to Bloomington anymore to buy this stuff,'" says Bob Gordon. "And Co-Op becomes this central hub for everything."[3]

"It was like our coffee shop . . . our hangout," suggests Jim Moran. "Bloody [Mess] worked there, Bob Gordon, Russell Hopkins, Bob Herington . . ."[4] In the pre-internet cultural landscape of middle America, they were the tastemakers and gatekeepers for those who sought more than the latest Wham! single. "These guys let us hang out all day, skateboard down the aisles, and basically buy nothing," adds Mike "C. P." O'Russa. "They sold our zines and tapes on consignment, and generally allowed us to use the store as our clubhouse. It was the epicenter of the Peoria scene, as Wax Trax was in the early '80s for kids in Chicago."[5]

With Owens Center no longer available for punk shows, the Peoria scene found itself in a familiar position: between viable venues. "There were a lot of shows in the Quad Cities," Herington recalls, "or I'd go down to Bloomington or Champaign. It just wasn't happening as much in Peoria." But Herington was in a position to help—and that's how a small, empty storefront next to Co-Op briefly came to host live music. "We weren't doing anything with it, so we decided to do some shows."[6]

"There were no lights, no stage, and the PA sucked, but there was room for people to dance and move around," says Bloody Mess. "It was like a New York warehouse/loft kind of vibe. It was weird, but I liked it."[7]

Stevie Stiletto and the Switchblades (from Jacksonville, Florida) came through Peoria on tour and played the Co-Op space alongside hardcore legends Life Sentence (Chicago), while Bloody's friends 10–96 (Kenosha) made another Peoria appearance: an intense evening fueled by whiskey and psychedelic mushrooms, which ended in dramatic fashion the following morning with Bloody in the ER getting thirty-two stitches, having sliced his arm open on a beer bottle. The Not (Boston)—the same moddish-punk band that played the Stepes' backyard half-pipe a year earlier—also returned to play Peoria. "The Not [at Co-Op] was my very first punk rock show," recalls Dollface singer-guitarist Matt Shane. "They sounded like the Jam. . . . They blew my mind."[8]

Although Main Street Co-Op hosted only a handful of shows, its connective influence on Peoria's early punk scene can hardly be overstated. And it was equally significant to a range of other eighties subcultures, both underground and otherwise. "We did all these in-stores with touring metal bands

. . . BulletBoys, Winger, L.A. Guns, Cinderella . . .," Herington says. "You look at the pictures now and think, 'Wow, people really dressed like that. We really did have a hundred dudes shopping there who wore spandex pants!'"[9]

It was indeed another time—an age in which fashion (or anti-fashion) proclaimed one's tribal identity. "People definitely dressed more like the music they were into," Herington continues. "You could really distinguish: these were punks, and these were goths, and these were metalheads. You don't see that so much anymore."[10]

"There was no internet, no Hot Topic," adds one Peoria scenester. "A t-shirt used to mean something because you had to actually work to get your hands on it."[11]

In 1986, hair metal was at its farcical peak. Punk had turned to post-punk, "college rock" was gaining traction, and "alternative" bands like R.E.M. were on the cusp of major-label stardom. "Things were starting to get more organized," says Bob Gordon. "That was the whole *Pretty in Pink* crowd, the 'cornchip' crowd. . . . I would work [at Co-Op] Friday and Saturday nights and play all the stuff they wanted to hear: Love and Rockets, the Cure . . . all that stuff."[12]

*   *   *

Cornchip. If you didn't grow up in Peoria or the Quad Cities in the late eighties, you've probably never heard the word outside of a Frito-Lay commercial. Yet somehow, this regional colloquialism became oddly ubiquitous across central Illinois, a label for anyone outside the cultural mainstream in the waning years before grunge swept the nation. As it migrated from high school to high school, various urban legends developed around its provenance, obscuring its true origins.

In fact, the word was coined in the cafeteria at East Peoria Community High School in 1985 by a close-knit female foursome who hung around with the Stepes and Caustic Defiance. The "Caustic D girls," as they were dubbed, would also become the original "Mutant Cornchips." Stacey Donovan (East Peoria, class of '86) explains:

> Amy [Berigtold] was the one who noticed she had a Frito that looked really weird. We called it a *mutant cornchip*. . . . We were talking about how "Mutant Cornchip" sounded like a comic book character and began thinking of titles, i.e. "The Mutant Cornchip Seeks Revenge." Janelle [Ryan] wrote one of the lines on a lunch tray and after that, we always wrote some random Mutant Cornchip

statement on a tray at lunch. . . . After a while, stupid kids at [East Peoria High School] started calling *us* mutant cornchips.[13]

It began as a pejorative of high school silliness—"what the jocks and creeps yelled at us . . . as we walked the halls," adds Tracey Bettermann Wetzstein. "None of us ever called ourselves 'cornchips!'"[14] It was a catchall phrase slung at anyone with a different haircut, who dressed unconventionally, or whose tastes were considered eccentric or weird. In the punk scene, however, the word "cornchip" was initially met with indifference or derision. "I hated that," chuckles local musician Jeff Gregory. "We all hated that."[15]

But as it migrated across the Illinois prairie, many so-called cornchips began to self-identify as such, reclaiming the slur as a badge of honor. And so this throwaway cafeteria joke became uniquely Peorian slang, its cultural import enduring long after the original "Mutant Cornchips" had graduated and moved on with their lives. As Kate Dusenbery (Peoria Manual High School, class of '91), recalls,

> I don't know exactly how the absurdist term caught on with the jocks and stoners, but I do know that by 1987, it was being jockeyed around the playground at Calvin Coolidge [Middle School in Peoria]. All of a sudden, if you listened to new wave (or in my case, the Stray Cats) and wore a lot of black . . . people followed you home from school screaming "CORNCHIP!!!! CORNCHIP!!!!" It was as perplexing as it was irritating. . . . Suffice it to say, if you were in any way different or weird . . . you were most definitely a cornchip. And, relentlessly, the school bullies made sure you paid dearly for your difference.[16]

It is perhaps no coincidence that, in the same year that birthed the word "cornchip," a movie then hitting theaters would come to define the high school narrative of a generation. Like *Pretty in Pink* (released one year later in 1986), *The Breakfast Club* was a John Hughes script, rich with poignant observations on the eternal struggle of teenagers to be understood. The film is not without flaws, especially in hindsight—among other concerns, it reflects a disturbingly misogynistic worldview—but it was an affecting allegory for its time. "A lot of people felt like it spoke to us," explains Eric Kingsbury (Illini Bluffs High School, class of '87). "It was shot in Chicago. Everyone in our high school world, in that generation, felt like [it] . . . in some kind of crude way, encapsulated the 'groups,' the social cliques [of high school]."[17]

In a similar coming-of-age spirit, the cornchip phenomenon offered a ticket to new worlds: an intersection of like-minded peers from different schools and different racial and socioeconomic backgrounds—and one in which women

Figure 6. *People*, pen and ink drawing by Juli Gittinger, 1987. Drawn during her senior year of high school, Gittinger's illustration depicts the various "cornchips"—new wavers, punkers, freaks, geeks, and weirdos—who came together at Fulton Plaza and Peoria's under-twenty-one dance clubs.

were a driving force. "As a black kid in East Peoria, I didn't find a lot of acceptance," notes Kimberly Luft (East Peoria High School, class of '85), who was affectionately known as "Sparky." "But my fellow cornchips always made me feel as if I was with my tribe."[18] For midwestern teenage misfits, cornchip camaraderie was a welcome respite from the demographic and cultural homogeneity they decried.

"[It] was such a GOOD thing," adds Joel Hess (Morton High School, class of '89). "I mostly grew up in uptight/lily-white Morton, Illinois. Meeting this incredibly diverse group of people was mind-blowing. . . . You could be or look however you wanted and it was cool. The more outside of the norm, the better."[19]

The coining of an expression, often by teenagers, for derisive ends—and its subsequent reclamation by the target—may not be all that uncommon. Think:

Bloody Mess being labeled a "skid," a "nickname in Chicago for a metal dude." Even the word "punk" (first used by Shakespeare in reference to a prostitute) has long been both a term of disparagement and a mark of pride, depending on the observer. Interestingly, another colloquialism analogous to "cornchips"— "megalos" or "megs," short for "megalomaniacs"—arose about this time in nearby Pekin, though it never really stretched beyond the city limits. "Cornchip," on the other hand, would follow a more expansive trajectory, taking root in another midwestern metro area some 100 miles to the northwest.

The Quad Cities (Bettendorf and Davenport, Iowa, and East Moline, Moline, and Rock Island, Illinois) were close enough to Peoria to share some cultural ties—including multiple Co-Op shops and the prevailing use of the term "cornchip." But how, exactly, did this distinctive slang make its way up the interstate into eastern Iowa? The answer can be found inside the era's teen dance clubs—where the aroma of Aqua Net was as distinctive as the crimped haircuts it held in place.

*　*　*

"The punk rock guys weren't into this at all, but [we] loved going out and dancing," recalls Stacey Donovan. "Confetti's was my favorite. At midnight every night, they'd do a countdown and yell 'Happy New Year' and throw confetti all over."[20]

The notion that teenagers, in all their awkward glories, need a place to go to stay out of trouble is perennial. In Peoria, alcohol-free clubs for the under-twenty-one set date back to the Kandy Kane, which hosted live music (and even boasted its own record label) for a brief time in the early sixties. Inevitably, more than a few curmudgeons would challenge the social value of the teen nightclub. An unintentionally hilarious 1962 review of a performance at the Kandy Kane, for instance, reveals an undisguised contempt for rock and roll—and by inference, the next generation—on the part of the establishment. Cue the *Peoria Journal Star*'s Jerry Klein: "A four-piece band begins slamming out a wild thumping number with a blast like atom bombs going off. The walls tremble as the sound roars out of a half a dozen speakers, amplified to the point of bedlam. And suddenly the cavernous dance floor is filled with writhing, gyrating, pulsating, undulating and hip swinging twisters who, when viewed en masse, look like Saturday night in Gomorrah, a voodoo bash in Haiti or Dante's vision of the tormented."[21]

52

Somehow, Peoria managed to survive this bout with adolescent purgatory. When the Kandy Kane closed its doors, the Static Attic (where the kids went wild for Jerry Lee Lewis in 1964) took its place, followed by the Teen Scene a couple of years later. Across the river in Pekin, the Let It Be Club popped up in the early 1970s, shortly after the Beatles released their final studio album of the same name. By the end of the decade, the grand opening of Tut's Tomb, Peoria's teenage disco, reflected the wave of Tut-mania that was then sweeping the na-tion—though its fleeting existence signaled disco's imminent demise as well.

Confetti's, the first of three Reagan-era teen nightclubs to open, was located in the former Second Chance, a north Peoria club that had hosted the likes of Cheap Trick, Budgie, and Van Halen several years earlier. It offered soft drinks on special nights designated for teens and quickly became known for catering to an underage clientele. Before long Confetti's had competition, as a second teen club opened in a space that had previously housed the Poison Apple, a once-popular adult disco (which also hosted soft-drink-only teen nights). Soon, Stage 2 was averaging 565 people on Friday, Saturday, and Sunday nights, according to a February 1986 *Journal Star* article: the club had "almost 18,000 square feet with a dance stage and two dance floors, game room, video, two bars, the world's largest selection of 8-foot-long Swatch watches (five), and at least 10,000 watts of lighting over the dance floors. . . . Top 40s, new wavers, punk, hard rock, you can tell what kind of music they're into by the way they dress."[22]

When Confetti's relocated and attempted to grow beyond the teenage market, most of its underage patrons migrated to Stage 2, and Confetti's soon closed its doors. In a game of musical chairs, Stage 2 then moved into the original Con-fetti's/Second Chance location, while the original Stage 2 became Thrills, yet another teen nightclub venture, and both operated in tandem for several years.

As legitimate businesses, these clubs naturally diverged from youth-run punk shows, to some degree seeking to cash in on teenage consumers. Never-theless, in mid-eighties Peoria, the teen nightclub (whether Confetti's, Stage 2, or Thrills) was as emblematic of youth culture as a John Hughes film: an ideal setting for smoking cloves or making out; for dancing to the latest hits or find-ing something new; for making one's tribal identity known through fashion. They were mainstream clubs yet generally welcomed the "alternative" scene (especially on "Alternative Night"); they were places where all kinds of kids— rich or poor, male or female, black or white, gay or straight or otherwise—could meet and mingle. Though to be sure, the cliques inevitably drew up their own

Figure 7. Stage 2, shown here ca. 1987, was Peoria's top under-twenty-one dance club in the late 1980s and early 1990s, a gathering place for teenagers from all over central Illinois. Courtesy of Sean Lervaag.

territorial positions: "cornchips under the stairs . . . metal kids over here, goths over there," and so on.[23]

For central Illinois's cornchips and alternative types—most of them isolated within their own schools—these clubs offered a potential point of connection. "There weren't enough of us in one place . . . so we kind of had to work to find each other," notes Eric Kingsbury, whose band Daed Kcis (pronounced "Dead Kiss") once played at Thrills. This was a rare opportunity, as live music was generally sidestepped in favor of DJs, who blended cutting-edge dance music with their favorite Top 40 hits.[24] As Matt Shane explains, "Wax Trax was huge in this town. Front 242, Nitzer Ebb, all the kick-ass dance music was being pumped out at Stage 2 and Thrills. When I worked at Co-Op, people would come in asking for [Chicago house pioneer] Frankie Knuckles. All these people were going to Chicago on the weekends, to Medusa's [dance club] . . . There were a lot of people from Peoria who were present for the birth of house music in Chicago."[25]

Dennis Cannon was one of those DJs—he started spinning records at Stage 2 in Peoria in 1985. When a second Stage 2 location opened its doors in Bettendorf,

Iowa, he took the opportunity to move up there and become *its* first DJ. And that appears to be how the word "cornchip" migrated to the Quad Cities—riding the coattails of Peoria's teen nightclubs.

* * *

Back in downtown Peoria, the old "Bum Box" was no longer earmarked for a small coterie of skaters—all the freaks hung out at Fulton Plaza. And if they weren't there, they could likely be found at the courthouse, another downtown hangout just a few blocks away. "It was goth kids, gay kids, punk rock kids, nerds and dorks . . . music people," explains Matt Shane. "It was a totally open, accepting scene. It incorporated the punk rock scene . . . but it was also like a gay scene. It was really cool."[26]

To be sure, the masses of kids congregating at Fulton Plaza had grown substantially since the Stepe brothers first made it their skateboarding home a few years earlier. "I remember going back there after I had been away at school," Barry Stepe recalls. "I was shocked to see the place filled with people. . . . It had definitely changed into a regular hangout scene on weekends."[27]

Among these various groups, solidarity was achieved through the shared experience of persecution for being different. But it wasn't easy being a freak in Peoria. "It was welcoming, but it was also intimidating," Matt explains. "And it was dangerous. Back then, if somebody wanted to fuck with you, they'd either punch you or call you 'faggot.' . . . There were lots of fights. You definitely had to take some punches if you were gonna hang out and be a cornchip."[28]

Cornchip. Despite isolated accounts of the word popping up in Arizona and New York (almost certainly brought there by Peoria transplants), it seems to have made its way only into the lexicon of two distinct locales. More than three decades later, both have Facebook groups dedicated to cornchip nostalgia: Peoria's "I Was a Mutant Cornchip and YOU WEREN'T!!!" and the Quad Cities' "I Remember the Corn Chip Days."[29] Here in the twenty-first-century cloud of social media—where the very idea of a regional colloquialism seems distant and quaint—the collective memories of big hair, black leather, and dramatic eyeliner live on in timeless perpetuity.

PART II

Building the Scene:
1986–1992

By the mid-1980s, Peoria's cornchips, punks, and other misfits had begun to find one another, whether at the area's teen dance clubs or at Fulton Plaza. Though the Stepe brothers and Bloody Mess remained involved on and off, the underground music scene slowly grew to encompass zines, promoters, and bands across a diverse range of punk/indie subgenres.

Stable venues remained nonexistent, but the Peoria scene began to draw occasional out-of-town acts and even some interest from national touring bands—though many others chose to drive right on through instead. Meanwhile, the veterans of Peoria's early punk scene, now out of high school, sought to broaden their horizons by moving to Colorado, California, or the nearby college town of Bloomington-Normal, effectively passing the torch to younger punks.

Nationally, the hardcore punk movement had flamed out. Minor Threat had broken up in 1983. The Dead Kennedys and Black Flag followed three years later. Because the music was so aggressive and militant, hardcore shows had routinely included a degree of violence, the admonishments of Minor Threat frontman Ian MacKaye notwithstanding. Some fights were thoughtless and petty, while others involved clashes between anti-racists and elements of the US neo-Nazi movement. Peoria's scene featured both varieties.[1]

This scourge of violence led many punks around the country—from the Bay Area, where the influential zine *Maximum RocknRoll* was published, to the scene around Dischord Records in Washington, DC—to push for clearer scene politics that included confrontational feminism, anti-racism, and anti-homophobia, as well as a united opposition to aggression at shows. The DC post-hardcore band Fugazi, formed by MacKaye in 1987, quickly became the standard-bearer for this message . . . eventually with direct implications for Peoria.[2]

In the meantime, the less macho and less abrasive independent music scene of the late 1980s allowed for vastly greater musical experimentation and invited a range of talented and quirky musicians to participate. This changed what played in Peoria and ultimately reshaped popular culture. Formerly underground "alternative" acts like Soul Asylum, Sonic Youth, R.E.M., and Nirvana achieved mega-success, while the Riot Grrrl movement ushered in a new wave of feminism, confronting sexism in the punk scene and beyond. As usual, Peoria arrived a bit late to the game, and with second- and thirdhand information—there may not have been any Riot Grrrls in the scene, per se. But the city soon caught up with the rest of the nation.

CHAPTER 6

Great Loser Bands and
Loosey-Goosey Backwash Gigs

> The Peoria scene, to me, was the Stepes, and that was about it. There
> was a guy named Doug Love who used to put on shows. And Bloody
> [Mess], of course. It seemed like they always wanted to come over here
> [Bloomington-Normal] rather than play in Peoria, because there were
> more people here that cared about it.
>
> —Jeff Wilson (of Naked Hippy, the Resinators, and others)

> We loved playing in Peoria. We'd drive to Peoria and hang out at Fulton
> Plaza, the courthouse and all that. One of my best friends [Becky
> Slane] was from Peoria, so I used to go hang out with her all the time.
> As a community, we were pretty tight.
>
> —Ed Young (of Semicids, the Resinators, and others)

For young people with cars, entertainment was not limited to Peoria proper. Chicago, St. Louis, and a half dozen other midwestern cities were within a reasonable driving distance, blurring the lines between scenes and tapping Peoria punks into national networks, at least periodically. Likewise, Peoria's music scene brought together youth from the surrounding region's small towns and rural communities: Bartonville, Chillicothe, Farmington, Lincoln, Metamora, Morton, Tremont, and more. Though at times resembling the childhood game of telephone, the growing scene offered central Illinois's youth access to new ideas and trends through face-to-face interactions—a step beyond what they could gather from zines and records.

High school kids provided a strong base for Peoria's punk scene, especially in its early years, but those kids grew up—and the scene grew with them. Eventually a network of expats spread across the country, scattering pieces of Peoria in Chicago, Atlanta, Los Angeles, Denver, San Francisco, Brooklyn, Portland, and elsewhere. Closer to home, this network loosely encompassed the major cities of central Illinois, including Springfield, Galesburg, and Champaign-Urbana. But it was in Bloomington-Normal where the ties to Peoria were strongest. Not only was it nearest in proximity, but the presence of a large state university ensured an endless sea of youth coming and going, including many Peoria-area punks.

"Caustic Defiance broke up basically because I went away to college," says Barry Stepe, who left Peoria for Illinois State University (ISU) in early 1986. "I soon started playing again in Bloomington-Normal with Naked Hippy. Chopper went on to play in the Outbreaks."[1] Both bands revealed the growth and development of punk rock in the post-hardcore era—as well as the routine straddling of the two music scenes.

"This was when we first started to learn how to actually play," notes Chopper Stepe. "I was still in Peoria . . . and some of these guys were from Bloomington. We had a firm grasp on the 1–4–5 chord progression and its offshoots . . . [and] a rudimentary idea of passing tones, etc. The songs actually have some melody. There's some highlights, and some cringes."[2]

In the spring of 1986, Naked Hippy played its first show—not in Bloomington-Normal but in Peoria—a benefit concert at Bradley University for the South African anti-apartheid movement. Just about every Peoria band in existence was on the bill that day. "We only played four songs," recalls Naked Hippy bassist Jeff Wilson. "The Outbreaks opened up . . . and we used their equipment."[3]

It was a unique affair, in that punk shows on the Bradley campus were relatively few and far between. Despite hosting larger rock concerts dating back to the sixties, Bradley stood aloof from Peoria's music scene—even as some of its own students were integral to it. They made their mark in spite of the general atmosphere on campus, where the "Bradley bubble" effectively served to isolate the student population from the rest of the city.

As a private university, Bradley was smaller than ISU, the state's oldest public university, whose property documents had been drawn up by Abraham Lincoln himself. And it was substantially smaller than the University of Illinois, an internationally renowned institution that drew students and faculty from all over the world. Because of this, Peoria lacked the "college town" vibe that infused both Bloomington-Normal and Champaign-Urbana, despite boasting a larger overall population. Absent that continuous influx of youthful energy—the kind that enables the building blocks of a local music scene—it's no wonder Peoria lagged behind.

Both Bloomington-Normal and Champaign-Urbana offered multiple venues for live music, radio stations that dared to play punk and post-punk, and record stores that supported the underground. But there were no comparable venues in Peoria. Even in the heyday of college radio, Bradley's public radio station confined itself to classical music. Peoria had Co-Op Records—though no punk haven, it was a modest oasis in a desert of stale rock and Top 40 drivel. But just a forty-five-minute drive down I-74, greener pastures beckoned.

"I spent a lot of time in Bloomington-Normal from the second I could get down there," recalls Becky Slane, who played bass in an early incarnation of Constant Vomit, a female musician in a space dominated by men. "The shows were better there. It was totally integral to the Peoria scene."[4]

Champaign-Urbana, though twice as far from Peoria, was also of central importance—a Big 10 destination with a campus bar scene hosting live music most days of the week. Its hometown bands, from Hot Glue Gun to Hum to Braid, played in Peoria and Bloomington-Normal and vice versa; Peorians would happily drive the ninety miles to shop at Record Swap (and if time permitted, Record Service) before catching a show at Mabel's. "I remember doing a lot of shows over there," affirms Jeff Wilson. "They had a better scene than us. So it kind of went Peoria, [Bloomington] and then Champaign."[5]

From shared band members to newly arrived college transplants, the Peoria and Bloomington-Normal music scenes were often and regularly intertwined. When Mike "C. P." O'Russa and Joe Borsberry graduated high school and left Peoria to join Barry Stepe at ISU in the fall of '86, they brought the satirical "puke rock" of Constant Vomit with them—and soon, their old friend signed on as their drummer. "Seeing the three of us perform was like going to the circus or a comedy club," Borsberry describes. "We were known for being entertainingly profane."[6]

Back in Peoria, Constant Vomit had released a handful of cassettes, but live shows were sporadic until the members' college years. Absurd stage props and drunken obscenity defined their distinctive brand of campus performance art, which extended mockery toward anything and everyone. "We made fun of ourselves the most," Borsberry laughs. "What we lacked in musical talent, we made up for with enthusiasm and [humor]."[7] The band's cartoonish repertoire was intended for entertainment more than offense (though it offered both), with lyrics often inspired by current events: "McMassmurder," for example, referenced a 1984 gun massacre at a California McDonald's. "Wake Up and Smell the Vomit," in contrast, depicted a routine dorm-room experience.

"We became pretty popular at ISU, mostly by putting on acoustic shows in the quad that would literally have 100 people sitting in the grass watching us," O'Russa explains. "We also played electric shows in our dorm, which we called the 'Puke Palace.' Constant Vomit became a lifestyle at ISU and was our calling card. It was a hilarious time for all of us."[8]

While the prolific Barry Stepe split his time among numerous bands, Naked Hippy stood paramount among them. Its self-titled LP—twenty-two songs put to tape on a single day in 1988—is an explosive shot of hardcore punk rock, issued on the band's own Smile or Die! Records the following year. Had it been released several years earlier, it might have secured the group's place in the hardcore canon, on par with the best of Minor Threat or Black Flag. Instead, Naked Hippy remains ripe for wider rediscovery, its lone record a lost masterpiece of the Midwest.

Semicids was Naked Hippy's slightly younger cousin, formed while the band's members were still in high school. Spraying minute-long songs like rapid-fire ammunition, they offered an equally ferocious take on hardcore. The two bands existed in tandem, sharing countless bills and laying a foundation for the rich DIY scene that took shape in Bloomington-Normal in the nineties. But punk rock in those twin cities dates back even further.

Another pair of bands, founded years earlier, were formidable influences on all who would follow. Both Dr. Butcher and the MDs and Nameless Dread were larger than life, comprising unique characters who successfully conjured wild performance art out of the flat midwestern landscape.

* * *

About fifteen miles northeast of Bloomington-Normal lies Lexington, Illinois, best known as a onetime stop along historic Route 66. That iconic symbol of freedom and mobility—the "Mother Road," as Steinbeck called it—defined the small town for decades, now replaced by a tourist-driven nostalgia for those glory days. Today, one can (quite literally) take a walk down "Memory Lane"—a mile-long stretch of the original highway turned interpretative walking trail, complete with refurbished 1940s-era billboards.

Toward the end of the seventies, right around the time Route 66's crumbling pavement was displaced by a brand-new interstate highway, a handful of Lexington youth were picking up instruments in spite of their lack of expertise, inspired to form what may have been the first punk band in all of central Illinois. Along with guitarists Tim Lindenbaum and Dan "Cube" Wilson, Dr. Butcher and the MDs (named for a schlocky B horror movie) included two brothers, drummer Patrick Dwyer and bassist Dennis Dwyer, better known as "the Dude"—a nickname that long predated *The Big Lebowski.*

"They were the first punk rockers [in Bloomington-Normal]," recalls Ed Young of Semicids. "The Dude and his brother were super-heavy into Devo, the Ramones and all that. Along with Jeff Warren and those cats, they were the early punks."[9]

"When I started, there *was* no scene," says Jeff Warren, who started playing punk rock in the early eighties under a slew of different names—most notably, Nameless Dread.[10] Beginning as a duo, he and drummer Mark Johnson infused punk's anarchic amateurism with avant-garde sensibilities, borrowing from Frank Zappa and Laurie Anderson as much as from the Sex Pistols. The result was a subversive but playful chaos, pure in its underground disposition. As Warren explains, "It's the wondrous discovery of music by somebody who doesn't know how to play. You don't know any of the rules—you just create like a child. . . . Everything was a discovery, and it usually came out of anger and sweat and energy. . . . It was like throwing paint against a wall."[11]

Dr. Butcher and the MDs were less artsy, more meat-and-potatoes, but shared with Nameless Dread an antiestablishment mindset and a theatrical bent of their own. "We were pretty wild," confirms Patrick Dwyer. "Our music was loud and fast, and we typically dressed the 'punk' style. We wrote our own music and basically just did our own thing."[12] One of Dr. Butcher's first shows, he recalls, took place in the tiny town of Girard, Illinois—an unusual gig that found the band cast in a high school play:

> They were supposed to have a punk band as part of the play, and they invited us down. At the time we had a lead singer. . . . He consumed a can of mushroom soup, came out onstage, and blew it out of his mouth as part of our act. . . . It caused quite a scene down there. One of the teachers got into a little trouble

because the parents thought it was too vulgar for high school students. The students loved it—they were yelling and screaming and everything else.[13]

Dr. Butcher and Nameless Dread were anomalies in their day—tempestuous punks among blues-based rockers and hair-metal acolytes, playing original music in a sea of cover bands. Joining them in bringing DIY to the masses was Toxic Shock, an all-female group whose "lack of expertise . . . didn't stop them from attempting to put a sound together," as the local newspaper wrote in 1983.[14] Additionally, there were hints of new wave in DiaTribe and the ska-influenced Uptown Rulers (featuring future members of the Jayhawks and Souled American) and, later, pop-minded alternative acts like Tricycle Thieves, That Hope, and the Something Brothers. An original local music scene was beginning to grow in Bloomington-Normal.

*   *   *

Powered by Reagan-era angst, Nameless Dread shows were confrontational "fight-or-flight" spectacles, describes band frontman Jeff Warren, differentiated by their highly visual performance art. "I remember thinking that if you had to pay to see a band, it ought to be something you've never seen before."[15] This stance fueled extreme performances that encompassed raw meat hanging from hooks, fake "blood" and "brains" splattered about, even "birth scenes [staged] on waterbeds in the middle of shows," he adds. "[We] would push the envelope so far, for what was socially acceptable."[16]

Seeking a home base for this artistic bedlam, Warren repurposed his loft apartment in downtown Bloomington into a makeshift venue called "Hell." Located on the fourth floor of the century-old Eddy Building, Hell soon emerged as a central hub for Bloomington-Normal's developing punk scene, hosting shows almost every weekend. Nameless Dread—now a trio with Diane Perris of Toxic Shock on bass—was at the forefront, passing the torch to the next generation. "These thirteen-year-old kids in leather jackets with Nameless Dread [painted] on them . . . they were the kids who became Semicids and the Outbreaks," Warren notes.[17]

With cheap rent, excess space, and little to no oversight, the Eddy Building—once home to physicians, attorneys, and other Bloomington professionals—became a center for starving artists and musicians. At age sixteen, Ed Young found a cheap apartment in the building and his band, Semicids, started practicing there—one of several acts that did so. "Our drummer, Rob Reed, lived there, and we got a space right next to his apartment. Jeff Warren and a bunch of artists lived there. . . . [It was] kind of a commune," Young laughs.[18]

After a couple of years, Hell gave way to a slightly more ambitious venture. Electric Coffee was a performance space, art gallery, and café on the second floor of the same building, run by an artists' collective that included Warren and his bandmates. The nonprofit cooperative, while it lasted, fostered a cross-pollination of artistic disciplines that was by then emblematic of the Eddy Building. "It was pretty amazing," Young says. "During the week you could go [and] there would be spoken word and free coffee. A guitar teacher in town used to bring students and let them perform. And then on the weekends, it was full-on punk rock madness."[19]

Once dubbed "the finest office building in Illinois outside of Chicago," the Eddy Building was indispensable to Bloomington's mid-eighties punk scene, offering a temporary autonomous zone for art-making and anarchy.[20] "You could get away with just about anything in there," affirms Jeff Wilson of Naked Hippy. "But then the place finally burned down."[21] It was St. Patrick's Day of 1990; the fire was deemed an arson. "Luckily, nobody was living there anymore," Young adds. "Semicids had an apartment in Normal and had started practicing in our basement. . . . We drove up and watched that fucker burn. It was really sad."[22]

Even as the Eddy went up in flames, Bloomington-Normal's most enduring music venue was going strong. Founded as a coffeehouse in 1967, the Galery (with one *l*) brought a taste of sixties counterculture to downtown Normal in the wake of the Summer of Love. Besides serving coffee and Chicago-style pizza (as well as the town's first draft beer; Normal was dry until 1973), it was a gathering place for artists, academics, and activists—a hub of activity encompassing folk, jazz, theater performances, poetry readings, art exhibitions, and the like. In the mid-seventies, amid the country's lingering hippie hangover, a second stage opened upstairs, and the venue's focus shifted to live rock and roll.

After a series of management changes and various business names (most notably Fink's), the Gallery, now with two *l*'s, reopened in 1988 under the auspices of Kup Tcheng. In addition to his day job as ISU's director of computer operations, Tcheng was an entrepreneur who took an active interest in fostering the local music scene, once declaring to the Bloomington newspaper that "a campus town without a good place for music is not a campus town."[23] Among his coterie of related businesses, Tcheng also owned Mother Murphy's (from 1985 to 1990), a record store and head shop just down the street—and another prime hangout for local punks.

Conveniently situated near the confluence of three interstate highways, the Gallery became a national destination for touring bands and a launchpad for local and regional acts, attracting showgoers from all over Illinois. Tcheng's son, Mike, had a punk band called the Free Radicals—"and that's probably how the Gallery ended up having punk rock bands," suggests Ed Young, whose Semicids played there many times. "It was really easy for everybody to just bounce in. There'd be several hundred people at some of these shows—it was incredible. We'd get Naked Raygun, Life Sentence . . . all these big bands. People from Chicago would come down, [from] Peoria, Champaign. The place was just fucking packed."[24]

*　　*　　*

Throughout the nineties, Bloomington-Normal was known far and wide for its incredibly fertile garage-punk scene—and Naked Hippy's Jeff Wilson was at the center of it all: "I started working at Mother Murphy's in '85, and I was really into the Cynics, Lyres, the Untamed Youth, all that shit. That's what I was into, so that's what we carried. We'd book all these cool garage bands at the Gallery. It was just good ol' rock and roll, you know. It was more fun to play that stuff than to play punk rock, I think."[25] Ed Young was a kindred spirit. "Max [Deutsch] and Brad [Christiansen] [from Semicids] were super into Minor Threat and Dischord, [hardcore] bands," he recalls. "I liked some of it . . . but I *really* liked '70s punk rock and '60s garage. MC5, the Stooges . . . that was more my thing."[26]

In 1990, even as Semicids and Naked Hippy were still active, Young and Wilson joined forces with some other heavy-hitter locals to form the Resinators—a Bloomington-Normal rock and roll supergroup. "We were just a garage cover band [at first]," Young explains. "We were doing 'Five Years ahead of My Time,' 'Action Woman,' a couple MC5 covers. . . . Everybody just dug the fuck out of it."[27]

Veering sharply from their hardcore roots, the Resinators were foundational in Bloomington-Normal's emergence as a nationally known garage-punk mecca. In addition, with Stevo Dobbins of Impetigo on guitar, the band's founding lineup reflected the habitual convergence of the local metal and punk scenes. Impetigo was a pioneer of the death/gore/grind-metal movement, world-renowned for pushing the extremes in both sound and subject matter but unique for its crust-punk influence. That was in part due to drummer Dan Malin, also of Naked Hippy, whose increasingly complex rhythms had pushed him away from punk toward metal.[28]

Malin wasn't the only Bloomington punk to go metal. Naked Hippy singer Shayson Clay went on to play in a string of metal bands, first with ex-Semicids guitarist Phil Karnats and Resinators drummer Tom Sparrow in Act of God, then with Stevo and Peoria transplant Ty Smith in Detest, a short-lived crust-core band, among other acts. He and Stevo then teamed up with ex–Naked Hippy guitarist Neil Hardesty (who had replaced Barry Stepe when he moved to Atlanta after graduating from ISU) in Church of Misery, later known as Insomnia— a doom-metal juggernaut that also included drummer Brett Fugate, a pivotal figure in Peoria's metal scene. Clay would also later join the Resinators . . . and on and on it goes, an intertwined, incestuous family tree of punk, metal, and garage rock ancestry. "We had a lot of bands," admits Ed Young. "That's one thing Bloomington-Normal was good for."[29]

The Resinators disbanded in 1992, but their reformation five years later— with former Peorian T. J. O'Brien replacing Stevo on guitar and a new drummer in Jered Gummere—signaled the staying power of Bloomington-Normal's fervor for loud, raucous, no-frills rock and roll. Between Mother Murphy's and the Gallery, and with Jeff Wilson as lead evangelist, a generation of punks came of age under this influence. Among them was Gummere, who later achieved indie rock success in Chicago as frontman of the Ponys, among many other bands. He calls Wilson "*thee* foremost Rock n' Roll guru there's ever been": "Just walking up all those crazy stairs at Mother Murphy's, you got the fever. You walk in and all the walls were covered in records curated by Jeff. He turned me on to so many records: garage rock, punk rock, '60s, '70s, psychedelic. He was probably the first person to play me 13th Floor Elevators. My record collection would be shit without him."[30]

Though barely out of his teens when he joined the Resinators, the multitalented Gummere was a scene veteran already, having sat behind the kit for both the Muggles and the Defilers while still in high school. The former played rowdy, fire-breathing punk rock à la the Damned; the latter were a scorching surf-rock trio. Both acts lit up central Illinois with their intense live shows, while other Bloomington-Normal bands like Chuck Seven and Teenage Timebomb were hatched from the same mid-nineties garage-punk incubator.

Most of these bands played in Peoria, and those influences no doubt rubbed off on their sister city. But because Peoria lacked anything like Mother Murphy's or the Gallery, it had less to offer—which in part explains its close ties to Bloomington-Normal. "The first shows I went to were probably at the Gallery," notes Brody Maag, a Pekin native and longtime stalwart of Peoria's punk scene. "Around that time, the late eighties and early nineties, there weren't a lot of shows in Peoria, other than metal shows."[31]

*   *   *

Eventually the Gallery was torn down to make way for a massive urban renewal project, but the Peoria and Bloomington-Normal music scenes remain inextricably linked even today. Young Peorians still head to ISU for college; bands continue to straddle the two areas; and for some, the bonds run even deeper.

When Brody's sister, Dallas Maag, called Ed Young to inquire about trying out for the Resinators, it was a no-brainer, Young explains, having seen her play many times in Rugg City and other bands. "I knew what she could do. Six months later, we fell in love."[32] The two played alongside one another until the Resinators finally broke up for good in 2009 (and later joined forces with another punk rock couple in Killshakes).

Likewise, when Jeff Warren married the younger sister of Dennis ("the Dude") and Patrick Dwyer, the founding fathers of Bloomington-Normal's punk scene became brothers-in-law—a familial thread connecting Dr. Butcher and Nameless Dread. And like so many of the early Bloomington-Normal punks, they're still kicking up musical dust decades later. As of the writing of this book, you can still find them—and a slice of their Peoria brethren—each summer at the Dude's "Route 666 Ranch" in rural Lexington, taking part in the annual festivities of Dudestalk, a beer-soaked celebration of rock and roll bacchanalia. (Its original name, Dude*stock*, was adjusted to distinguish it from a glut of post-*Lebowski* tributes.)

The Dude and "Cube" Wilson—the songwriting half of Dr. Butcher and the MDs—still play "loud, dirty, stupid and amped up" rock and roll in Demolition Derby, and they even do some Dr. Butcher songs. Jeff Wilson still pushes rock and roll records into the ears of central Illinois's youth, but now from his own shop, North Street Records—just down the block from Mother Murphy's, which celebrated its fiftieth anniversary in 2018. Jeff Warren continues to push the envelope in his own way, joining a rotating cast of old-school punks (including members of Semicids and Dr. Butcher) in a semi-improvisational experimental project known as Putin's Cock. All of this proves there's plenty of life left in old punks.

"The things I was writing about Reagan in 1980 certainly haven't gone out of style today," Warren notes. "In fact, they've come full circle and are more prophetic than ever."[33]

While the riches of Bloomington-Normal's DIY punk scene could hardly be summarized in a single chapter, its cameo in the Peoria story is an essential one. Perhaps most significantly, Bloomington-Normal's superior capacity for hosting touring bands was indispensable to many Peoria punks. It's no wonder it was cited as one of the 1990s' "Unsung Punk Hotbeds" in *The Official Punk Rock Book of Lists* by New Bomb Turks singer Eric Davidson, whose band played in both cities on numerous occasions. Davidson's terse recommendation mentioned the "great loser bands who never released much[,] . . . loosey-goosey backwash gigs from Chicago, and the great Mother Murphy's record store."[34]

CHAPTER 7

What Played (and Didn't Play) in Peoria

Chris [Hall] and Walter [Flakus] . . . lived outside of Peoria in their
formative years. [They] came to Macomb, started the band, went
through a bunch of different band members, and then decided that in
order to actually succeed, one cannot be from Peoria.

—Andy Kubiszewski (of Stabbing Westward)

Why would Dag Nasty, of all bands, come to Peoria anyway?

—Doug Love

Meanwhile back in Peoria, much of the original punk scene had scattered by
1987, off to college or elsewhere. The space next to Co-Op was no longer available for shows, and Bloody Mess sold off his soundboard, microphones, and
other equipment. Doug Love purchased Bloody's gear so he could promote
shows, embracing the DIY ethic that had made such an impact on him: "When
[Peoria band] Concilatory [*sic*] Resentment put out their cassette, I remember
being so amped up about it. And I had already bought the Caustic Defiance
cassette. So I thought, yeah, I want to do that, too. Things were happening . . .
and if you could get a band together, you could play out."[1]

With Bloody's gear, Love was now equipped to do shows (and soon had his
own band), but he lacked a venue. "I lobbied Thrills [dance club] and a few other
places . . . but they wouldn't have it," he recalls. "I kept looking for someone to
partner up with, and that's when I landed the ICC gigs."[2] Nestled high among
the river bluffs of East Peoria, Illinois Central College was the region's two-
year community college. As an ICC student, Love discovered he could secure
the gymnasium to host bands. The space was huge, the rent was cheap, and

the college even provided a stage and risers. "For the first time, bands weren't playing on the ground," he notes.[3]

Love's first ICC show, in March 1987, was a veritable showcase for the next wave of Peoria-area punk/indie bands. Though worlds apart musically, Kill City Boys, Daed Kcis, and All Desires were connected by more than local geography; each group represented an alternative escape route out of its midwestern confines, as well as a departure from the straightforward hardcore punk of the scene's early years.

Featuring two former members of Caustic Defiance and the Outbreaks—Chopper Stepe on guitar and vocals and Doug "Happy" Chasteen on bass—Kill City Boys signaled one response to hardcore's musical stalemate: punk rockers gone glam. Dressed in pseudo-drag and eyeliner, they were Peoria's own Hanoi Rocks or New York Dolls, mining much the same territory as Guns N' Roses, whose landmark debut would come out later that summer.

Today, Chopper downplays the band as "schlocky, cheesy-ass rock n' roll," but for Peoria punks, Kill City Boys represented more than a mere stylistic shift.[4] "In my opinion, they were the first 'legitimate' band to come up in the Peoria

Figure 8. After playing together in Caustic Defiance and the Outbreaks, Doug "Happy" Chasteen (*left*) and Chopper Stepe displayed glam rock influences in Kill City Boys. Here they are performing in the Illinois Central College gymnasium, ca. 1987. Courtesy of Doug Love.

scene," Doug Love suggests. "You could see the musical growth, the maturity. It was no longer three-chord speed punk. . . . It wasn't just about raw aggression or teenage angst."[5]

Daed Kcis embodied the gloomier side of Peoria youth, the "goths," echoing Bauhaus and the Misfits with deathly serious artistic ambitions. In an early bio, the band earnestly described itself as "a four-piece collection of thought and emotion . . . with an intense stage show . . . all about love, hate, bitterness, pain, laughter, boredom, and all those things that make life what it is."[6]

"I think we were full of ourselves a little bit," laughs frontman Eric Kingsbury. "We felt like big ideas mattered. We read a lot of books, and we liked the David Bowies of the world."[7] In a previous incarnation as the Wine of Violence, they had released a demo tape in 1986, but the band didn't really come together until Rockford, Illinois, transplant Matt McDonough signed on as drummer. That's when they became Daed Kcis.

"It was just . . . a name that sounded cool and seemed to fit. For me, it means a sort of social apathy that we are constantly up against," McDonough explained in a 1988 fanzine interview.[8] "To me, it means a kind of dark and screwed-up passion," Kingsbury added years later. "We used to joke that if you read our name backwards ['Sick Dead'], you got a good description of the scene in Peoria."[9]

"At the time, they were pretty shocking," recalls Matt Shane, who played with Dollface. "They were really angular and aggressive, but also kind of spidery. No power chords—they weren't metal . . . but they were kind of confrontational."[10]

All Desires aimed for a more uplifting commercial appeal, despite hints of foreboding in some of their original numbers. As the Duran Duran or Depeche Mode of Peoria's cornchip scene, the group's teased hair and dance-rock ambitions had some believing they could become stars at the national level. "They were way too good-looking and really good musicians," Shane notes, "into the whole Brian Eno/Japan [thing]."[11]

Led by vocalist Todd Clifton, who combined the showmanship of David Lee Roth with a heart-on-sleeve emotional presence, All Desires staged an impressive show, with catchy originals mingling with covers of INXS, the Cure, A Flock of Seagulls, and other '80s staples. "They were a really, really good synth band," notes Bob Gordon. "Great frontman—he could dance and pull in everybody."[12]

Glam, goth, and synth: in a larger city, these disparate acts might not have brushed elbows. But in Peoria circa 1987, a shared sense of "otherness" was enough to bind them.

*   *   *

While shows at ICC were well-attended, the college's cavernous gymnasium wasn't ideal for punk rock, nor could its availability be counted on. So when a potential new venue came to Doug Love's attention, he jumped on the opportunity. Tucked away in the village of Peoria Heights, the Juice Bar was a so-called dry bar, owned by a recovering alcoholic looking to attract new patrons. "Business was bad," Love recalls, "and he was desperate for an infusion of people."[13]

Throughout the summer of '87, the Juice Bar hosted shows on a weekly basis, and Love had a hand in most of them. The Peoria scene was growing and new bands were popping up, each different from the next. Along with Daed Kcis, All Desires, and Kill City Boys, the Juice Bar hosted local acts like Despondent Youth (skate punk), the Valley Dolls (trash/glam), Leviathan (thrash metal), and Love's own band, pavlovsdogs (post-punk/goth), as well as numerous touring bands, including Suburban Death Trip and Iowa Beef Experience (from Iowa), Dissent (South Dakota), and Dead Silence (Colorado).

At the same time, Love had become friendly with an up-and-coming band out of Western Illinois University in Macomb whose singer had spent some of his formative years in Peoria. "The goth/new wave kids took me in . . . introduced me to new types of music, and did weird things to my hair," recalls Christopher Hall of Stabbing Westward.[14] In the mid-nineties, the band's polished industrial rock would become a fixture of Chicagoland's post-grunge alternative scene, but "they were much more Cure-ish back then," notes Love, who brought the fledgling band to Peoria several times in 1987.[15]

Although Love was finding success as a DIY promoter, the work was all-consuming and often thankless. Between taking money at the door, running sound, and overseeing other details, he found little time to enjoy his own shows. With that in mind, he joined forces with T. J. O'Brien and Bob Gordon to form G.O.D. Productions, but the alliance quickly fell apart, as did Love's own band. There were other problems as well: sometimes the bands Love booked wouldn't show up at all, or the *wrong* band would show. Rights of the Accused was supposed to play at ICC in April 1987, for example, but some sort of bait and switch—"one of Chopper [Stepe]'s little pranks," Love suggests—brought Denied Remarks down from Chicago instead.[16]

Still, though his motivation was beginning to wane, Love pressed on. He was especially excited for a hardcore show at the Juice Bar in July, which he arranged through a series of long-distance phone calls to a fast-talking New York City promoter. "Johnny Stiff was supposed to send us the Asexuals, Life Sentence, Face First and Underdog as a package deal," Love recalls. "I was like *whoa, jackpot!* And then . . . nothing. They didn't show up."[17] The no-show appeared to jibe with Stiff's modus operandi, immortalized by the Dayglo Abortions that same year in their classic revenge song "Kill Johnny Stiff":

> We got gigs over here, we got gigs over there
> We got gigs everywhere, we ain't playin' nowhere
> Kill Johnny Stiff, do it now
> Kick him in the head, stamp him in the ground . . .[18]

It wasn't the first time Peoria had been stiffed, and it wouldn't be the last. If the old vaudeville phrase "Will it play in Peoria?" is a timeworn cliché, a more poignant metaphor may lie in what *almost* played Peoria: in the opportunities missed and potential unfulfilled.[19]

Just one year earlier, the city was slated as a stop on Black Flag's now-legendary final tour, along with SST labelmates Painted Willie and Gone. The show was scheduled for Expo Gardens—where the Who had played eighteen years earlier—but it fell apart when its young promoters balked at the bands' contract and rider. Though a bust, tour dates on the back of Painted Willie's *Live from Van Nuys* EP list June 18, 1986, as the Peoria show that could have been.[20]

But what didn't play in Peoria *did* play elsewhere. Up in the Quad Cities, Black Flag played two gigs on June 17 alone—the night before it was supposed to play Peoria—while the canceled Peoria gig found the band lingering in Iowa for an extra day. One week later, the band played its final show.[21] For Peoria, it was simply another missed opportunity.

Like Black Flag in 1986 (and Samhain before it), Dag Nasty—Washington, DC's preeminent hardcore band in the post–Minor Threat era—*almost* played Peoria in 1987. But its July 23 date with Naked Hippy, scheduled for a downtown American Legion hall, also fell through. Doug Love explains:

> I believe it was the morning of the show when a friend called: "Hey, I just want you to know that [a DJ from Thrills] and his friends are calling everybody in the scene and telling them the Dag Nasty concert has been canceled."
> *Why would they do that?* It had something to do with Thrills[, which] was either going to close, or they were going to cancel "Alternative Night" . . . and they wanted all the kids from the scene to come out to Thrills and support his [the

DJ's] gig. So I'm told, they spent a couple of days calling everyone they could think of and told them the show was off.

And really, it wasn't that hard to believe. Rights of the Accused didn't show up, and the Asexuals and Life Sentence didn't show up two weeks earlier. Why would Dag Nasty, of all bands, come to Peoria anyway?

Well, we didn't have cell phones, texting or computers back in those days. Getting mass information out was painstakingly time-consuming. What was I going to do in a few hours?

I asked my friend if he could call some people and let them know it was on. I don't know if he did or not; I don't remember seeing him at the venue. Then again, that whole day was kind of a nightmarish blur.

I called Dag Nasty's agent and told him what was going on. He, like me, couldn't contact the band; again, no cell phone, no texting, no computers. They were in a van driving across America. The only way I was going to hear from them is if they called me at the American Legion or when they showed up.

About thirty kids showed up for the concert. None of the usual help was there. I was trying to set up the PA and take money at the door. To that end, it was obvious I had burnt my own bridge.

Brian Baker of Dag Nasty did call when they were close to town. I tried to explain the situation. As you can imagine, they were perplexed. They said they'd come to the hall and check it out for themselves.

They did. And they left.

That was it. It was over. I was heartbroken; and it was my birthday, to top it off.[22]

Adding to Love's disappointment, the Juice Bar was finished as a concert venue—the crowds "get too rowdy," claimed a club spokesperson in Bradley University's student newspaper.[23] Between that and the no-shows, the breakup of his own band, and numerous frayed friendships, Love grew despondent. "There's a point where you think, *I've done all this work . . . and this is it? This is what I get?* There was a sense of hurt . . . so I did not intend to do any more shows."[24]

As it turned out, Love had one final show left in him. Ironically, it would be his greatest accomplishment as a promoter, forever securing his place in Peoria punk folklore.

*   *   *

With the fall semester about to start, Doug Love found himself back on the ICC campus, and another chance to rent the school's gymnasium fell into his

Figure 9. The legendary Chicago punk band Naked Raygun played in the ICC gym in August 1987, a tumultuous yet well-attended show that was documented by a local Peoria TV station. Though listed on the bill, Stabbing Westward was unable to play. Courtesy of Doug Love.

lap. "I only had a couple weeks to put the whole thing together. I didn't know who to call, but I knew it had to be someone close."[25] Naked Raygun was Chicago's biggest punk band—and one of the top punk bands in the country—but it didn't tour often. So when the group accepted Love's invitation to come down to Peoria, it was a fairly remarkable coup. And this time, the band showed up.

August 28, 1987, would go down as a seminal moment in Peoria punk history, as the legendary Naked Raygun lit up the ICC gym with its melodic rock anthems. Though listed on the flyer, Stabbing Westward couldn't make the date. Peoria's own Smoldering Remains played in its place, while Bloody Mess assembled another new lineup of Hate, including Doug Love himself "fumbling around" on bass.[26]

"I came out in a suit and tie and opened the show to a cassette tape . . . doing Bing Crosby's 'White Christmas'—just a straight, normal version," Bloody recalls. "Then I left the stage and two minutes later, they introduced Bloody Mess and Hate."[27]

"[Bloody] came out in a straitjacket; it was all the Alice Cooper [shock rock] stuff you would want from him," Love adds. "I couldn't keep time to save my life—and I was getting spit on, *literally*."[28]

Hate's rousing "Spit on My Face" was by now a local tradition, and the slam-dancing crowd once again obliged. ("Singin' in the rain," Bloody called it.)[29] As luck would have it, Channel 19 News was also in the house. It was a slow news day in the dead of summer, and the station was rolling tape for a special feature on punk rock in Peoria. "There's this crazy footage of me wearing a straitjacket—all these people are spitting on me, and I'm kicking them in the teeth," Bloody notes.[30] For the media, it could hardly have been more of a spectacle, confirming viewers' worst fears about youth gone astray.

To add to the chaotic atmosphere, no one was there to run sound, so Co-Op's Bob Herington was asked to step in. "I'd never touched a mixing board in my life!" he laughs. "It was just total feedback and noise. . . . Then the lead singer for Naked Raygun [Jeff Pezzati] went, 'Dude, get out of the way'—and he ran sound after that."[31]

Bloody Mess and Hate were thoroughly unrehearsed, and after a handful of songs, the band's own drummer had had enough. "He just got up in the middle of the show and left!" Bloody exclaims. "I turned around, and there was no drummer."[32] Jim Moran recounts the tumultuous scene from the audience:

> We were all just kind of looking around. So Barry [Stepe] comes up onstage, and he tries playing drums. Then some kid in the audience comes up—he had to be fourteen at the oldest—and he was actually playing along. So [Hate] did a few more songs . . . and somehow at the end, Barry had gotten a guitar, and he was in the crowd doing this fake "heavy metal" thing. . . . [Guitarist] Kevin Offend kind of stomps out and grabs the guitar from Barry, like, "I'm taking my ball and

going home." And that was how the set ended. The Naked Raygun guys were going, 'What the fuck is this?'"[33]

"The Rayguns hated our performance," Bloody laughs, and the band's manager admitted as much to the TV camera crew.[34] In contrast, the Chicago band was tight and professional, the crowd appreciative and enthusiastic. "They were fantastic," Love says. "They were up on the riser, leaning over the crowd, putting the microphone down . . . and people knew the songs. Somebody said it was kind of the pinnacle—the high point of everything that had happened [in the scene] up to that point."[35]

"Hearing 'Rat Patrol' in the ICC gym," Amee Snyder Suydam agrees, "was truly classic."[36]

"It was the first time a lot of us saw a real headliner punk band," adds Kami Tripp LaVallier. "And [we] also saw how big the punk rock community was in our area."[37]

"More than the show itself, I remember being impressed at how this was like a *real show*," recalls Mike "C. P." O'Russa, who was back in town from Bloomington-Normal. "There was a stage and lots of people. It surprised me. Peoria had expanded."[38]

Channel 19's feature on the Peoria punk scene would air in three parts, its narrator introducing the first segment with a familiar piece of slang: "Call them by any number of names—punks, posers, cornchips—they're here with makeup, Mohawks, and black leather to have a good time."[39] If punk culture was depicted as decidedly foreign, the coverage was a relatively positive portrayal—"earnest journalism in ironic contrast to the subject," as one viewer suggests upon watching the footage years later.[40] "The best part is how they treat it like they're tracking the Yanomami [indigenous tribe] in the Amazon, but really it's just a bunch of kids in a gym," offers another.[41]

In spite of the turmoil, the Naked Raygun show was a high-water mark for Peoria's early punk scene. But it was the end of the line for Doug Love, who moved to Chicago after the fall semester. "I dropped out of the scene," he explains. "I lost some friendships I didn't intend to lose. I lost some money I didn't intend to lose. . . . I kind of felt that I needed to move on. I thought a fresh start was where it was at."[42]

CHAPTER 8

Public Enemy Number One

I don't think I ever saw him perform until I joined the Skabs. He had gotten pretty notorious for the GG Allin stuff and also for burning the American flag. He was Public Enemy Number One in Peoria for a minute.

—Matt Shane (of Dollface)

I once saw him piss on an adoring fan at a house party in Peoria. That freaked my shit.

—Max Deutsch (of Semicids)

Nothing worse than the smell of burnt pubic hair.

—Bob Gordon

Shortly after the Naked Raygun show in August 1987, Bloody Mess announced his retirement from punk rock and left Peoria behind. As he recalls,

> I was just tired of it. I moved to Colorado, to the mountains, and tried to put together a band like Crosby, Stills and Nash. . . . I wanted to do kind of a hippie sing-along thing—no violence, no negativity. . . . That lasted about six months.
> Then I had a party at my house. I was watching *The Grateful Dead Movie* with forty Deadheads, and I got drunk and just snapped. I put on Black Flag, and within minutes everyone was gone. I was like, *fuck everything*—I'm gonna go back to Peoria and raise hell.[1]

From his jet-black Mohawk and studded leather jacket to his very name, Bloody F. Mess embodied the antisocial trappings of punk. He was the guy with

Figure 10. Bloody F. Mess: Peoria's most notorious punk rocker, ca. 1985. Courtesy of Bloody Mess.

Glenn Danzig's phone number—a pivotal figure with an unquestionable mystique who booked bands, published fanzines, toured the country, and released a string of records that pushed the Peoria scene beyond the demo tape.

He's been in the trenches for decades and garnered some measure of respect for his achievements. But while subsequent generations of Peoria punks marveled from afar, few were compelled to follow in his footsteps. Perhaps his personality was too singular, his music overshadowed by the controversy he courted. Indeed, there's only one Bloody Mess.

By all accounts, he was a Jekyll-and-Hyde type—like a drug-fueled Whitman, he contained multitudes. "I was always a very contradictory personality," he explains, citing the symbol of his Pisces nature: "two fish swimming in opposite directions." Looking back, that duality may be his most distinguishing characteristic.

Most everyone who knew Bloody in his early years acknowledges his dark side. He's remembered by some as a pathological liar and manipulative sociopath who used his overindulgences as cover for bad behavior. "He could always get people to do whatever he wants," recalls one acquaintance. "He was one of those people who just goes and does it, and doesn't think about the consequences."[2] To some he was a thorn in the side of the scene; in fact, some who knew him prefer not to comment on him at all.

Yet many others are quick to add that he could be quite thoughtful, even gentle—that he was intelligent and fun and had great taste in music. "Bloody could rub people the wrong way, and yes, he was a hard-living, self-abusive dude," notes Mike "C. P." O'Russa. "But he was actually and remains a very sincere and caring person. He has changed over the years, yet has always stayed true to himself."[3]

"I'm not sure he was the most musically talented person in the world, but God, that motherfucker could promote," adds Jason Pellegrino of Leviathan. "He was an amazing showman. . . . I've never seen anyone who could network like he could."[4]

"He was into being the center of attention—pushing the limits and seeing how far things could go," recalls another associate. "He was a legend in his own mind."[5] There's no doubt that Bloody basked in the spotlight as a rock and roll frontman.

* * *

The mythology of Bloody Mess—how he became this larger-than-life character—could probably be the subject of its own book. "I thought it was fun to have a 'punk name' . . . and it just stuck," he says. "I think the persona created itself: 'Here's this crazy, manic guy screaming onstage . . . and his name's *Bloody Mess*.' But I never tried to do that on purpose. It just happened."

The oft-repeated story that he legally changed his name is just a rumor, Bloody acknowledges. On the other hand, reports that he dislikes being called by his birth name are accurate. That was reserved for his mom, he explains. "All my life, from the punk days on, it was always *Bloody*. And then when I started doing radio in 1999 . . . I created the Reverend Derek Moody [character] and became an actual minister. Those people in that world have no clue that I've ever even done music. So I've literally lived my life as three different people."

Born and raised in Peoria, Bloody says his dad was a right-wing, alcoholic business type, his mom "more of a saintly person." Growing up in a fantasy world, his escape was music. "I didn't play sports; I didn't work on cars; I was a music fanatic," he explains. "Country, pop, rock and roll . . . I was into all of it, but I was really attracted to things that were extreme: Alice Cooper, Kiss, Jim Morrison, Keith Moon, drug addicts and alcoholics . . . people like that."

Like many kids, he craved self-expression and enjoyed putting on a show. "I used to pretend I had my own radio station. I would put headphones on and pretend I was a DJ for hours." At eleven or twelve, he started a "band" with a friend, lip-syncing to records in his backyard. "We'd charge kids fifty cents, and we actually made money!" Bloody laughs. That lifelong penchant for showmanship was a critical ingredient in his formula for performance art:

> I liked people who dressed up onstage. I always thought it was boring to watch people get up there with their T-shirts and jeans and . . . look like everyone else. And, being from Peoria, I was into the history of vaudeville and all that.
>
> I think if you pay money to be entertained, let's be entertained—starting with the visual aspect. I'd be wearing women's underwear and a pink feather boa, striped shirts, flapper shoes, makeup, whatever . . .

Like his taste for theatrical excess, Bloody's affinity for mind-altering substances developed early on. "I was the kid that grew a beard really easily . . . so I could get alcohol anywhere," he remembers. "I was a total alcoholic by the age of fourteen or fifteen. I smoked pot and did a lot of acid."

At the local record stores, he'd come across flyers for bands in need of a vocalist, but nothing clicked until he answered the Stepes' ad at Co-Op—the encounter that ignited Peoria's punk scene. Since their days in Chips Patroll and Unaccepted, Bloody's relationship with the Stepe brothers has been contentious at times, yet he acknowledges their early influence: "Even though there was this weird rivalry . . . I will honestly say they were a huge inspiration on my life. They inspired me to get into doing fanzines, which opened up another world for me. They inspired me to 'do it yourself' in my own way. Regardless of our not always getting along, I still retain a level of respect for what they showed me."

*   *   *

Bloody Mess and the Skabs formed soon after Bloody's return from Colorado. It was Halloween of 1988 "in one of the most unlikely of places: conservative Peoria, Illinois, U.S.A. (the heart of the Midwestern United States and the anus of the world!!!)," as he once described his hometown. The objective, as it was with Hate, was to start "a really obnoxious punk rock band. But this time, I wanted to tour, make records and really do it up," he explains. "I met a bunch of biker dudes . . . so I'm like, fuck it: we'll have a biker punk rock band."

Fittingly, "Biker Punks from Hell" was the second track on the Skabs' 1989 debut single, which showcased their original lineup: Ugly Ted (bass), Gabby Skab ("skinz"), Fish (guitar), and Bloody F. Mess (vocals, "Master of Disaster"). "After that, it was a revolving door of musicians and utter chaos for the next eight years."

Controversy followed the Skabs from their inception, not only due to their obnoxious music and stage act but because of the cover of that first single, which featured original artwork from the notorious serial killer John Wayne Gacy. "I was pen pals with Lynette 'Squeaky' Fromme, John Hinckley Jr., Charles Manson, Ottis Toole, Kenneth Bianchi, and John Wayne Gacy," Bloody explains. "I visited Gacy three times on death row . . . and have hundreds of letters from him." In fact, one of Gacy's final interviews prior to his 1994 execution was published in Bloody's *Fanatic* zine, which sought to spotlight "the fringe . . . the dark underbelly of the American Dream."[6] And when the Skabs' *Empty* EP came out in 1992, it included a poster designed by Bianchi, also known as the Hillside Strangler.

Elements within punk rock had always blurred the line between the shocking and the repugnant—sometimes going too far in attempts to troll "straight" society. The Sex Pistols recorded a song with train robber Ronnie Biggs, for example, while SST Records nearly released an album by Charles Manson. In Bloody's case, his fascination with serial killers earned local, national, and even international media attention, from appearances on BBC Radio to various TV talk shows, including the *Phil Donahue Show*. (Backstage at NBC Studios, the late comedian Chris Farley's dressing room served as his "green room." According to Bloody, he and a friend stole a script from the forthcoming episode of *Saturday Night Live* and replaced it with a Skabs tape.) "I do *not* condone serial killers," he clarifies years later. "These days, I have zero interest in those dark, negative people and actions. But, I cannot erase history."

Likewise, Bloody's friendship with GG Allin brought him notoriety. It also got the Skabs signed to Black and Blue Records, which issued *6th Grade Field Trip* in 1990. It was the first full-length LP to come out of Peoria's punk scene: "a juvenile romp through drug addiction, self-hate and . . . good old-fashioned punk-rock decadence," wrote Jeff Gregory in *People of Peoria* magazine.[7]

As their fan base grew, Bloody Mess and the Skabs pursued disrepute at every opportunity, onstage and off. "There wasn't much difference between a really out-of-control party and our stage show," Bloody admits. "We pretty

83

much lived how we were." Extreme living and extreme art were intertwined, flouting authority and ginning up the shock value. But to sustain shock value for any length of time is to perpetually raise the bar for sheer offensiveness.

In hindsight, the censorship battles and "Satanic Panic"[8] of the 1980s seem harmless, even amusing, relics of a distant time. To be sure, the perceived occult powers of Ozzy Osbourne were no match for GG Allin, who proved that shock rock had come a long way since the days of Kiss and Alice Cooper. Years later, in an age of gonzo porn and a vile, reality-show presidency, not much remains truly shocking—but GG still does. Despite leaving a trail of clubs trashed and stages defiled, Bloody, though kindred in spirit, never sank to such disgusting lows.

"I used to set my hair on fire . . . and there were quite a few shows that I passed out at," he says. "We would trip [acid] onstage, so we would always do weird shit that really didn't make any sense. To us, it was funny; but everybody else was like, 'You guys are fucked!'"

Matt Shane was among the three dozen or so musicians who did time in the Skabs over the years. "I knew it was confrontational," he says of joining the band. "I probably knew, maybe, that bodily fluids were potentially involved. I knew it was punk rock—the real deal. And [Bloody] was really a cool dude. We totally hit it off. I think I did three, maybe four shows with him. . . . [Then] I bailed because it got a little intense."[9]

With their anarchic stage show, the Skabs were banned, more often than not, from whatever place would have them. The liner notes to the band's 1994 *Live EP* boast of a dozen venues that banned them—and eleven different reasons why. "That was my entire goal for most of my career: 'let's just play here *once*,'" Bloody laughs. Beyond the serial killer connection, he garnered the most notoriety out of his flag-burning act, including one incident in Davenport, Iowa, that made the front page of several midwestern newspapers. On July 8, 1989, the *Des Moines Register* reported,

> Members of the band Bloody Mess and the Skabs, from Peoria, announced in a radio interview . . . that they had burned a flag in a Thursday night performance at the Tri-Lighter Tavern and planned to do it again Friday. The announcement started telephones ringing with calls of protest to the radio station, the tavern, the Davenport Police Department, the city fire marshal's office and Davenport American Legion Post 26.
>
> Mike Fox, a co-owner of the Tri-Lighter, said the tavern canceled the Friday night performance after learning of the flag burning. . . . [He] said the tavern's

owners had no idea flag burning was part of the band's act and wouldn't have booked the band if they'd known. The four-member band mutilated at least one˜ foot-long U.S. flag and burned another as part of their act Thursday. Twenty to thirty people saw the act and more than a half-dozen walked out. . . .

Even without the flag burning, Fox described the band's act as garbage. "They swear and talk bad about government and school and religion. . . . It's not music and it's not entertainment unless you're warped or something," he said. Bloody Mess is the name adopted by the group's lead singer. Other members of the group go by the names Ugly Ted, Gabby Skab and Tyrone Brown. . . . "All you veterans come on down," Mess taunted during the broadcast interview. "We think Iowa deserves to be burned a little."[10]

In 1989, flag burning was part of the national zeitgeist—that summer, the US Supreme Court declared the act a protected form of political speech. But legal or not, it didn't play in Peoria, Davenport, or anywhere else, really. From Nashville, where he burned a Confederate flag onstage, to Staten Island, where he was chased out of a club by angry skinheads, Bloody had discovered a surefire way to elicit outrage—and he indulged.[11]

The outlines of another outlandish Skabs gig (they are plentiful) were detailed in a book about the Rockford, Illinois, punk scene. The story goes that Bloody performed oral sex on "a surprised young fan that jumped on stage," outraging the soundman, who shut the show down.[12] In response, singer Dean Dirt of the opening band, 10-96, threatened the soundman, lifting his shirt to show a gun in his belt, and everyone scattered. The book describes it as the low point of the Rockford punk scene—and it was consummated by a product of Peoria.

"True story," Bloody responds. "But it happened in [nearby] Beloit, not Rockford." Later, he adds, "the guy who booked that show supplied my best friend Dean [Dirt] with the drugs that killed him. . . . We were a little crazy back then."

After years of hard living, with Peoria as their home base, Bloody Mess and the Skabs broke up on the road in the mid-1990s.

We were on our *Hungover and Stoned* tour, and we had spent all of our money on heroin and acid and booze and drugs. We were completely fucked up—not only as a band, but as human beings. I had just had a kid, and it was time for me to change, and it just imploded.

I quit in the middle of a gig in Delaware after three songs. I got tired of people calling me a faggot because I had tight pants on or whatever. I was like . . . "I'm sick of this punk rock crap." That was like my tenth [time] retiring.

* * *

Reflecting on his own band's notoriety, Sex Pistols drummer Paul Cook says they were "public enemy number one" in the late-1970s UK. After all, they swore on television and mocked the queen of England.[13] Perhaps it is unsurprising that the same moniker would be employed to describe Bloody F. Mess for turning American norms on their heads a decade later.

With the paranoia and pearl clutching of the conservative culture wars at a fever pitch, Bloody both inflamed and mocked them. Ronald Reagan had employed the American flag to stir up patriotic nationalism and win presidential elections—there were three flag-raisings in his sixty-second "Morning in America" commercial, for example. Bloody burned it instead. While Reagan ignored the AIDS crisis and promoted abstinence-only education, Bloody performed live sex acts onstage. Reagan launched the "War on Drugs"; Bloody imbibed a little of everything.

Whether his intent was even political or just shocking for its own sake, Bloody Mess was the very antithesis of Peoria's "All-American" mythology. He was everything the bipartisan Parents Music Resource Center, champions of the "Parental Advisory" sticker, warned Americans that rock and roll had become. And like his predecessors, he knew just the right buttons to push.[14]

As the Skabs era came to a close, so did Bloody's more provocative stage antics. He became obsessed with outlaw country music, first releasing a single as Bloody and the Country Trash Punks, then touring with the Renegades, playing honky-tonks and roadhouses.

> Then I started the Vaynes, a cover band doing Blondie, T-Rex, David Bowie, and stuff. And then I decided I wanted to do punk rock again, so we changed it to Bloody and the Vaynes. Then it was Bloody and the Transfusions, and then Bloody and the New Disease. . . .
>
> When I came to Oregon, I joined Bloody Mess and the Hollowbodys. We did a tour, two records and a couple soundtracks. I did a couple films . . . and then started the Bloody Mess Rock Circus. Then I had Bloody and the Backstabbers, and now I'm at my last band, finally, in my career. And we're just called Divine Dirt.

Whether or not Divine Dirt remains the final word on Bloody's musical career, the band's name is well suited for his present, for both its spiritual implications and lack of a possessive ("Bloody Mess and the . . .")—a departure that echoes his life's turn. Now content in sobriety, Bloody will always be a rocker, but he appears to have grown beyond the relentless pursuit of outrage and darkness.

> I discovered that I had been viewing everything incorrectly my entire physical life, and it opened up a whole new way of thinking. My entire belief system completely changed. I started subscribing to the Hindu way of life, and that's pretty much my life.
>
> I used to worship things like women, money, rock and roll . . . and then I realized that real energy—this thing called God—is really *us*. We are God; combined collective consciousness is God; there is no separate entity that's God. And it blew my mind.

But is this new identity just another mask to hide behind, or an attempt to make up for past excess? "No, I think I just woke up," he declares. "And I'm seeing things the way I *should* be seeing them."

For some of his older fans, Bloody's evolution beyond his "dive bar superstar" persona has been confounding. One social media encounter "got really weird and intense," he recalls. "I'm like, dude, why do you expect me to live some fucking image? What kind of human being do you think I am, outside of this picture frame that you put me in?"

Though some question his sincerity, it's really just the latest chapter in the enigmatic Bloody Mess story. He's changed, to be sure, but he hasn't rejected or played down his past life. "I regret nothing," he explains. "You live your life, and you just go on."

"I love the past," he adds. "I think there was some great magic and music and memories—but I was a completely different person then. I really believe the good ol' days are *right now*."

Often crazy, occasionally profound, and always inimitable, it's been one wild ride for Peoria's most notorious punk rocker. Whether you love him or hate him, Bloody F. Mess, unlike many of punk's larger-than-life characters, is a survivor. And it seems like he's finally found peace, perhaps for the very first time.

> I have a great band, a great family, a good life out here in Oregon. . . . There's still people who will try to haunt me—certain people that haven't let go of the past. . . . [My daughter] is like, "Well, when you named yourself 'Bloody F. Mess' and created the energy you created for all those years, it really added up. That whole scene is drawn to you because you're fucking nuts, like they are."
>
> We create our own realities, and that's what I did. It fucked me up: I created kind of a crazy one.

CHAPTER 9

Montage of Madness

I saw Leviathan play once in a barn in utter darkness, in the pouring rain. That do-it-yourself spirit was the most significant—and most enduring—facet of the cornchips and punk rockers of Peoria. . . . That "stick together" philosophy also explains why we had shows where there would be a folk band, a goth band, a metal band and a Jim Morrison impersonator on the same bill. We couldn't afford to be picky about genre.

—Kate Dusenbery (of Walpurgis Nacht)

I will never forget hearing and seeing Dollface for the first time. How could I? I would compare it to breathing some improbably pure blast of fresh mountain air, or tasting some favorite meal for the first time.

—John San Juan (of Hushdrops)

"Opportunities to play in Peoria have been scarce recently because the main hardcore venue, the Juice Bar in Peoria Heights, no longer books bands." The account in Bradley University's student newspaper, published February 12, 1988, highlighted a perennial problem for the local punk scene. "When asked why [Daed Kcis] has difficulty getting booked at other places in Peoria, [drummer Matt] McDonough remarked bitterly on the stifling conservatism of his hometown."[1] This dispiriting predicament, coupled with the college-town draw of Illinois State University, eventually drove the band to move en masse to Bloomington-Normal.

While the Bradley paper crowned it "the vanguard of underground rock in Peoria," Daed Kcis struggled to find a local audience for its "unique brand of raw, unforgiving music." So, the band took to the road. "Other parts of the state were more receptive," explains vocalist Eric Kingsbury. "We got a '73 Dodge Sportsman van and started going on these little tours."[2] Trekking all over Illinois,

Iowa, and Wisconsin, the group opened for national acts like SNFU, Shudder to Think, and the Accused while garnering modest attention with its six-song demo tape of dark, simmering punk rock.

Over time, the band's catalog of influences would encompass everything from classic rock and metal to folk, classical, and even dance music. Guitarist Steve Awl's music theory training brought new complexities to the group, while McDonough's drumming grew highly sophisticated. With the addition of a second guitarist, "[we] became a very elaborate band—almost like a fusion of punk, goth, and prog rock," Kingsbury notes.[3] But even as Daed Kcis progressed musically, members' ambitions continued to hit a wall—a proverbial midwestern dilemma. The band, according to an old bio sheet, felt "stuck in limbo between an underground audience that doesn't like the music we write now, and a standard rock audience that expects imitation of certain well-known styles."[4]

Though a follow-up demo more faithfully depicted the multifaceted band Daed Kcis had become, it failed to conjure record label interest. With lives and interests naturally diverging, momentum subsided and the bandmates eventually went their separate ways—an amicable split, Kingsbury says, adding, "Matt's the one who really succeeded musically."[5] To be sure, McDonough—after a stint drumming for Peoria speed-metal pioneers Leviathan—would rise from Peoria's underground to find fame in Mudvayne, one of the metal world's biggest acts in the late 1990s and into the next decade, selling over six million records worldwide. While Mudvayne went on indefinite hiatus in 2010, McDonough remains an active musician: a rock star from Peoria who cut his teeth on the local punk scene, one of the few who really "made it."[6]

*　　*　　*

In contrast with Bloomington-Normal, where the Gallery catered to underground bands, there were no such venues in Peoria. The Juice Bar had gone the way of Illinois Central College and Owens Center; bands that strayed from the blues-rock/cover-band formula were forced to create their own opportunities. It was the dawn of the "hall show era," as musician Kate Dusenbery explains:

> The M.O. of the time was to rent local halls-for-hire, like VFW or American Legion halls that didn't have much other revenue and didn't really know what we were up to, pay the deposit fee of a couple hundred bucks, and promise there would be no trouble.
>
> To see live music at that point in Peoria, you had to be willing to put it on yourself. If you weren't going to be solely responsible, you were going to have to go

to every stinkin' VFW show (even if you didn't like the bands playing), because without the three or four bucks they were charging at the door, the next show wouldn't happen. This sucked at the time, but it made us more creative people.[7]

Each activity happened from the ground up: renting the hall and PA, tacking homemade flyers up to telephone poles, calling people on the phone to spread the word, taking money at the door, and cleaning up afterward—and a community was carved out of what little they had. "The establishment had no idea what to do with any of us," says Jason Pellegrino, bassist for Leviathan and Smoldering Remains. "They basically said, 'Fuck you; what you guys offer is garbage; we're not interested.' And we all, kind of together, said, 'Fuck *you*, we don't need you!' We'd promote our own shows, book our own places, and have combos of bands. There weren't so many options . . . so you kind of build relationships that way."[8]

Pellegrino stood at the intersection of Peoria's punk and metal scenes, both relatively new creations. Prior to the explosion of death metal in the nineties, Peoria's underground metal scene started and ended with Leviathan. Formed in 1983, they called themselves Critical Mass—high school kids playing Iron Maiden, Def Leppard, and Scorpions covers. Then came the revelation: hearing Metallica for the first time. "We were like, holy fuck, how do they play this fast?" Pellegrino laughs. "So we ditched most of the covers and focused on writing original material . . . We became Armageddon; then we switched it to Leviathan. We played *every day*—full band, full volume—for hours and hours and hours," he adds. "That's how we got chops: we played all the damn time!"[9]

When former Daed Kcis drummer Matt McDonough joined the band, Leviathan morphed into far more technical beast: "math metal" before such a term existed. In the eighties, however, it was a full-on thrash band. Founding member Ty Smith brought a hardcore edge to the group, Pellegrino explains—he was "a monster back there on the drums" and a pivotal figure in the punk-metal cross-pollination that was taking place in Peoria and across the nation.[10] Besides publishing a well-regarded underground zine, *Poison Planet*, Smith also briefly played with Bloody Mess and the Skabs, straddling the two genres.

As Ty drifted away from metal, he left Leviathan to form Smoldering Remains with frontman Matt Ziegler, guitarist Marty Gray, and Pellegrino on bass. Their rapid-fire blasts of hardcore—informed by Corrosion of Conformity, Suicidal Tendencies, and other punk-metal crossover acts—were well-received, though the band was relatively short-lived. Ty eventually moved to the West Coast, where he continued to play in hardcore bands and expanded *Poison Planet* into a "distro" (a punk rock distribution company) "dedicated to promoting the DIY anarchist punk/HC/grind movement." His tragic death of heart failure in 2011, at just forty-two years old, was a tremendous blow to everyone who knew and loved him.

In Peoria, Leviathan and Smoldering Remains brought thrash to the same circuit as the so-called punk scene—more accurately described as a nebulous assemblage of punks, metalheads, goths, new wavers, and cornchips. "At the time, there weren't four speed-metal bands where you could do an all-speed-metal show," explains Matt Shane. "It was just these weirdos—and some of the weirdos did heavy metal, some of the weirdos did Duran Duran disco-rock . . . and nobody gave a shit. Everybody was wearing black leather coats," he chuckles, "so it didn't matter."[11]

"We were literally just trying to find other bands that existed," adds Jeff Gregory. "It didn't matter what kind of music they played."[12] "Punk" was effectively not a genre but a catchall for the underground—and that inadvertent eclecticism, notes Dusenbery, was one of the best things about the Peoria scene:

> One of the early shows I went to (to interview Bloody [Mess] for my first zine) had the Skabs (shock rock/punk), Smoldering Remains (hardcore-thrash), even Bu Khara Bu (TV news anchor Garry Moore's African-jazz fusion band) and Leviathan (speed metal) as the lineup. . . . You never knew exactly what you were going to see. . . . You heard music you probably would have never sought out, and met people you would have never interacted with. . . . It forced us all together, but that was a great thing.

These alliances were not without tension, however, whether due to personality conflicts, musical differences, choice of drugs, or innate tribal animosities. "Often there were fights, unfortunately more often than not," Dusenbery adds. "It happens when you throw extremely disparate and warring groups together at the same show. . . . Sometimes I think fights happened more in Peoria because we were trying to bring all of these different music scenes together into one 'anti-top 40' scene."[13]

Though it's easy to romanticize in hindsight, the Peoria scene's sparring factions, lack of venues, and relatively small numbers (which seem to have dwindled somewhat since Naked Raygun played ICC) were obstacles enough to cause one to question whether it was worth all the trouble. In a 1989 *Thrashcore* interview, Smoldering Remains remarked derisively on the state of the Peoria scene: "In a word . . . pathetic! No shows, a couple of good bands, no active people. Mostly fashion punks who could care less about the music!"[14]

Shows were relatively sporadic in the "hall show era"—they demanded sweat and initiative, and no single venue would have them for long. "We booked the Italian American Hall a bunch of times—then somebody pulled the sink off one of the walls," Pellegrino recounts. "That was kind of the way it worked. We'd play a couple of times and the place would get wrecked. . . . Slowly, we eliminated every place we could play."[15]

Without rules or formal authority, it took little for a minor disturbance to get out of hand. In spite of (or perhaps because of) this volatility, hall shows possessed a unique kind of charm; the work and dedication they entailed seemed to count for more. They served as temporary spaces of community and freedom in an increasingly disposable world—a lifeline for many who needed one—forged inside buildings designed for that very purpose.[16]

The halls that hosted Peoria punk bands were gathering places for war vets (VFWs, American Legions); for nonprofits (Peoria Blind People's Center); and for ethnic and cultural organizations (Itoo Hall, German American Hall, Italian American Hall). The Itoo Hall—where Peoria's first "rock and roll dances" were held in 1957—is still home to the city's Lebanese population today, albeit in a different building on the other end of town. Many of the others no longer stand, or they exist as shadows of their former selves: institutions that once stitched neighborhoods together now parceled off, passed on, torn down, or left to crumble—symbols of a simpler time, harbingers of a collapsing American empire. But the ghosts of old halls live on.

There were also house shows in Peoria and even more unlikely venues for punk rock: remote country barns, small-town roller rinks, even a shotgun range. "We would play these barn parties . . . because we couldn't rent anywhere anymore," Pellegrino says. "The big one we really liked was the [Big Hollow] Sportsman's Club. When it rained, the whole place became a mud pit. There was this tiny little clubhouse, and we would just pack everyone in there."[17]

"The 'stage' was where you stood to shoot your guns, and you watched the bands from out in the field," adds Jim Moran, noting the uniquely Peorian absurdity of having once attended a "peace festival" at a shotgun range. "There were broken clay pigeons everywhere."[18]

Incongruity was a calling card, like the time Smoldering Remains and Leviathan inexplicably found themselves among a lineup of R&B acts at a talent show in the 2,200-seat Peoria Civic Center Theater. "We got through one song and they dropped the curtain," Pellegrino chuckles.[19]

A charming snapshot of this period appeared in the *Peoria Journal Star* a few weeks before Christmas 1989. While the lead photograph—a full-page portrait of a pensive-looking, Mohawked punk against a vaguely graffiti-ridden, concrete wall—feels a bit too on the money, "Peoria's Wild Things" was actually a thoughtful, sympathetic account. It linked punk rock to the surrealists, characterized slam dancing as an "industrial-barbaric tribal rite," and generally took its subject seriously as a harbinger of societal change. Bill Knight, the same journalist who introduced Peoria to Caustic Defiance and the straight-edge movement some four years earlier, concluded his case with an intergenerational nod to the sovereignty of youth: "Despite the shock effects of appearance, the impassive distance in the eyes, the ruthless fury of much of the music, the Wild Things are a celebration. Of life and liberty."[20]

*   *   *

As the nineties approached, the Peoria scene was turning over again: new bands, new promoters, new kids cutting their teeth on DIY punk. In August 1989, a group calling itself the Disgusted Youth Organization planned a show in downtown Peoria. "We put on the first DYO (sort of inspired by the BYO—Better Youth Organization) show at the YWCA . . . featuring [punk bands] Sub 13, Semicids, Circus 76, and a band from Galesburg whose name I can't remember or was unclear on even at the time," recalls Kate Dusenbery.[21]

The DYO put a name to a loose-knit group of high schoolers who bonded over skateboarding, straight edge, and hardcore, much like the Stepes and their crew had done several years earlier. Along with Dusenbery, they included Tom Nieukirk and Chris Hauk, the prime movers behind *I Used to Be Disgusted*, a skate/ hardcore zine defined by their aggressive straight-edge and anti-racist views, and later the Peoria chapter of Skinheads Against Racial Prejudice (SHARP).

Though not a skateboarder herself, Dusenbery was already a zine veteran, having contributed to *Maximum RocknRoll*, San Francisco's long-running punk rock bible, as well as publishing her own, *Void Where Prohibited*. She also had experience fronting the short-lived punk band Despondent Youth. It was her next group, however, that would become a staple of the Peoria scene in the new decade. "Walpurgis Nacht was goth-punk with a heavy dose of synth," Dusenbery describes. "Our biggest influences were Joy Division, Christian Death,

Figure 11. *I Used to Be Disgusted*, a zine focused on skateboarding, straight edge, and hardcore punk rock, produced by Tom Nieukirk and Chris Hauk in the late 1980s and early '90s. From the collection of Jonathan Wright.

TSOL and My Life with the Thrill Kill Kult—although we also covered Minor Threat."[22]

"We didn't want to do the straight punk thing, which was kind of what everybody else had been doing," adds bassist Sean Pope. "Paul [Basinger] was really into Pink Floyd and Hawkwind, so he had that psychedelic thing going with guitar. My tastes were eclectic . . . Misfits, Bauhaus, Siouxsie and the Banshees. . . . Jane's Addiction was a big influence. We had Matt [Eisele] on keyboards—the first alternative/punk band in Peoria other than Saint Sirus [with a keyboard player]."[23]

Fittingly, Walpurgis Nacht played its first show on Halloween night of 1990. ICC was once again the setting for a bill that included Saint Sirus, a new wave band featuring members of All Desires, and Geek Love, the immediate precursor to a band that would come to define the nineties Peoria scene. "They were a little bit funkier," Pope describes, "not the straight-up rock and roll of Dollface."[24]

Along with bassist John Kiley, Geek Love featured three future members of Dollface: a pair of gifted brothers, Matt and Josh Shane, and their preternaturally talented neighbor Scott Ligon. "We did 'Groove Is in the Heart' by Deee-Lite, 'If You Want Me to Stay' and 'Que Sera, Sera' by Sly [and the Family Stone], and a deconstructed medley of Kiss songs. We also did a totally pornographic version of 'Roundabout' by Yes," laughs Matt Shane. "We had really learned our

Figure 12. Kate Dusenbery of Walpurgis Nacht in an abandoned cemetery north of Peoria, 1989. Courtesy of Kate Dusenbery.

instruments by that point . . . so it was kind of like a bad-joke jam band. But we kicked those songs' ass. 'Groove Is in the Heart' sounded like Jimi Hendrix."[25]

Matt, Josh, and Scott were natural performers who grew up playing music together in Morton, a relatively affluent suburban community across the river from Peoria. Long before Geek Love, they had their own band (with Matt Choberka, later of All Desires) called the Jam. They were eleven- and twelve-year-olds, unaware of the influential British punk band of the same name, doing mostly Beatles covers—"except we did throw in some Ramones and Big Country," Matt notes. With the Shanes' parents as willing chauffeurs, the Jam played talent shows around central Illinois and even a smattering of dive bars (where they were once, hilariously, paid in pork sandwiches). For two years running (in 1983 and '84), they took first place at Beatlefest in Chicago, outdoing dozens of Fab Four soundalike bands, some more than twice their age. "But Josh and Scott were these cute little kids and they sang their asses off," Matt adds. "So we won."[26]

The Dollface story begins several years later at Co-Op Records, where store clerk Matt Shane and Jeff Gregory, a regular customer, first conceived of forming a "heavy indie band" in the vein of Mudhoney or the Afghan Whigs. Both were fluent in Peoria's music underground: Gregory as guitarist for Circus 76, One-Dimensional Man, and the Bugs (a lo-fi, psychedelic pop project); Shane drumming with Kill City Boys and Geek Love; and both, at one time or another, having played with Bloody Mess and the Skabs. With Shane moving to guitar and Gregory to bass and with Scott Ligon on drums, Dollface's founding three-piece lineup was in place.

Beyond the trio's instrumental dexterity and songwriting acumen, which quickly set them apart from the average punk band, another ingredient was essential to Dollface's identity: an instinctual kinship with America's rich musical heritage—the line that runs through Leadbelly and Kurt Cobain alike. Matt Shane recalls the band's origins:

> I had gotten seriously into *Bleach* by Nirvana and had been learning to play guitar a little bit. I started jamming in my parents' basement with Scott Ligon . . . and I knew Jeff Gregory from a blues project he had done with Josh [Shane] called A Egg. It was Josh, Jeff, and a guy named "Flea" [Dave Wagner] played drums. Dave and Josh got really into the blues and started going to these blues open mics.
>
> On the south side of Peoria, the blues jams were at this place called D. R.'s, which was owned by a guy named Johnie [Rayford] and his wife, Weezy; I believe he was [blues legend] James Cotton's brother. So the blues jams down there were *serious*. Josh hooked up with a guy named Maestro Sanders [longtime guitarist for Koko Taylor]. He couldn't drive yet, so my parents would take him and eventually Scott [Ligon] over for these jams. Maestro at the time was probably fifty, fifty-five, and he was a mentor to Josh and Scott.
>
> So that was going on, I was jamming with Scott . . . and I asked Jeff to come over: "Hey, we should start a punk-rock band." And that's how it started.[27]

Equally steeped in pop and punk—with knowing dashes of sixties rock, R&B, blues, and soul—the Dollface sound began to coalesce, proclaims Ben Ruddell of the band Frozen at Sea: "Sharing an affinity for feedback, distortion, and loud, detuned guitars with the Sub Pop [Records] bands they admired, the songs they produced were highly melodic and displayed a direct, engaging, and unpretentious lyrical sensibility and wicked sense of humor. Scott, Matt, and Jeff traded off lead vocals freely and frequently added soaring harmonies to their spastic racket. Their snotty, exuberant brand of rock and roll steamrolled over the supposed boundaries between the Stooges and the Beatles, Devo and the Who, amalgamating these influences, and many others, with a stylish inventiveness."[28]

*　*　*

Ed Carper was one of Matt Shane's coworkers at Co-Op, a huge proponent of local music and a musician himself who had built a small recording studio in the basement of his Canton home, about thirty miles outside of Peoria. In December 1990, Ed released *Montage of Madness,* a cassette-tape compilation of central Illinois performers that slotted Bloody Mess and the Skabs' notorious "Burn the Flag" alongside slightly more radio-friendly sounds. "All of these bands did *original* music, which was key," Matt Shane stresses. "There was not one venue in town that hosted original music."[29]

A second volume of *Montage of Madness* arrived the following year, the first release on Carper's new label, Ed Records. It featured the recording debut of Dollface, alongside noteworthy tracks from Walpurgis Nacht, the Bugs, and Bloody Mess and the Skabs. But equally significant to the tape itself was the daylong party Carper hosted that preceded its release. "That was Dollface's first show," Shane explains.[30]

"It was sometime during the summer of 1991," Carper says. "To my recollection, the acts that performed were Str8 Sounds, Ed Carper, Dollface, Bloody Mess and the Skabs, Leviathan, and Walpurgis Nacht. I recall it being very hot and no one wanting to play first. I remember Dollface really had quite the following and put on quite an electric set."[31]

"Between me and Jeff [Gregory], Scott Ligon and his girlfriend, and Rockin' Billy from [blues-rock band] Rockin' Billy and the Rhythm Riot, we polished off an entire bottle of Jägermeister before we played," Shane laughs. "At the time, we had about four songs—but we played ten!"[32]

"So Jeff, Matt, and Scott come out with Dollface," recalls Sean Pope of Walpurgis Nacht, attempting to put into words the musical tour de force that was the band's live debut. It was gloriously shambolic rock and roll, not unlike the Replacements at their drunken peak. "Matt had been drinking freakin' Jäger the whole time, [he was] puking off the side of the stage . . . and they deliver this blow-away performance. Everybody was just like, wow! Nobody knew that was going to happen."[33]

"[Walpurgis Nacht] had just gotten off stage," Pope adds with a laugh, "and we were like, *nobody's* gonna remember *us.*"[34]

"There weren't that many people there, and I don't think we really played that awesome of a show because as usual, there were no monitors or anything," says Kate Dusenbery. "But I knew as soon as Dollface launched into 'Kick the Ball' that music in Peoria had forever changed. The audience didn't clue into what a watershed moment this was, but that wasn't unusual. People have a way of not noticing the genius that's right in front of them."[35]

CHAPTER 10

Nazi Punks Fuck Off

Remembrance of things past is not necessarily the remembrance of things as they were.
—Marcel Proust, *In Search of Lost Time*

I hate Illinois Nazis.
—Jake Elwood, *The Blues Brothers*

Throughout the 1980s, the arrival of police had been a Peoria punk tradition, from the first house show to the final performance at Owens Center and beyond. Even with bands like Dollface exuding world-class musicianship and songwriting, Peoria shows in the final decade of the twentieth century were still better known for the violence—and/or police action—that sometimes ended them. "The music wasn't always that good," admits Jim Moran, "but at every show something crazy happened."[1] Dollface formed amid this turbulence, and as a result its pop songs carried an unmistakable grit, grounded in the notion that rock and roll could still be a daring proposition. Following its memorable debut at Ed Carper's Montage of Madness party, the band was more than ready for its first Peoria hall show.

The German American Hall show of July 1991—featuring Dollface, Walpurgis Nacht, Str8 Sounds, and Bloody Mess and the Skabs—remains legendary for its premature conclusion, still marveled at decades later. The newspaper would describe it as a "slam-dancing melee" that spilled onto Knoxville Avenue on a Friday night and left several days of media coverage in its wake.[2]

Tensions spiraled out of control during the Skabs' set, as a handful of slam-dancing punks faced off with the "kind of redneck" guys Bloody hired for security.[3] One of these "bouncers" was allegedly itching for a fight and found his opportunity when one of the punks bumped into him. Bloody was a ringmaster in this rock and roll circus, his alcohol-fueled performance revving up the crowd as hostilities somehow escalated into an all-out, animated brawl. "It was like a big ball of twenty people that looked like a cartoon cloud of fighting, with little arms sticking out," Dollface singer and guitarist Matt Shane describes. "And it moved from the stage, all the way through the hall, out the front door, onto one of the busiest streets in Peoria. And it shut that street down."[4]

The unfortunate episode garnered multiple articles in the *Journal Star*, which conflated the fighting with slam dancing itself. "It's arms slashing and people crashing into each other," one Peoria police officer told the paper. "If this were happening out on the street, we'd call it battery." The "frenetic activity," he added, may have given the bouncers "an excuse to just go after people."[5]

Though no one involved in this melee was charged, Peoria police instead cited the show's three organizers—Matt Shane, Bloody Mess, and Steven Streight—as well as the bartender, a German American Hall trustee. "I got charged with 'mob action' and paid an eighty-dollar fine," Shane recalls. "Bloody was also charged with mob action; he fought it and got it dismissed."[6] The hall trustee, meanwhile, vowed "never to let a punk rock band use [the hall] again."[7]

Whatever the perceived merits of slam dancing, there's no doubt that violence had become a huge problem at Peoria shows. "There were almost always fights," notes Kate Dusenbery, "a phenomenon which, if you weren't actively being attacked, made the whole scene take on a carnivalesque demeanor."[8] This pandemonium ranged from simple drunken idiocy, to self-destructive nihilism, to more serious quasi-ideological concerns—like the rise of Nazi-sympathizing punks.

In October, several months after the German American Hall fiasco, a VFW show on Pioneer Parkway in north Peoria ended in similar epic fashion. It was a typically odd Peoria lineup, slotting three metal bands (Leviathan, Coma, and Denial) alongside the gritty pop hooks of Dollface. And in classic Peoria style, Dollface's set abruptly ground to a premature halt. "Some skinhead came up while we were playing and did the Nazi salute right in front of me," recalls Jeff Gregory. "I took off my bass and tried to take his head off with it."[9]

"I look over and Jeff has the bass guitar above his head . . . getting ready to smash it down on this guy," describes Matt Shane. "At this point the sound guy intervened and dove into the mix; it's like four or five people fighting now. He grabs Jeff, takes him down and just pounds his head into the ground . . . and his guitar pedals. He didn't realize Jeff was in the band. And that was the end of *that* show."[10]

*　*　*

Despite the state's "Land of Lincoln" identity, central Illinois was no stranger to the dark underbelly of American racism and white nationalism. In addition to Peoria's own history of segregation, discrimination, and police violence, nearby Pekin had once been regional headquarters of the Ku Klux Klan—and its high school mascot was a racial epithet until 1980. In the early 1990s, East Peoria native Matt Hale was one of the most prominent white supremacists in the country, already with a sizable criminal record in his early twenties. Long before his forty-year prison sentence for soliciting an undercover FBI informant to murder a federal judge, Hale and a small band of acolytes preached racial holy war at rallies in and around Peoria, triggering vehement protests from area residents, including many in the local punk scene.

Hale's narcissism and delusions of grandeur ran nearly as deep as his well of bigotry. He organized his first hate group, the "New Reich," in eighth grade. When his attempt to form a white student union at Bradley University was unsuccessful, he founded the American White Supremacist Party instead. As former KKK grand wizard David Duke gained national notoriety for his political efforts (including a 1992 presidential bid in the Republican primaries), Hale proclaimed himself the local leader of Duke's National Association for the Advancement of White People. He then formed the National Socialist White Americans Party and ran openly as a white supremacist for the East Peoria City Council, receiving a disturbingly high 16 percent of the vote. Finally, he established the World Church of the Creator, bestowing upon himself the preposterous title of "Pontifex Maximus": chief high priest of the mumbo-jumbo neo-Nazi group.[11]

The string of hate groups founded by Matt Hale is comically absurd, in spite of his deadly serious intents. Setting aside his deplorable worldview, Hale's organizing efforts also demonstrate a more universal human yearning: the desire for group belongingness, especially among the young and disaffected. Even at the opposite end of the sociopolitical spectrum, one might find a delicate parallel. Having identified a common adversary in the racist skinheads on the periphery of Peoria's punk scene, a small circle of friends was prompted to start a local chapter of Skinheads Against Racial Prejudice, or SHARP. Many of them, including Chris Hauk, Tom Nieukirk, and Jeff Keller, had previously been affiliated with the Disgusted Youth Organization, active in booking DIY shows and making zines and outspoken in their beliefs.

With members spanning the United States and Europe, SHARP was a global movement that sought to wrestle away the widespread image of skinheads from its neo-Nazi hijackers. The original skinhead movement—a union of working-class whites and Jamaican immigrants in 1960s London—was emphatically *anti*-racist, they explained, bound by their mutual love for ska music. "Nazis with short hair are not skinheads," declared Chris Hauk in the February 1990 zine *I Used to Be Disgusted*. "They are bald racists and should be called that."[12] But more often than not, that message fell on deaf ears, as the media failed to make this critical distinction.[13]

While SHARP was a welcome counterpoint to racist skinheads, the two groups shared a street-gang mentality that could be problematic of its own accord. "Back in the day you showed up as a crew," explains Tom Nieukirk. "We all had jackets that said 'SHARP' on them and things of that nature, so you're very identifiable."[14] On the opposing side—with "Aryan Nation" and the like painted on their own studded leather jackets—were the racist skinheads, the Nazi punks. Neither group shied away from violence. When they showed up in the same place, it took little to light the fuse.

For many in the punk scene, the phrase "Nazi punks" became shorthand for the recurring potential for violence at Peoria shows. But it was rarely clear—then or now—who was "actually" a Nazi and who was merely an aggressive jerk or drunken buffoon. Ben Ruddell was at the infamous "Dollface and the metal bands" show: "I don't remember seeing any Nazi salutes at the Pioneer Parkway VFW, but something like that might've happened. I do have a pretty vivid recollection of a metal dude who had a tattoo of a drunken Pink Panther on his shoulder, acting a fool and getting all up in the band's face while they played, and Jeff whacking him with the headstock of his bass, after which a scuffle ensued."[15]

Irrespective of labels, punk rock was unquestionably a vehicle for anger and aggression and a magnet for alienated youth—often for better, but sometimes for worse. "Peoria had a weird hybrid of good ol' boys/Pantera metalheads/ Front 242 guys who seemed influenced by Matt Hale and Clark Martell's [former leader of CASH—Chicago Area Skinheads] hate movements," explains Peoria musician Jason Teegarden-Downs. He recalls "the most violent mosh pit I ever saw" at the Italian American Hall in April 1992—ironically, another mismatch of Dollface and three metal bands (Leviathan, Sid Ripster, and Act of God): "A bunch of guys were there with screws in combat boots and razors between their fingers. I'm pretty sure it is more gruesome in my head, now, than it actually was. But scary nonetheless. I remember a lot of it was more about self-mutilation. I was only fifteen years old and seeing guys purposely bleeding was quite an impression."[16]

Of those on the fringes who openly hailed Hitler, it is difficult to say who were true believers like Matt Hale and who were flirting with fascist imagery for its shock value. If their numbers were small, their presence alone was still enough to stir up trouble. For Dollface, an opportunity to play a large community festival on the Peoria Riverfront—the band's biggest gig to date—found yet another set disrupted by violence. It would conclude in an extraordinary showdown between SHARP adherents and neo-Nazi skinheads, according to Andrew Wisecarver, who founded still another skinhead group, SANS (Skins Aren't Nazi Sympathizers), upon moving to Chicago in the mid-nineties:

> A group of Chicago SHARPs came down; they had heard that a pro-Nazi group from Pekin had plans to start trouble. . . . Dollface was on stage. . . . The Nazis, some in scout uniforms they'd modified to look like Brownshirts [the violent paramilitary group that aided Hitler's rise to power], started shouting and trying to drown out the band with their *Sieg Heil* chant. This, of course, caused a bunch of us to start shouting them down. . . . The band started to balk, then their singer started to change the song to [Dead Kennedys'] 'Nazi Punks Fuck Off.' Well, that's when the trouble really started. . . .
>
> Rather than the Nazis rushing the stage (the action that the band, the SHARPs and the police were waiting for), the SHARPs (all twenty of them) took the stage, knocking over the bassist, the drum kit and the "monitor" amps. . . . The slow-witted police rushed the stage, but by now the SHARPs had started offstage onto the Nazi shites (all 10 of them) . . . full-scale battle. . . . When it was over . . . so was the show and any future shows. . . .
>
> The next day, what do you suppose was reported in the papers? You guessed it: "NEO-NAZI SKINHEADS DISRUPT RIVERBOAT DAYS" . . . not "Skinheads Against Racial Prejudice Takes on Neo-Nazis," not "Police Arrest Neo-Nazis for Disrupting . . ." Nope, *skinheads*. Once again the media associated the neo-Nazis with the skinheads . . . and once again, there was no one there to explain the difference.[17]

It should be noted there are conflicting memories of this show; just how deeply it devolved into violent spectacle remains unclear. But if the details are in question, the outline of the story rings true nonetheless. While Nazi punks continued to be an on-and-off concern at Peoria shows for years, the SHARP movement in Peoria was short-lived. "We kind of faded out of it," Nieukirk explains. "Basically, we just got tired of being a magnet for fights all the time."[18]

In May 1993, *Journal Star* reporter Pam Adams profiled the former SHARP crew and the exchange of their acronym-emblazoned jackets for hip-hop fashion: "the shoes, the baggy pants, the [Negro League] baseball caps, the haircuts." It was the same group of friends, still skateboarders, a little older and wiser—still realizing their group identity and proclaiming it to the world. "Keep in mind, youth is fluid," Adams wrote.[19] The yearning for human connection, however, is unchanging.

*   *   *

Despite being a consistent thorn in the side of the scene, Nazi punks were far from the only reason Peoria shows got shut down. In August 1992, the Hopewell Grange Hall near Washington, Illinois, hosted Beautiful Bert and the Luscious Ones and 10–96 (two Kenosha, Wisconsin, punk bands playing Peoria again) along with local acts Bloody Mess and the Skabs, World's End, and PND (whose then-singer, Tom Twomey, formerly of Sub 13, had been a key participant in the raucous German American Hall brawl the previous summer). For fourteen-year-old Nick Lippert of Washington, attending his first show, it was quite an eventful evening: "I got doused in beer, clobbered by a sweaty shirtless drunken obese man, rode on the running board of a Volkswagen van, accidentally drank Jägermeister from a cooler jug, talked to a shirtless guy with a Mohawk and chest tattoos, saw some great music, and then the cops came and shut it down. I was hooked."[20]

The place was packed. A couple hundred people congregated in and around the otherwise-isolated hall, located a few miles outside of town. Bloody Mess and the Skabs were about to perform when the cops showed up, explains Jeff Gregory, a Skab at the time, who was backstage tuning his guitar: "I just remember coming out through the curtain, and everyone was gone. Bloody and the entire band were gone. The audience was gone. There were just cops . . . and garbage and empties everywhere. I was like, what the fuck happened?"[21]

What happened was slapstick—a Keystone Cops routine. As law enforcement descended upon the hall, scores of kids scattered among the cornfields, while Gabby Skab, sporting a blue wig, hurled his drum set at the uninvited guests. He then ran backstage, ditched the wig, and headed for the exit, Gregory recalls. "The cops coming in the back were like, 'Did you see some guy with blue hair?' [Gabby] was like, 'Yeah [pointing], he went that way!'"[22]

As red and blue lights flickered through the dust clouds of August, a more cringe-inducing story made the rounds. This one starred Beautiful Bert—the (now-deceased) 300-pound frontman with a stage act not unlike Bloody's or GG Allin's—who allegedly bent over and stuck the mic where the sun don't shine: a disappearing "magic trick" for the benefit of Washington's finest. "I wouldn't be surprised," Bloody admits. "He used to do that shit all the time. Bert played at a party in Peoria once, where he did something [like that], only he used a Barbie doll."[23]

Whatever Beautiful Bert did or did not do, this outrageous account was enshrined in legend—just one of many wild stories spawned at the Grange Hall that night. Vans plowed through the darkness, combing for hidden cases of beer in the cornfields. One band member, high on something, allegedly ran off with the door money. And the hall itself was vandalized; someone broke all the windows. One erroneous account blamed Bloody—not just for the broken windows but for proceeding to "douse the interior with animal blood," evoking the debunked satanic ritual scare of several years earlier.[24]

"One hundred percent fabricated lie—lots of those floating around," Bloody declares, though he does plead guilty to peeing into an ashtray at a party later that night.[25]

Memory is a tricky thing, and history is always subjective. Legends conform to preconceptions; thus Bloody takes the blame. Truths are stretched into tall tales—ergo, animal blood. Many tall tales came out of the Grange Hall show of 1992, but whatever hijinks followed the arrival of the police, everyone seems to agree on one thing: there were no fights—and no Nazis. "I think that was a peaceful show," Bloody muses. "I think everybody was having a good time."[26]

PART III

The Next Nirvana: 1992–1997

The catapulting of Nirvana onto the world stage in the fall of 1991 almost singlehandedly upended youth culture. Practically overnight, three-chord punk songs topped the charts, and flannel shirts, ripped jeans, and Chuck Taylor sneakers could be found at suburban shopping malls as well as thrift stores. *Rolling Stone* declared Seattle "the new Liverpool," and record labels began scouring the country for "the next Nirvana."[1]

As it turned out, the Berkeley, California, punks in Green Day were next in line for fame, sparking new corporate hopes of cashing in on "the next Green Day." Dozens of other underground bands were swept up and signed to major label recording contracts, including Jawbreaker, Samiam, Jawbox, Chicago's Smoking Popes, and Champaign-Urbana's Hum. In Peoria, most of the buzz centered around Dollface, which ultimately did not make the jump to a major label but did sign with the Minnesota-based indie label Crackpot Records.[2]

As punk "broke" nationwide in the early 1990s, ever-greater numbers of young people were drawn to DIY shows and inspired to start their own bands. This singular moment of cultural popularity coincided with the emergence of the Peoria punk scene's first steady venue, Airwaves Skate Park, as well as a showcase of local "alternative" acts at the historic and giant (by punk standards) Madison Theater.

As the Peoria scene grew in size and apparent cohesion, it became more ambitious as well. Under the banner of Naked Bums, Inc., one promoter began recruiting major touring acts, including two of the biggest underground bands in the country, Fugazi and the Jesus Lizard—bands, as it happens, that Kurt Cobain regularly hyped in the national media.

By 1997, however, the cultural winds had clearly shifted. For better or worse, the major-label feeding frenzy largely fizzled out, and one of the alternative era's iconic accomplishments, the Lollapalooza tour, came to an unceremonious end. The mainstream diverged from the underground once again. But in the meantime, the nineties punk explosion created a tsunami of independent record labels and musicians—and Peoria was not to be left out.

CHAPTER 11

Teenage Airwaves

> The Peoria music scene truly "happened" at Airwaves. No other venue
> even came close to capturing the energy, fun, and freedom of that
> place. I never missed a show there, even if it meant quitting a job.
>
> —Ben Leitch (of Frozen at Sea)

Despite its perennial problems, the Peoria scene was growing quickly. Kiss
This Productions, launched by Kami Tripp LaVallier and Amee Snyder Suydam,
booked a number of prominent shows in the early nineties, bringing to Peoria
bands like Hum, Sixteen Tons, and Hot Glue Gun from Champaign-Urbana and
Bruce Lee's 4" of Destruction (featuring members of Semicids) from Bloomington-Normal. It was the height of the grunge era, and the Reagan-Bush years
would soon be supplanted by a rising politician from Arkansas, Bill Clinton,
a Democrat.[1]

Meanwhile, the Midwest continued to shed manufacturing jobs. In Peoria,
the peak years of "alternative" overlapped with exceedingly contentious strikes
at Caterpillar from 1991 to 1992 and again from 1994 to 1995, which ended in
a humiliating defeat for union workers. Even as a youth countercultural wave
swept the country—echoed, somewhat, by American politics—the economic
and cultural shifts of the 1980s continued their rightward drift.

Documenting Peoria's musical output in the new decade was Ed Records,
which had a banner year in 1992, issuing two more *Montage of Madness* cassettes
(volumes 3 and 4, released concurrently à la Guns N' Roses' *Use Your Illusion* I and
II), a pair of Dollface tapes (self-titled in February, *Corvette Summer* in June), and
the debuts of two new Peoria bands: Nora Hate and Three Boyfriends. Having

inspired a new generation of Peoria's teenagers to take up guitars and start their own bands, Dollface found its hometown legacy falling into place, setting the stage for the remainder of the nineties. There would be many more bands and a much larger scene—and no one would do more to make it all happen than Brody Maag.

Brody's first punk band, the Creeps, played just a handful of shows, but they sparked the seeds for Nora Hate, who would become ubiquitous on the Peoria scene. A December 1991 show inside a shuttered grocery store in Pekin would prove pivotal—that's where Brody met Chris Cowgill, a Washington, Illinois, native who had recently joined members of Walpurgis Nacht in an even shorter-lived punk band, the obnoxiously named Midget Toss. Cowgill made quite an impression that night with his boyish energy and furry, jet-black "gorilla pants"—not to mention the Cabbage Patch doll dangling curiously from the end of his guitar.

As the Creeps morphed into Nora Hate (named for the rundown VW Bug that carried its members to practice), Cowgill was tapped to play bass, and a friend from the Chicago suburbs stepped in for original singer Chad Belvill. Brian Berg's atonal, Ian Curtis–like deadpan and stock-still stage presence proved an excellent foil for the band's unnerving, off-kilter brand of punk rock. The classic Nora Hate lineup (with Brody on guitar and Chad Trone on drums) was set.

Three Boyfriends exuded more celestial sensibilities, exploring layers of psychedelia from '60s San Francisco to '90s Manchester with youthful abandon. "For me, it was a capricious, offbeat experiment for introverted teenage psychonauts," offers drummer John Williams.[2] From their original form as a trio of high schoolers (with Brian Gould on bass and Justin Hartman on guitar), the band shapeshifted as various Boyfriends came and went. In their five-piece form, an army of guitarists accompanied the rhythm section, conjuring a "twee-paisley-grunge" wall of sound.[3] Prior to joining the band as a second guitarist, Jeremy Kerner was already a devoted fan: "I was a total metalhead and I remember being surprised how much I loved those weird sons-of-bitches. I listened to their demo tape constantly. I made my own Three Boyfriends shirt based on their song 'Butterfly.' I painted a giant butterfly on the back and the body of the insect was a syringe with some green *Re-Animator*-type concoction loaded up. I wore it to their next show and Brian commented on it, and we struck up a conversation."[4]

In the summer of 1992, a local news article touted the rising popularity of Dollface and the scene growing around the band, citing a crowd of 300 at a recent Washington VFW show: "Local band hopes to make it big," went the axiomatic headline.[5] A wave of new Peoria bands was echoing the national explosion of the post-Nirvana underground in microcosm—each inspired by Dollface, none sounding alike. Along with Nora Hate and Three Boyfriends, they included Frozen at Sea, Terata, the Dave Moe Band, the Busy Plaids, and Resin.

"I wanted to be in a band that sounded like Guns N' Roses, until I saw Three Boyfriends and Dollface," explains Dave Moe. "We were enthusiastic kids trying to figure out how to play rock n' roll."[6] And they were about to find a home at Airwaves Skate Park.

* * *

"My brother had a boy who was into skateboarding . . . and we just saw it as something for the kids to do," explains Gary Thomas, founder and owner of Airwaves. "Peoria police had been giving street skateboarders a hard time. I ran a bar and grill in East Peoria—I had a little bit of money and wanted something else to do."[7] After a brief search, Thomas found an old warehouse on the south side of Peoria, spacious enough to convert into an indoor skate park.

"We had a construction crew do the big ramp—we had a big half-pipe inside," he recalls. "Everything else was done by skateboarders: a street course and a little mini-ramp with a spine in it. Mainly it was a group called SHARP—Chris Hauk, Tom Nieukirk, Jeff Keller . . . and they had friends, too. They helped set up most of the street course."[8]

Upon opening its doors in the fall of 1990, Airwaves immediately became Peoria's skateboarding headquarters. Clearly the sport had grown substantially since the days of Fulton Plaza and the Stepe brothers. "The first year, business was pretty good," Thomas recalls. "It wasn't making any money, but it wasn't losing money either. Then the economy started to take a slide and the money started drying up. We were looking for other revenue streams."[9]

Offering plenty of elbow room and relative seclusion from any potentially hostile neighbors, Airwaves was an ideal setting for punk shows. "Skateboarding and music: it just made sense," declares John Williams, who along with Brody Maag was one of the main promoters at Airwaves. "We did one to see what would happen and it went over well. From there on out, it was easy to book a show there."[10]

Figure 13. Located on Peoria's south end, Airwaves Skate Park started hosting all-ages punk shows to build an ancillary revenue stream in the wake of a national recession. Its reign as Peoria's punk rock mecca lasted less than a year before the venue closed in 1993. Courtesy of Brody Maag.

More than the Juice Bar, ICC, Owens Center, or any VFW hall, Airwaves was a creation of, for, and by Peoria's DIY underground. A mercurial zone of youth autonomy developed around the venue—a communal bonding experience facilitated by Thomas's laissez-faire approach to oversight. "Hundreds of people came to those shows," Brody notes. "It was a mess of a party and everyone got into everything."[11] And somehow it worked. Compared with hall shows, fights at Airwaves were few and far between; police visits were rare.

"That place was amazing—you could fit so many people in there," says Julie Maag, who met Brody, her future husband, as he was working the door. Musical diversity, she adds, remained an endearing hallmark of the Peoria scene. "You'd have metal and punk and ska, all at one show, and everyone was digging all of it."[12]

"The bands would set up on the floor, and there was a natural auditorium with the ramps and everything," describes Dollface bassist Jeff Gregory. The sound was shoddy more often than not, but that hardly mattered—the smell of teen spirit was everywhere. Showgoers sprawled across the ramps, surrounded the bands as they played, joined in on backing vocals, and skated during shows. "It

Figure 14. Ben Ruddell (*left*) and Ben Leitch of Frozen at Sea, playing at Airwaves Skate Park, ca. 1992–93. Showgoers at Airwaves would sprawl across the skate ramps, surrounding bands as they played. Courtesy of Chasity Marini.

was a totally all-ages vibe," Gregory adds. "That was when we started reaching critical mass with the crowds."[13]

No newspaper or internet touted its existence, not a word of promotion was published institutionally. Like a secret society, it was all word of mouth and flyers at record stores: scrawled and scribbled, cut and pasted, splashed with inside jokes, misspellings be damned. Two or three or even four flyers would be lovingly created for the same show, as each band put its own artistic stamp on the experience. And with hundreds of kids paying five dollars each, the bands could make real money—sometimes $300 or $400 each at a single show, an astounding figure for a bunch of (mostly) teenage punks. Nearly three decades later, Airwaves remains in showgoers' memories a veritable Shangri-la of punk rock possibility.

*   *   *

In the early 1990s, the Seattle music scene—through Nirvana, Pearl Jam, Soundgarden, and others—provided a major windfall for the music industry.

111

In its wake, the Geffens and Warner Bros. of the world were snatching up underground bands across the country in a post-grunge frenzy.

The major record labels "took a relatively indiscriminate approach to buying up budding talent," as sociologist Ryan Moore notes, descending upon "bohemian enclaves" and "college towns" from Portland to San Diego to Chapel Hill. Desperate to cash in on the next big thing, the mainstream media and city boosters alike speculated that an absurdly long list of music scenes might well be "the next Seattle." In addition to the aforementioned, they included Brooklyn and Chicago, as well as Norman, Oklahoma, and Halifax, Nova Scotia. Even Champaign, Illinois, was described by *Rolling Stone* as a "fledgling music Mecca."[14]

Though surprising to most outside of the underground, the Nirvana phenomenon had actually been building for years, just waiting for the right torchbearers. In addition to the DIY touring networks built by bands from Black Flag to Fugazi, the 1980s also witnessed a growing number of college radio stations that supported slightly off-kilter independent bands: Soul Asylum and the Replacements (from Minneapolis) and R.E.M. and the B-52s (from Athens, Georgia) among them. In the 1990s, this so-called alternative music was folded into popular culture, introducing millions of young Gen Xers to the world of punk rock—or a modest slice of it.[15]

Pervasive tropes about the "next Nirvana" or the "next Seattle" were revealing of the music industry's derivative and plundering nature. Yet they also testify to a cultural moment in which underground music scenes all over the country were absolutely exploding. As the Peoria scene rode its Airwaves high, punk shows in similarly sized cities in Iowa and South Dakota, for example, were regularly drawing 200 to 400 people.[16]

Un-hip hometown aside, Peoria's Dollface seemed to have as good a shot as any at being the next band to "make it." Its songs were as good as or better than anyone else's on MTV's *Alternative Nation*, and with the addition of Josh Shane on bass, the band—now a quartet—was better than ever. This was the classic lineup that produced the landmark *Corvette Summer* record.

"Josh's arrival both tightened and expanded the band's sound," notes Ben Ruddell. "He also possessed a lovely and soulful tenor, taking the group's already sublime harmonies to even greater heights."[17] With the 1992 Ed Records release of *Corvette Summer* on cassette, it was clear Dollface was onto something big.

Figure 15. The classic four-piece lineup of Dollface, from the band's *Corvette Summer* CD, 1994. Courtesy of Matt Shane/Dollface.

The tape, submitted as an unsolicited demo, soon landed the band a deal with Minneapolis's Crackpot Records, as Matt Shane explains:

> When we did our demo-tape version of *Corvette Summer*, we knew it kicked ass. We considered it a *record*; we didn't consider it a "demo tape." So it had good packaging. We had fun; we liked doing imagery and stuff. . . . We put a press pack together that didn't have any press in it—we stole all the words from the back of Nancy Sinatra's *Boots Are Made for Walkin'* record and sent it out. And we got a response from two labels: Crackpot and Mammoth.
>
> Mammoth called and they were a little more standoffish, whereas Crackpot was like, "Book a show—we want to come see you. We love your record." . . . They came down to an Airwaves show, through the ass end of Peoria to this abandoned warehouse . . . and there were like 500 kids. No security. No adults.

No bar. Some kid at the door saying "five bucks." They'd never seen anything like it.

Minneapolis was a town that had venues—if you wrote some songs, you could play them out at a bar with a proper sound system. Peoria did not have that. It blew their minds.[18]

With Dollface poised for wider success, 1993 brought another slew of releases from Ed Records—including follow-up efforts from Three Boyfriends (*Touched*) and Nora Hate (*Stacy Looes Shakey*), as well as the debut of another quirky Peoria group. "Frozen at Sea began in my bedroom with [vocalist] Ben Ruddell and I doing a boom-box recording of a cover of They Might Be Giants," explains guitarist Ben Leitch. "After witnessing the first Airwaves gig, I knew that I wanted to be a bigger part of this than just an audience member."[19]

Finding inspiration in the school of Devo (and taking its name from a box of North Atlantic cod at the Long John Silver's where Leitch worked), Frozen at Sea was a decidedly odd concoction. There was long-haired bassist (and occasional trombone player) Nathan "Norm" Sales, freshly fired from death metal band Terata for refusing to play with a pick. There was professionally trained multi-instrumentalist Laraine Kaizer, whose talents on violin really differentiated the band's sound. And there was Kwaku Anakwa, who assisted with "non-musical" elements—"namely by making a spectacle out of himself (e.g., thrashing around in a straitjacket while we played)," Ruddell explains. "One time at Airwaves, we were the only non–death metal band on the bill, and we opened our set with Kwaku inverting a big wooden cross we'd assembled while the band played the riff from 'Black Sabbath.'"[20]

With its unique instrumentation and circus-like performances, Frozen at Sea quickly cemented a reputation far removed from the typical rock band. Likewise, Airwaves was far from an ordinary venue. It was truly beloved—a unique space for youth fellowship—though its heyday lasted less than a year. On April 17, 1993, Chicago's Hushdrops joined Dollface and Three Boyfriends for the final show at Airwaves—and "probably the best Airwaves show overall," Leitch suggests. "Place was going to explode!"[21] That unbottled energy marked the end of an era, as if the crowd somehow suspected they'd never feel anything quite like it again.

"The insurance [costs] doubled, which put the kibosh on the whole thing," recalls Gary Thomas. "There was no way we could make it work."[22] Forced to close the skate park, Thomas moved the operation across town and reinvented

Airwaves as a retail shop. With its dedicated owner and loyal clientele, Airwaves Skate Works would serve the local skateboarding community for a quarter of a century before finally closing for good in 2015.

* * *

Airwaves' reign as Peoria's punk rock mecca was short, but its legacy has long outlived it, recalled years later as one of those rare moments when the stars align just right. "A part of me never left Airwaves," declares Ben Leitch, whose efforts to continue shows in the building after Thomas moved out were similarly thwarted by the cost of insurance. "It is amazing how close-knit the players still are today. We are bonded because we went through something very special that was bigger than all of us individually."[23]

"My best memories revolve around how music was responsible for uniting hundreds of kids who were social outcasts in their immediate areas and/or schools," adds Jason Teegarden-Downs, who soon formed his own ska band, the MIBs. "It was amazing to have the community we had, and I am forever grateful for all of the friends I made."[24]

Considering its outsized impact, it is striking how few Airwaves shows there actually were (barely more than a dozen) "and in such a short amount of time," muses Sam Dantone, who attended most of them. "It all seemed so much bigger to me."[25] What seemed like years to some was really just nine or ten months. Time, it seems, moves slowly when you're young; spaces take on greater significance, their formative shadows cast across a lifetime.

Today, while Gary Thomas is pleased to hear of Airwaves' enduring significance, he mostly shrugs. "It wasn't my kind of music, so I didn't pay much attention," he admits. "It didn't seem that important at the time."[26] But for those who came of age watching Dollface, Nora Hate, Three Boyfriends, and Frozen at Sea at the skate park, the word "Airwaves" is practically hallowed, stamped forever onto adolescent memories—a foundation that paved the way for another new generation of Peoria punks. Jared Madigan was just twelve years old when his older brother took him to his first show at Airwaves. "I remember almost every detail, because I honestly feel like it changed my life," he says.

> Joel and I had to plot and scheme . . . [to] convince my parents that it was okay. . . . We had frequented Airwaves to skate, but this was my first experience at a show. The place was fucking packed. . . . We had to wade through the kids just to get into the area where the show was. . . .

More than anything about this night, I remember the feeling. This wasn't my first concert, but it was my first *show*. . . . There was no separation between the bands and the crowd. It was emotional and raw. It was more about the connection you had with the band. I walked away . . . wanting to feel that connection again very soon. I thought about it all the time and did everything I could to be at every single show after that.[27]

Airwaves came and went, but its fleeting existence announced the arrival in Peoria of a national trend that would be far bigger than the punk rock that paved its way: "alternative."

CHAPTER 12

For God and Country

This next song . . . is for God and country.
—David Yow (of the Jesus Lizard)

You know what they say: "If it'll play in Peoria, it'll play anywhere."
Well, we played in Peoria, and it wasn't a bad thing.
—Duane Denison (of the Jesus Lizard)

The Peoria scene—an ever-changing ebb and flow of bands, friends, supporters, and hangers-on—was constantly turning over, and those who made up the scene were generally unaware of what came before. When Airwaves closed, Peoria carried on without it, reverting to the familiar hodgepodge of one-off shows at various halls, bars, and community centers. "We continued playing wherever we could, and released our second record, *Maggot Dance, in My Pants*," says Ben Leitch of Frozen at Sea. "This went on to sell well enough to put us on the Co-Op Records top ten list."[1]

Meanwhile, a historic theater in downtown Peoria was being reinvented as a live music venue—after having sat mostly vacant for nearly a decade amid on-again/off-again development plans. "Word got out to the manager at the Madison Theater that I was [promoting shows], and he hired me as a stage manager for a while," recalls John Williams of Three Boyfriends.[2]

The Madison—a sprawling structure, ornate and lavish in design—was Peoria's first "movie palace." Built in 1920, it signaled the end of vaudeville as film took over. Sixty years later, a citizen-led preservation effort led to its successful listing on the National Register of Historic Places, sparing its marble pillars, crystal chandeliers, and classical reliefs from demolition. By 1983, however, the

1,800-seat theater had screened its last film. For years afterward, the 70mm reel of *Superman III* (the original superhero franchise, transformed into a slapstick vehicle for Peoria's own Richard Pryor) remained intact on the projection booth floor.

In the fall of 1992, the Madison reopened briefly as a dinner theater, and soon it was hosting live music for the very first time. The "Restoration Concert Series" kicked off in February 1993 with a performance by the Marshall Tucker Band, followed by more typical Peoria fare: Cheap Trick, .38 Special, Foghat, Three Dog Night, Steppenwolf. But as management latched on to the burgeoning "alternative" scene, the likes of Concrete Blonde and the Violent Femmes could be found commingling with the dinosaur acts. Before long, a local showcase, dubbed "The Madhouse," materialized, presenting a unique opportunity for Peoria bands.

The Madison's Old World splendor, ornamental details, and cavernous size exuded an air of grandeur that was not easy to come by in Peoria. Of all the theaters from the city's vaunted vaudevillian past, it was the one still standing. Shows there felt like stepping back in time—or like Chicago. "It felt pretty great to be on a proper stage with hundreds watching," recalls Paul Gentile of Three Boyfriends, who played the first Madhouse showcase. "I remember thinking that our scene had 'graduated' somehow, no longer reduced to playing skate parks and basements."[3]

Dollface continued to ascend as well, logging hundreds of miles in a VW station wagon in support of its Crackpot Records debut. Recorded by Brian Paulson (Slint, Superchunk, Wilco) in the Minneapolis offices of the venerated Rykodisc label, *Corvette Summer* built on the group's same-titled Ed Records release, retaining its artwork and basic sequence while rerecording most of the songs, along with four older numbers. Unveiled in February 1994, the album showcased a band at its peak—another proverbial "next Nirvana" with a seemingly limitless trajectory that stretched well beyond the local scene.

From Minneapolis to Detroit to Cleveland and beyond, Dollface played just about every major midwestern city and most of its midsized college towns, even traveling to Austin for the South by Southwest music festival, then in its eighth year. Back in Peoria, the band members were bona fide rock stars with strong record sales, local radio play, and well-attended shows at the Madison Theater—where photographs of the era reveal a sea of flannel dotted with islands of hoodies, baggy pants, and baseball caps. It's a time capsule of the post-grunge

"Alternative Nation," just prior to being washed away by boy bands, nü metal, and Britney Spears.

*　　*　　*

With Dollface on the rise, its influence on another up-and-coming Peoria band—in style, quirk, and ambition—was unmistakable. The delightfully catchy garage-pop of the Neptunes was right in line with the melodic genius of *Corvette Summer*. Drawing members from Three Boyfriends, PND, and the Busy Plaids, the trio of Justin Hartman, Chris Riley, and Larry Keach played their first show at Peoria's One World Coffee and Cargo on April 8, 1994—the same day the world discovered that Kurt Cobain was dead.

By midsummer, the Neptunes were the "it" band of the moment, and their ten-song demo tape, *Transparent Divorce*, was selling hundreds of copies across central Illinois, from Peoria to Bloomington to Springfield. An exciting live act, the band packed the house at One World and drew large crowds to Sneakers, the new teen dance club in the old Stage 2 location, which had started hosting occasional shows.

Meanwhile, a new promotional outfit was about to shake up the Peoria scene. Jon Wright of Morton (one of this book's authors) and his friend Doug Hoepker had launched Naked Bums, Inc., as high school seniors, primarily as a vehicle for publishing their poetry. But with Hoepker away at college, Naked Bums became Wright's by default. It wasn't a huge leap from poetry chapbooks and spoken word performances to music promotion, and if the Beat influence was a bit obvious (conjoining Burroughs's *Naked Lunch* with Kerouac's *Dharma Bums*), the earnestness behind it was genuine—fuel for the DIY fire. Wright describes his introduction to the local music scene after landing a job at East Peoria Co-Op one week into his freshman year at Bradley University:

> I could hardly believe my good fortune. To work at a record store was my dream, and with Matt Shane of Dollface—I was in the company of rock stars. I scored a copy of the new Dollface 7", signed and personalized by the band: "*Good luck at Hardee's Jon—YOU'RE FIRED*." It was just Matt hazing the new guy, but it couldn't help but tap into some of my latent insecurities. I wasn't a punk. I'd never been to Airwaves. I felt like an outsider, like I had to build my "credibility."[4]

Then there was Chris Cowgill, bassist for Nora Hate, who also worked at East Peoria Co-Op—and seemed to have come out of the womb listening to

119

the Damned. As Cowgill converted his cassette tape collection to CD, Wright snatched up his discarded cassettes: classics on the Touch & Go, AmRep, SST, and Dischord labels. "Working with Chris was an informal seminar on punk rock and the Peoria scene," Wright notes. "Practically every night I would meet new friends. I was regaled with meditations on Airwaves, schooled on the 'glory days' of hall shows. And together we lamented the lack of a steady venue in Peoria."[5]

While occasional shows were happening at Sneakers dance club and the Madison Theater, hall shows had become nonexistent. As "alternative" music continued to grow in popularity, the loose-knit Peoria scene was ready for more. *So why don't we have hall shows anymore?* There was no good answer to that question. Airwaves had been closed just a year and a half, but it felt like a whole different era. In the fall of 1994, during downtime at Co-Op, the question for Wright and Cowgill soon became *What are we going to do about it?*

A couple of phone calls was all it took to rent the American Legion hall in downtown Peoria, just a few blocks from the Madison. It was the same venue Dag Nasty nearly played seven years earlier, though neither Wright nor Cowgill were aware of that lineage at the time. "Chris drew up a flyer and brought in the Muggles from Bloomington-Normal," says Wright. "Nora Hate was a no-brainer. We knew the Neptunes would draw a crowd, and we added some old friends of mine from Morton, Hampton Wick, to the bill."[6] This was Naked Bums' first "Four Bands for Four Bucks" all-ages hall show. It was November 26, 1994, and for the next year, the downtown Legion hall on Monroe Street was Wright's go-to venue.

Meanwhile, the Madison Theater's local showcase continued into the spring of 1995 and encompassed three Naked Bums shows, the last of which marked the Madhouse's demise, in what *Journal Star* reporter Clarence White called "one of the strangest events I've seen during my short time as a critic":

> The small crowd . . . seemed to be enjoying [the] Factory until its lead singer, Mark Thunehorst, 21, decided to do a little "crowd surfing." Unfortunately, he seemed to forget that crowd surfing only works when you've got people in front of the stage who are willing to catch you. . . . Thunehorst dived from the stage and into the crowd, hoping that they'd catch him. But as he was falling, the crowd parted and Thunehorst landed on his head on the theater's concrete floor.
>
> Needless to say, the stunt ended [the] Factory's part of the show. Security personnel helped Thunehorst to his feet and carried him out to the lobby, where

local paramedics were summoned. Thunehorst was taken to Saint Francis Medical Center, where he was treated and later released.[7]

It took just a day for the theater's manager to make the announcement: that was the end of the Madhouse. The Madison continued to host live music until 2003—including acts ranging from Béla Fleck to Linkin Park to Slayer—but the local showcase was dead, another opportunity for Peoria bands up in flames. Over time, the historic building would be shuttered and fall into disrepair, its future likely destined for the wrecking ball despite periodic calls to "Save the Madison."

But in the spring of 1995, shows at Peoria's downtown American Legion hall were just getting started, and Naked Bums had larger acts in its sights. The nearby Champaign-Urbana scene was red-hot, and Hum was riding that wave when it returned to Peoria with fellow Champaign-Urbana rockers Steakdaddy Six. It was only two months before the release of Hum's major label debut, *You'd Prefer an Astronaut*, and to this day some claim it was the loudest show they've ever attended.[8] It was also Wright's first time signing a contract, an arrangement that nearly went awry: "The guarantee was a reasonable $400, and we had a decent-enough turnout. But after the hall rental and sound were paid for, I

Figure 16. Inside the Madison Theater, early 1995. A sea of flannel exemplifies the post-grunge "alternative" scene, while ornamental details reflect the golden age of Peoria's old movie houses. Courtesy of Eric Peterson.

had just $25 left—barely enough to fill [the band's] gas tank for the ride back to Champaign. As I contemplated a visit to the ATM, I found myself explaining the situation to Hum frontman Matt Talbott, who insisted on accepting the $25 as full payment. I will never forget this generous act of kindness to a young promoter who'd gotten in over his head."[9] If Hum had demanded the guarantee that was contractually theirs, Wright adds, he might never have taken a chance on booking another bigger act—like when Tar brought its aluminum-body guitars and post-punk precision down from Chicago two months later. Likewise, the *Now Playing in Peoria* compilation CD might not have come to fruition.

At this point only a small slice of Peoria's underground bands had released music on CD—namely, Bloody Mess and the Skabs and Dollface—and both had independent labels behind them. In the years before CD-Rs and Napster democratized digital music, CDs were expensive to produce; cassettes were still the affordable medium of choice. But as Naked Bums' shows proved more and more successful, a "comp" CD seemed like the next logical step.

Released in April 1995, *Now Playing in Peoria* was a milestone document of the post-Airwaves music scene. "Landing two exclusive Dollface tracks felt like a coup," Wright says; by central Illinois standards, Dollface was a "big" band. Amid standout tracks by the Neptunes and Fast Food Revolution and a mélange of punk, goth, and psychedelic pop from local mainstays (Nora Hate, Dismiss, the Factory, John Toilet and the Bugs), Infect's epic death metal anthem "Fucking Death" was another unexpected highlight of the compilation. "And the Fast Food Revolution tracks still linger in my head years later," Wright adds.[10]

Peoria's music scene was growing larger and more multidimensional, and Wright's ambitions were growing as well. Besides promoting three to four shows a month, Naked Bums was now a small record label, and its next project—a four-song 7"-single from the Peoria pop-punk band Dismiss—soon added a second release to its catalog. Meanwhile, national acts were about to make their mark on Peoria.

* * *

In June, Naked Bums brought the Jesus Lizard to town. The veteran Chicago noise rockers—later described by recording engineer Steve Albini as "the greatest band I've ever seen [and] the best musicians I've ever worked with"—were fresh from striking a deal with Capitol Records.[11] They were going to try their luck in the big leagues, and Peoria was a warm-up show for their slot on the upcoming Lollapalooza tour—and by far Wright's biggest show to date. The band promptly commenced to drinking upon their arrival, pleasantly surprised that the young promoter had actually purchased *all* the food, beer, and liquor requested in their contract rider. "I was nineteen and didn't even drink at the time," Wright says. "I had to get a friend to buy $200 of alcohol for me."[12]

Five hundred people packed into the downtown American Legion hall—a huge number for a hall show. Peoria's own Nora Hate and Chicago's Sidekick Kato were the opening acts. And then, watching the quartet file onstage and launch into their set, the masses bobbing up and down to "Destroy before Reading," it seemed hard to believe: the Jesus Lizard was playing an all-ages punk show in Peoria, at a veterans' hall of all places. *How did this happen?* The audience, the band members, and the vets in the adjacent bar were likely wondering the same thing. Underneath a giant bingo board and a banner proclaiming "For God and Country," the American Legion motto became the evening's central theme and frontman David Yow its madman patron saint, as he proclaimed again and again, "This next song . . . is for God and country."

Bassist David Wm. Sims struck a menacing stance, daring the persistent queue of stage divers to come within striking distance of his steel-toe boots. (This time, no potential crowd surfers landed on their heads—unlike at the final show at the Madison, the crowd was dense enough to catch them.) Silver-maned guitarist Duane Denison was the jazzman—calm, cool, collected; drummer Mac McNeilly the workhorse, relentlessly pounding, holding it all together. It was a typical Yow performance—prowling the stage, hurling himself into the crowd, his body a weapon, all sweat and scratches, spit and bruises. At one point he spotted a wooden pulpit just offstage, carried it out front, and became a reverend,

Figure 17. Advance ticket for the Jesus Lizard show in Peoria, 1995. From the collection of Jonathan Wright.

preaching to the awed congregation. The band's stage act was a perfect match for the anxious tension of the music, Wright explains: "As the pulpit teetered back and forth in Yow's hands, I held my breath, just waiting for it to fall and splinter into pieces. As a fan, I was thrilled; but as the promoter, I worried that I'd be paying for the damage. Sure enough, it ultimately toppled to the ground, yet fortunately for me, remained intact. Between songs Yow dragged it back where it came from. And I exhaled."[13]

At the same time, knowing fans speculated on whether Yow would unveil the so-called Tight and Shiny—"the *pièce de résistance* of the many party tricks he can perform with his male member . . . his testicles [twisted] into a form resembling a sweaty, shriveled kiwi," as the act was later described in the pages of *Rolling Stone*. He would indeed . . . as did one member of the audience, a Peoria kid whose audacity threw the Jesus Lizard frontman for a loop. David Yow was "the first naked man I ever saw in person," Erin Page, fourteen at the time, recalls:

> It was hot and sticky and I remember the smell: like a barnyard of kids who aren't good at showering or doing laundry, mixed with weed and stale incense and beer. David Yow was up on stage screaming and ranting, writhing his sweaty, rubbery body around stage. I had never heard anything like this band before—it was a weird juxtaposition of surfy guitars and driving bass and drums and David's creepy stage antics. And then, he got his junk out. I was shocked. The most I had done is kissed a boy. Next thing I know, Stan Wood [in the crowd] was also naked. I couldn't believe what I was seeing.[14]

It was over in an instant—most of the crowd never witnessed Yow's friendly bit of exhibitionism nor Wood's copycat counterpart. Given the band's surgical performance, it was hardly the highlight of the evening. The bedlam was measured if not disciplined and, like the music itself, far more substantive than shock for its own value. "Even then, all of us knew we were experiencing something we'd remember for the rest of our lives," Wright explains.[15] The band was paid handsomely, and for the first time, Naked Bums actually made some money.

After the show, as Wright basked in the afterglow, someone began peppering him with questions, after introducing himself as a reporter. "I finally asked who he wrote for . . . expecting the name of some small fanzine," he recalls. "'*Rolling Stone,*' came the response. I couldn't believe it. THE *Rolling Stone*?"[16]

Sure enough, the iconic music magazine—still a cultural force in the mid-nineties—ran a lengthy cover story about the Jesus Lizard on the cusp of their major-label coming-out on that summer's Lollapalooza tour. The opening line, in big block letters, was straight from Peoria: "For God and Country." In the article, Yow shrugs off the Tight and Shiny as "just a treat for the local kids . . . because we'd never played Peoria, and we probably never will again."[17]

All of this national attention attracted the wrath of longtime *Peoria Journal Star* columnist Jerry Klein, who began his editorial rebuke, "Freedom of expression? Much of today's music is more like raw sewage." As Peoria's own version of Andy Rooney, Klein derided the young people of the 1990s for "becoming increasingly wild and undisciplined," echoing his own description of 1960s teens "writhing, gyrating, [and] pulsating" to rock and roll like a "Saturday night in Gomorrah."[18]

Admittedly, by the time Klein's piece on the Jesus Lizard went to print, David Yow had been arrested following a Lollapalooza gig in Cincinnati for the same trick he'd pulled in Peoria. To Klein, for whom the Jesus Lizard's name alone was "an abominable blasphemy," Yow's "treat" was a clear indicator of the decline of Western civilization—or at least that of Peoria's midcentury salad days. It was good he hadn't been privy to the GG Allin show of ten years earlier.

In the same editorial, penned just after Jerry Garcia's death, Klein expressed surprise at the "monstrous outpouring of grief" for the beloved Grateful Dead leader. Garcia's passing—one month after the Dead's final show at Soldier Field in Chicago—"could hardly be called surprising," he wrote, "considering the kind of life he and so many rock stars led."[19]

Tributes to Garcia were everywhere in August 1995. At the same time, the schism separating punk rock from hippie culture was also at its peak, fans of the former convinced that members of the latter had sold out their utopian roots and become just another capitalist tool in the hands of greedy baby boomers. This was the general mindset that led to Naked Bums' infamous "Tribute to Jerry Garcia" show that month.

The show was no tribute, despite what its flyer teased: the Norms, delivering a doom-rock take on the Dead's *American Beauty*; the Factory, backed by a thirty-piece orchestra, painting *Aoxomoxoa* in goth; Superego's hardcore paired with guitarist Bob Weir; and Chicago's MK Ultra, thrashing out a Dead-inspired rock opera. The flyer also promised a preshow screening of rare footage from Jerry's funeral—"so get there early!" it suggested.

"It was supposed to be a funny flyer, an inside joke," Wright notes. "Looking back, I can see how it felt mean-spirited."[20]

For many young people in 1995, music was a stand-in for their very identity, just as it had been in the cornchip era: "your" bands represented *who you are.*

125

Punk's longtime disdain for commercial success, coupled with a proclaimed antipathy for the Dead, was a powerful driver of behavior. But as Wright explains, a lot of people didn't get the joke:

> The phone at Co-Op rang all week. And with every Deadhead we let down—bewildered, disappointed or angry—I began to realize the show could be a fiasco. When I arrived at the Legion hall, the parking lot was already full of hippies, blissfully unaware of the prank. Blankets stretched across the front lawn; the smell of patchouli filled the air. As word trickled out, the crowds slowly dissolved, and refunds were given to the trickle of Deadheads who'd paid to get inside. There was some anger, but no physical altercations—unlike many of the shows back then.[21]

For many punks, Johnny Rotten's warning to "never trust a hippie" was something of a commandment, despite being fairly anachronistic beyond its late-1970s context (and being derivative of the sixties counterculture's own warning against trusting anyone over thirty). But it was no coincidence that punks and hippies were disparaged in the same Peoria newspaper editorial. For all their differences, the two countercultures were in fact kindred spirits—remarkably similar expressions of opposition to the status quo, separated by barely a generation. Both were existential threats to the powers that be, or at least collective pains in the ass of the ruling class. This was particularly true in the 1990s, when the "alternative" umbrella merged the politics of underground punk rock with the culture of Pacific Northwest coffee shops before quickly becoming another hollow marketing term.

Perhaps Jerry Klein recognized something that even the punks did not. While the Jesus Lizard was altogether too much to appeal to many Deadheads, the band's guitar and drum work was only shades away from Led Zeppelin. David Yow's "Tight and Shiny," meanwhile, mirrored an alleged act that landed Jim Morrison of the Doors in a Florida jail cell in 1970. Even Wright's Naked Bums took its name from the hippie-influencing beatniks. Klein's worst sixties nightmare had returned with a vengeance. And if the Jesus Lizard were playing in Peoria, who knew what youth might be brewing up elsewhere?

CHAPTER 13

This Is Not a Fugazi Chapter

Let's try to think of a more creative way to deal with this.
. . . One idea is that everybody just sit the fuck down on the
ground. . . . Or, maybe everyone who wants to watch the band
could go stand on the sides, and then we'll face sideways and
the people who need to "mosh" in the so-called pit can be
by themselves in the middle. . . . What do you all think?

—Ian MacKaye (of Fugazi)

After Peoria's cameo appearance in *Rolling Stone*, David Yow's "For God and Country" sermon hung in the air like a triumphant battle cry. In the age of "alternative," bigger and better things seemed not only possible but probable. As Naked Bums aspired to become a formidable independent record label, it made sense to borrow Yow's motto—stolen from the Legionnaires—for the title of its next release. The planned *For God and Country* 7″ was to feature a quartet of heavy hitters: Nora Hate (punk rock), Fast Food Revolution (indie rock), Mingus Council (math rock), and the Norms (Sabbath worship), sound quality be damned. A benefit show with the four bands was scheduled to raise funds for the project—but perhaps more memorable than the show itself was the venue that hosted it.

*   *   *

Crazy's was another historic space inherited by punks, located in the village of Bartonville, a blue-collar industrial town on the southern outskirts of Peoria. The short-lived, all-ages nightclub stood on the grounds of the former Peoria State Hospital, better known to local youth as the "insane asylum." It was a curious setting for a club, to say nothing of its dubious moniker—thoughtless and borderline offensive in retrospect, though in line with punk rock's often on-the-nose political incorrectness. No one questioned it at the time.

When it opened its doors in 1902, the Illinois Hospital for the Incurable Insane was virtually a small village of its own, encompassing several dozen buildings on 215 acres overlooking the Illinois River valley. ("Incurable" was dropped from its name in 1907; it became the Peoria State Hospital two years later.) At its center loomed the Bowen Building, an imposing, three-story hulk of gray limestone. Though merely an administrative building, its haunting presence sparked the imagination of ghost hunters and curious teenagers alike for decades.[1]

Under Dr. George Zeller's leadership, the Bartonville hospital was a pioneer in the treatment of the mentally ill. It was among the first to eliminate restraining devices, remove bars and gratings from doors and windows, and abolish the dispensation of narcotic drugs. Yet this significant history had long been eclipsed by tales of the supernatural—fueled by Zeller himself, who published a book detailing his own inexplicable experiences at the complex.[2]

After the hospital closed in 1973, it became a magnet for thrill seekers, who broke into its shuttered buildings and surveyed its network of underground tunnels, making off with beds, wheelchairs, gurneys, and other "souvenirs." As tall tales of their provenance magnified widespread ignorance of the hospital's past progressivism, the proverbial ghost stories proved irresistible. For decades, exploring the "insane asylum" was a rite of passage for Peoria-area teenagers and a perennial headache for Bartonville police, even as the village worked to convert the old hospital grounds into an industrial park. (The iconic Bowen Building, however, was eventually deemed beyond repair. Despite years of restoration talk and multiple efforts to turn it into a "haunted" tourist attraction, it was finally reduced to rubble in 2017.)

Situated within the former hospital's gymnasium/activity center, one of its newer buildings, Crazy's was unlikely to lead any revival of industry. But it sufficed for a punk venue, hosting half a dozen all-ages shows in 1995. "I don't [remember] how we came across it, but these two guys . . . had leased it and wanted to start a club," explains promoter Brian White. "So my brother and I worked our way in to do shows. They never really got it off the ground. We did a few shows and it got weird with those guys, so we moved on."[3]

Under the banner of Freekshow Records, White booked shows and released cassettes by a number of local bands, just as Jon Wright was doing with Naked

Bums. Besides bringing several major ska acts to Peoria, White was responsible for promoting the first show at Crazy's in July 1995. With no air conditioning in the building, the bands played outside in the adjacent courtyard—an inadvertent throwback to the Cramps' fabled set at California's Napa State Mental Hospital seventeen years earlier (minus the cavorting of delighted psychiatric patients). But there was no lack of youthful passion, and the night proved to be a decisive prologue for at least one Peoria punk. "I [found] something special in the band that I had been invited to see," recalls Jared Grabb, a high school freshman attending his first show:

> The band was Fast Food Revolution and they played a brand of indie rock similar to bands like Sebadoh, Pavement, and the Flaming Lips. In fact, that night they played a Flaming Lips cover. . . . What really struck me about this local band onstage, though, was their original songs. The band was awkward, yet authentic. Here were four "losers" (as Beck had lovingly coined us all recently) on a stage playing their own songs with their own words, chords and beats, and people were listening. People were feeling it.
>
> I remember being uncomfortable and self-conscious, leaning against the outside rail of the courtyard with my shaggy bowl haircut and oversized T-shirt. I thought this thing that I was doing (going to a punk show) was cool. I wanted to fit into that. Soon after, I would set my sights on joining a rock band—not to become famous or to get girls—but to be this local band that fifty kids actually cared about.[4]

Naked Bums' "For God and Country" fundraiser came a couple of months later, though it raised few funds for the ill-fated record. Unsurprisingly, Crazy's soon closed its doors. Meanwhile, Jon Wright and Brian White were each separately pursuing the same goal: bringing Fugazi to town. The renowned Washington, DC, band's October 1995 performance would be the biggest DIY punk show in Peoria history—though it would come with its own conflicted legacy.

"Having the chance to work with Fugazi, even unsuccessfully, was awesome," Brian says. "Ian MacKaye told me later that they went with Jon because I was pitching my venue as a club, and he [Jon] seemed more of an independent. What he [Ian] didn't know was we were the same thing—[and] it [the "club"] just was in the gym of the old mental hospital in Bartonville."[5]

*　*　*

"What's the first thing that comes to mind when you think of Peoria, Illinois?" It's nine years after the infamous Fugazi show, and Jon Wright is on the

129

phone with Ian MacKaye, interviewing the legendary musician for a magazine article about punk rock's role in the 2004 presidential election. Before posing his questions, however, Wright leads with the Peoria reference.

"Crazy skinhead kids!" MacKaye replies without hesitation, and Wright reminds the bemused frontman of the last time they met. *"That was* you*? What a fucking gig that was! What a crazy night."*[6]

MacKaye's previous band Minor Threat, an acknowledged influence on the Stepe brothers, had indirectly played a foundational role in Peoria's punk scene (and many others), while straight edge, a term coined by the band, continued to find periodic renewed interest. Though sonically quite different, Fugazi had a similar impact on US punk rock.

The band was (and is) admired for consistently living up to the high standards for which its members advocated. They played five-dollar all-ages shows almost exclusively; eschewed corporate clubs for smaller and more unique venues; ran their own label, Dischord Records; and exemplified strict DIY principles in all of their dealings. Their music is potent and timeless: the dual vocal interplay and interlocking, angular guitars; the experimental stretching of their punk roots; the firm grounding of a dub-inspired rhythm section. Though on hiatus since 2002, Fugazi's sterling identity remains powerful and affective—and members' progressive politics are "as frighteningly relevant today as they were in 1988. What sticks out most, though, remains the band's interaction with its audiences," wrote Mason Adams in a 2015 article for Vice: "Early on, Fugazi developed a reputation for verbally challenging aggressive crowd members in service of providing a safe space for everyone. Usually that took the form of verbal reprimands but occasionally required going a bit farther. After stopping several times because of crowd fights during a 1995 show in Peoria, Illinois, the band requested the audience all sit down and allow the guys causing problems to mosh by themselves until they grew uncomfortable and left."[7]

Fugazi's Peoria show took place inside the Youth Building at Exposition Gardens—the same large hall where the Who played in 1968, where Black Sabbath played in 1971, and where Black Flag *almost* played in 1986. But these titans of rock were the exception rather than the rule. As home of the Heart of Illinois Fair, Expo Gardens was more acquainted with over-the-hill rockers, tame country acts, second-tier pop singers, and other marginally unfashionable groups. It was certainly not a regular venue for local punk bands. Nevertheless, Peoria's own Mingus Council found itself on the bill alongside the Make-Up, a fellow

Dischord band on tour with Fugazi. In a formidable display of esprit de corps, the touring musicians made it a point to watch the local act, while other interactions revealed a mindset that was "almost like mentoring in a lot of ways," recalls Mingus Council guitarist Stan Wood:

> That night changed my life forever. I wanted to play music really bad before that . . . but talking to Ian, he was so encouraging . . . it blew my mind. It gave me a stronger conviction to do it and a greater interest in it—much greater. And the Make-Up—they were super-encouraging and awesome, too . . . very inspiring.
>
> For newbie musicians at that time, especially in Peoria, we had so little exposure to this stuff. . . . It was a big deal. And to have them be such down-to-earth dudes . . . it opened my mind and made me see that the world could be more than I thought it was.[8]

Around 900 people awaited the headlining act in varying states of anticipation and disbelief. It was Naked Bums' biggest show ever—by far. Then a familiar voice boomed into the mic. "Good evening, ladies and gentlemen," proclaimed Ian MacKaye. "We are Fugazi from Washington, DC."[9]

The excitement in the air was palpable, and from the first chords of "Birthday Pony," the restless audience let loose. But inside an already intense physical

Figure 18. More than 900 central Illinoisans were in attendance to watch Washington, DC's post-punk quartet Fugazi at Expo Gardens in Peoria on October 9, 1995. Courtesy of Eric Peterson.

environment, scattered acts of moshing quickly became stray elbows thrown, and the aggressiveness kicked up a notch. The people up front were being crushed against the rented stage, a rickety island of wooden risers that seemed to have little chance of surviving such force. Within the first ten minutes, the whole platform was pushed backward several feet. If it were to collapse, the show would be derailed entirely, as MacKaye reminded the crowd while scanning the room for provocateurs.

The band cut multiple songs short, stopping periodically to admonish a number of individuals for stoking the chaos. All the while, a steady string of aggressors were being escorted out of the venue by Wright and his makeshift crew of "security," composed solely of willing friends. At some point a large man in a Pantera shirt broke free of Wright's bear hug and landed a punch. "I ended up with cuts and bruises on my face, a ripped T-shirt, holes in my jeans, and I lost a contact lens," he recalls.[10] It wasn't his first scuffle as a promoter—that seemed to come with the territory back then—but it was his first significant injury.

With characteristic magnanimity, Fugazi's Guy Picciotto even invited one of the troublemakers—a shirtless man in red suspenders—onto the stage, handing him the microphone to express his grievances. It wasn't a sophisticated performance. As the band's continued efforts grew more exasperated, Wright retreated to the foyer to catch his breath: "I was discouraged. One of my favorite bands in the world was playing in the very next room—*in Peoria!* But my shirt was literally in tatters, I could only see out of one eye, and I was still worried the stage would collapse altogether. Then a friend grabbed me and said, 'You *have* to see this. The ENTIRE crowd is sitting on the floor.'"[11]

Sure enough, having failed to appeal to reason, a frustrated MacKaye had casually requested that the entire crowd sit down. Like children following their teacher's instruction, nearly everyone dutifully complied—aside from "a handful of men clad in combat boots, black leather jackets and spiked jewelry," as the newspaper later reported.[12] It was an astonishing scene, no doubt. "You could hear a pin drop," recalls one attendee. "I was standing off to the side and made eye contact with the singer from the Make-Up a few feet away—we began laughing our asses off!"[13]

"Is everybody comfortable?" MacKaye inquired, semi-incredulously. "You might think this sucks. . . . I think it's about the coolest fucking thing I've ever seen."[14] And on that note, the show started up again. The crowd soon returned to their feet, and the band completed its set without further incident.

What happened after the show, Wright stresses, validated his already sky-high regard for the DC band. "After paying the bands, Ian and I discussed the surreal events of the evening. Then he gave me $100, unsolicited, out of their share to help replace my contact lens." It was a generous gesture—the spirit of DIY punk at its best—not unlike what Matt Talbott of Hum had done for Wright several months earlier in accepting a mere $25 for Hum's show. "They truly got it," he explains, "and I'll never forget that."[15]

At least three newspaper articles referenced the show over the next ten days, rendering accounts of two arrests (including of one person bizarrely accused of "biting another man's waist so hard he drew blood") as well as of a third showgoer who was treated at the hospital for injuries sustained in the mosh pit. "Fugazi . . . usually has no problem controlling crowds at its shows," the *Journal Star* reported, noting one significant exception: "The band has performed in Peoria, Bloomington and Champaign five times and run into minor conflicts with the audience on each occasion."[16]

It was an ignominious distinction for central Illinois, and it wouldn't be forgotten by anyone, including the band members. The Peoria show was among the first twenty gigs handpicked for digital release in the Fugazi Live Series—"because it was such incredible fucking madness," as MacKaye explained in 2004.[17] It remains a landmark performance, even if the continual interruptions grow tiresome on the recording. This was Peoria, simultaneously at its best and worst—a conjoined duality of hometown shame and pride, a scene that proved routinely prone to ruining a good thing.

The reaction from showgoers was mixed as well. "I came home from ISU with out-of-town friends for that show," recalls Jen Boniger Dixon. "I'd never been more embarrassed for Peoria. People love to talk that show up. I don't get why."[18] But where some saw power and purpose in the band's stand against crowd violence, others viewed it as political correctness run amok. "I thought it was a rip-off," says Jeff Gregory of Dollface. "Ian was there to lecture, not to play music."[19]

And yet plenty of others felt differently. More than a few were able to see a magnificent band in its prime, some for the first or only time. For many, the experience was life-altering. "In spite of the chaos, it felt like a triumph," Wright says. That the show remains a topic of discussion more than two decades later is proof enough of that. "To this day, some people know me as the man who brought Fugazi to Peoria," he laughs.[20] Love it or hate it, it was a seminal moment in Peoria music history, on par with the Who's explosive set in the very same room a generation earlier.

Ian MacKaye's behind-the-scenes goodwill wasn't limited to the night of the show, either. A couple of weeks later, Wright received the following postcard in the mail:

Dear Jon

We're slowly making our way west. Tonight we're playing a crazy rock joint called "the Pomp Room" in Sioux Falls, S.D. It's a tradition for me to write notes of thanks to promoters, but I want you to know that I particularly appreciate the work and sacrifice you put into the Peoria gig. I hope all things turn good for you. Take care. IAN*Fugazi[21]

Upon writing back, a second postcard arrived for Wright in January 1996. "I hope all is well in Peoria and there hasn't been any unpleasant fallout from the show we did there. Did you ever run into those dopes again?"[22]

*　*　*

With Naked Bums' shows drawing increasingly larger audiences, bands like Hum and the Jesus Lizard signing to major labels, and Dollface ostensibly not far behind, the upward trajectory of underground music, both locally and nationally, seemed well secured. "After the Fugazi show, I felt like I could book anybody," recalls Wright, whose ambitions briefly found him pursuing country legend Johnny Cash for a concert at the Peoria Civic Center.[23] But the cultural winds would soon shift.

Like their stint with Capitol Records, the Jesus Lizard's much-touted slot on the 1995 Lollapalooza festival tour was mostly a bust. Their intimate performances were not exactly stadium-friendly, and the band's early time slot ensured they played to plenty of empty seats. The *Washington Post* dubbed the tour "Alternative Nation's Last Stand," marking both the peak of alternative rock as a significant cultural force and the beginning of its decline.[24] This dynamic was mirrored in central Illinois as well.

If the Fugazi show was a high-water mark for mid-nineties Peoria, there were plenty of triumphs to come. In the early months of 1996, Naked Bums brought a wide-ranging mix of talent to town, including the Promise Ring (Milwaukee emo), Man or Astro-man? (Alabama surf), C-Clamp (Champaign indie rock), and U.S. Maple (Chicago avant-noise). "[Wright] was a master curator," says

Tyson Markley of the band Ham. "He brought in a wide variety of top-notch indie touring acts and then paired them up with the best punk/indie bands Peoria had to offer at that time. . . . You knew that when Naked Bums put on a show, there was going to be a certain level of quality to it."[25]

But it was getting more and more difficult to sustain the crowds of just a year earlier, and the downtown American Legion hall had become unaffordable. All-ages shows during this time migrated to smaller, less expensive venues across the Illinois River, including a Legion hall just outside of Washington. Back in Peoria, a house full of college students started hosting large, eclectic parties featuring live music, which presented another option for local shows. At 808 North University Street, DJs spun dance music in the attic, indie/punk bands played in the basement, and all four floors (and often each individual room) catered to a slightly different audience.

"I was in charge of booking the basement," explains Sharon Berardino. "We had such a great space to throw parties in, and it was an alternative to the hall shows that were happening around town. [It] gave bands new audiences to play to as well—not many university folks would make it out to the hall shows, but our house was packed with them."[26]

Forced to seek out ever-cheaper venues, Wright booked a handful of touring acts at the 808 house in the spring and summer of '96, including Champaign-Urbana emo icons Braid; another DC/Dischord post-hardcore act, Bluetip; and an experimental jazz/hardcore ensemble from Salt Lake City, Iceburn. Still, many of his shows were bigger than 808's basement could comfortably handle.

No longer able to rely on the established halls, Wright thought he had found a solution in Inn Cahoots, a dive bar on the edge of Creve Coeur that (somehow or another) agreed to host all-ages shows. The wishful arrangement lasted all of one evening. When New Orleans sludge-metal masters EyeHateGod rolled through town in May 1996—one month after the release of their classic third album, *Dopesick*—they proceeded to pulverize the mishmash of faithful met-alheads, baffled barflies, and indie/punk kids in attendance. "Thankfully, the police didn't show up until the end of their set," Wright explains. "Unfortunately, the bar's owner immediately canceled all further shows."[27] It was back to the drawing board again.

With punk rock supergroup Pegboy scheduled to come down from Chicago in less than two weeks, a scramble ensued to find a replacement venue. Eventually Wright settled on the Romeo B. Garrett Cultural Center, a carpeted auditorium on the Bradley University campus, just a block from his dorm room. It was a sedate space, more accustomed to aspiring poets than punk bands, though it had hosted occasional local shows at least as early as 1986, when Barry Stepe's Naked Hippy made its stage debut at an anti-apartheid festival.

Pegboy offered an illustrious punk pedigree, with former members of Naked Raygun, the Effigies, and Bhopal Stiffs, and shared with those bands an ear for melody that was uncommon in most punk rock. The show also marked the return to Peoria of guitarist John Haggerty and bassist Pierre Kezdy, who'd played the ICC gym with Naked Raygun nearly a decade earlier.

"Pegboy was fantastic—an incredibly energetic performance," Wright recalls. "As soon as they finished their set, I remember [vocalist] Larry Damore walked offstage, out the side door, and puked his guts out. But more than anything, I remember losing $1,000 on the band's guarantee."[28] Despite his best efforts, not enough people showed up to break even on the show. For a nineteen-year-old college student on a shoestring budget, the financial loss stung. But he had little time to dwell on it: Tortoise, the Sea and Cake, and 5ive Style loomed just around the corner—a triple bill of mid-nineties Chicago "post-rock" all-stars booked for early June.

In 1996, Tortoise was pushing the boundaries of indie rock with an approach that fused jazz, dub, and electronica with prog, krautrock, and world music influences. Its sophomore album, *Millions Now Living Will Never Die*, released earlier that year, is considered a post-rock landmark, pointing toward a future in which any musical influence could be sliced, diced, combined, and rearranged—and the very idea of "punk credibility" rendered obsolete. The Sea and Cake and 5ive Style were standouts on their own, exceptional musicians skewing their post-rock lenses toward jazz and funk, respectively.

For Tortoise bassist and Peoria/Pekin native Douglas McCombs, the June 5, 1996, show was an unlikely homecoming. It was the last date of a lengthy US tour that found the band playing each of its members' hometowns, he explains, and it was almost called off at the last minute:

> Everyone else in Tortoise comes from a town that is on a "normal" tour circuit: Asheville, Louisville, Portland, Madison. The only friends I had who had EVER played in Peoria were the Jesus Lizard, and they said it was a good show. After two months on tour and being two hours away from Chicago, everyone in all three bands wanted to blow off the Peoria show. At the risk of sounding heroic,

I told them that they were all a bunch of pathetic pussies and we were doing the show no matter what. Historic. HA![29]

Collective memories of this show revolve around the Chicago bands' extraordinary musicianship and astonishing surplus of gear; one audience member recalls being "kind of dumbfounded by how well [Tortoise] played."[30] However, the relatively low turnout wiped out what remained of Wright's savings account, and with it the ability to take risks on larger acts or support a record label. That August brought the final Naked Bums show—another stellar lineup featuring Lifetime (New Jersey emo/hardcore) and Weston (Pennsylvania pop-punk), which at least managed to break even. But after promoting shows nonstop for two years, Wright was ready to reassess his energies. As others had discovered before him, the intense work of DIY music promotion proved too emotionally and financially draining to sustain indefinitely.

The euphoria of the Jesus Lizard and Fugazi shows had worn off, and ambitions had to be reeled in. The *For God and Country* 7" never came to fruition, nor did a proposed Dollface record. Naked Bums, Inc. never became a Polyvinyl Records or a Jade Tree, much less a Sub Pop or a Dischord. The label discography Wright envisioned never made it out of his head, but he wasn't quite done yet. The decision to drop the Naked Bums moniker in favor of "Desperate Acts" (borrowed from a Jawbreaker song) was both an attempt to signal a new start and a reflection of Wright's own evolving musical tastes. The mid-nineties return of straight-edge hardcore, now sounding more metal than punk, had conjoined with the rise of second-wave emo (via Jawbreaker, Sunny Day Real Estate, and other faithful acolytes)—and the Midwest was a stronghold for it. As music critic Andy Greenwald notes, "The best and most lasting of these bands emerged from the perceived cultural no-man's-land of Middle America, from the forgotten cities in the flyover states. Braid from Champaign-Urbana. Christie Front Drive from Denver. . . . The Get Up Kids from Kansas. The Promise Ring from Milwaukee."[31]

In Peoria, bands like Superego and Headstrong were paving the way for a whole new wave of hardcore, and pop-punk groups like the Manleys and Shazzam were morphing into emocore acts Trainfare and Keepsake, while Fairmont straddled the line between the two—equal parts heavy and melodic. Meanwhile, with the addition of Superego's Matt Bellinger on guitar (amid a series of lineup changes), Dismiss had transformed from a snotty bubblegum-punk trio, à la

Green Day, into a dense, guitar-driven quartet bursting with tinges of emotional hardcore. Unreleased recordings of the band in its later stages reveal the path that Bellinger and frontman Gared O'Donnell would follow in their next outfit— a direction they hinted at from the very beginning. In her zine *Between the Covers,* Sharon Berardino's 1994 review of an early Dismiss show proved remarkably prescient: "While thoughts of Green Day come to mind . . . Dismiss's music is both harder and faster, but still has the catchy lyrics and riffs. Try as they may, Dismiss is too cute to be hardcore, but given a few years, that could all change."[32]

CHAPTER 14

Rock Over London, Rock On Peoria

You had great local acts like Dollface, the Neptunes, the MIBs,
Nora Hate, and Frozen at Sea making very different, very awesome
music. And then Naked Bums would bring in really amazing
touring acts like Sweep the Leg Johnny, MK Ultra, Man or Astro-
man? and so many more. These great bands inspired so many
kids to pick up guitars and make their own weird bands.
—Tyson Markley (of Ham)

Ham really whips a llama's ass.
—Wesley Willis

The very notion of a unified, all-ages scene was of course utopian, but it didn't
stop successive generations of punks from trying. Like the Peoria BYO, the Disgusted Youth Organization, and others before them, both Jon Wright's Naked
Bums, Inc., and Brian White's Freekshow Records came from the same place
and followed the same trajectory. If the young promoters' loftiest goals were not
successful, their efforts were hardly failures. Their competitive rivalry, despite
its tensions, pushed them both to be better, White explains, and "to dig deeper
and be on point."[1] And a lot of other young people came along with them.

After losing a couple thousand dollars on the Pegboy and Tortoise shows,
Wright took a six-month hiatus from booking. As for White, "I guess you could
say, I went to jail, found Jesus and moved to Idaho," he says, summarizing a
much longer personal journey. But the principles he found in punk's DIY culture stayed with him for life: "Making things happen, building community,
working together . . . it was life-changing . . . the music, the ethos, the work.

I am part of city planning, government, etc. [today] because of this idea of building community. My thoughts of church—and what that community looks like as a pastor—come from that. How I carry myself in the school I work at . . . dealing with kids—hopefully inspiring them to do what we did, and do still."[2]

And yet, for everyone who bonded over their shared experience, others felt left out. Among any group of so-called outsiders, some will become insiders—and this was the unavoidable paradox of the Peoria scene as well. Naked Bums' booking success, for example, at times carried with it a perceived cliquishness, suggests Tyson Markley of Ham. "Because their shows were so well-curated, it was also very exclusive. It was a club," he explains. "They had the tendency to book only a handful of local bands to open for the touring acts. At the time, us younger folk didn't understand why it worked that way."[3]

But not everyone could open for Fugazi or the Jesus Lizard. With contracts, guarantees, and real money on the line, local bands of a certain caliber were naturally invited to play more often. Punk rock was not about making money, but a scene that relied on renting other people's venues did have a built-in overhead. "Looking back, it's clear we just weren't that good yet," admits Ham drummer Tom "Atomic" Satterfield. "Plus, we were writing goofy pop-punk songs about cartoon characters and small-town weirdos—not the 'deep' subjects our peers were writing about. This was a time of political punk and post-hardcore/emo bands. . . . Songs about Nickelodeon TV shows were not the topic du jour."[4]

For those on the outside looking in, the feeling of exclusion could invert the sense of community that so many found in the punk scene. But it also drove people to create their own niche—and to discover they were better off for it. "Every DIY story starts with some outsider feeling like there is no outlet for their interests, and the established groups are not supportive of [them], so they take control of the situation," Satterfield explains. "[But in this case] the 'established' group that was being rebelled against were *also* a bunch of outsiders taking control of *their* art."[5]

While this dynamic sometimes felt counterproductive, it was inevitable for a group outgrowing its confines. Peoria's "punk" scene, a hodgepodge of outsiders, was beginning to splinter into its constituent forms—multiple, overlapping micro-scenes—even before the internet accelerated the phenomenon. There were more bands and shows than ever, but they came at the expense of a wider sense of camaraderie. It was a far cry from the cultural desperation that brought

Bloody Mess and the Stepes together and a marked departure from the Airwaves days of just three years earlier, when there was effectively a single scene whose constituents came to nearly every show no matter who was playing.

With Naked Bums and Freekshow Records out of the booking picture, numerous others stepped up to fill the void. "I felt like somebody had to pick up the slack," recalls Mike Perveiler, aka Mike Rugg, who promoted dozens of shows around Peoria in the late nineties and into the next decade.[6] A Chicago-area transplant, he teamed up with Brody Maag (of Nora Hate) and Brody's sister Dallas Maag ("a lady Lemmy with a Mae West twang to her sang") to form Rugg City, a raw, sometimes ferocious rock and roll trio and a fixture on the Peoria scene during their three-year existence.[7] Rugg went on to play in Pootinanny, the Wet Spots, and 52 Blue Candy Hearts while bringing prominent acts like the Red Aunts, Gaza Strippers, and New Bomb Turks (twice) to Peoria. "Some of it's born out of necessity," he explains. "You want to play a show and you want to bring a band to town, so you just go out and do it."[8]

Eric Williamson, aka Suit and Tie Guy, started booking and playing shows about the same time—and for similar reasons. "Jon [Wright] and Brian [White] were not in a position to keep doing shows the way they had been," he explains. "So I was like, I guess I have to put on a show, if I want to play a show."[9]

Meanwhile, Ham's first bass player, Ryan Hovind, had started promoting shows as Lame Productions, named in response to his view that Naked Bums wouldn't book "oddball dorky bands," recalls Tom Satterfield. "Ryan was a bit of his own type . . . [an] outsider Christian oddball promoter dude."[10]

New sets of outsiders were doing their own thing—the very essence of punk's DIY ethos. "There was a new crop of new kids making new music and trying to form their own scene," Markley explains. "It was not as unified, and the quality control of well-curated shows was gone . . . but there was something cool about this scene because it was scrappy, not polished, and in my mind it was not exclusive."[11]

*   *   *

After hosting live music for about a year, shows at the 808 North University house ended abruptly on September 13, 1996, the night the Chicago band Lustre King (math rock) and Peoria's Danse Macabre (avant-goth) opened for a much-hyped touring band from Brooklyn, New York. The organ-fueled psych rock of Jonathan Fire*Eater was then at the center of a major-label bidding

141

war—though you wouldn't have known it from the modest house show the band played in Peoria.

The troubles began the day before the show. "I came home to find that our landlords had built a wall in the middle of our basement," recalls Sharon Berardino. "I guess they got wind of us having shows there." With their basement split in half and no time to find a new venue, she and her roommates moved the show to the attic, which was dangerous because of the massive holes in the floor. With all the people and heavy equipment, "I'm still surprised nothing or no one fell through," she admits.[12]

While both opening acts were able to play full sets, the Peoria police arrived just a few songs into Jonathan Fire*Eater and pulled the plug. It wasn't 808's first run-in with the cops—a prior noise violation had already landed Berardino and her housemates in court, though the charge was tossed out. "I remember Brody [Maag] showing up to our court date with a few other folks saying they'd throw benefit shows to pay off our fines," Berardino recalls. "But we never even got there, thankfully."[13]

With the inexplicably constructed wall in the 808 basement, however, she was forced to redirect her booking efforts to the Bradley University campus. As for Jonathan Fire*Eater, the band soon imploded in dramatic fashion, just like the nineties alternative gold rush that had fed the group's hype. But its legacy helped stoke the Brooklyn rock revival soon after: besides inspiring the likes of the Strokes and Interpol, three-fifths of the band went on to find indie success as the Walkmen.[14]

Even as another short-lived Peoria venue vanished, yet another teen nightclub in the Sneakers/Stage 2/Confetti's location started hosting shows again. From the summer of 1996 into early 1997, the Twilight Zone regularly showcased the Peoria scene's continued eclecticism: the off-kilter psychedelic rock of Solar Wimp Trio (ex–Fast Food Revolution) and the flute-laden darkness of Danse Macabre (ex–the Factory); the Hives' poppy punk and the MIBs' peppy ska; the measured slowcore of Recuerdo and the brutal metalcore of Erebus; and the last days of Dollface and Dismiss. No two bands were quite alike, and though their bonds were steadily weakening, Peoria remained small enough to bring them together. "It was hard to find two other people who liked the same stuff . . . so you had to compromise," notes Kevin Dixon. "I always saw that as an asset of Peoria. . . . The problem was that none of those bands were going to get out and tour and let people know that this weirdo scene exists."[15]

Dixon had just returned from touring the country with Mustard Plug, a nationally known ska band from Grand Rapids, Michigan, where he had moved for the opportunity to make a living as a full-time musician. After quitting the band and returning to Peoria ("I realized that I didn't really like ska," he admits), he brought back a wider sense of possibility—the knowledge that there was more out there for bands ambitious enough to venture beyond their hometown.[16]

And Dixon quickly put this insight to work, first in the indie rock band 21 Union Square, which did some modest regional touring, and later and more successfully in Brief Candles, the long-running shoegaze-pop band he and his wife, Jen Boniger Dixon, started in the late nineties and eventually moved to Milwaukee. Deeply rooted DIY sensibilities also informed Silent Film Soundtracks—the couple's record label, and the first Peoria-based label to build a respectable discography—as well as their efforts to bring touring bands to town. "People tell me now, 'I'm so glad you set up these shows,' but . . . I always felt like nobody was really paying attention," Kevin recalls. "I was just doing things because I wanted to do things."[17]

Kevin's influence had also been critical in getting his younger brother, Corey Dixon, and Corey's friend Tim Beck into the music scene several years earlier. "Like most kids our age, we gravitated to grunge first, identifying as 'outsiders,' and then punk rock, then ska," Tim explains.[18] The quirky joke songs he and Corey wrote together in junior high paved the way for their band, the Skamedians, and both went on to play in the MIBs and Corey Dixon and the Zvooks, helping to sustain Peoria's small but steady ska presence.

A versatile instrumentalist, Tim also played drums for the Hives (*not* the Swedish band of the same name) and joined with another fellow Skamedian, Zak Piper, in Wheelchair Sex (WCS)—"a relatively over-the-top, inappropriate" hip hop act.[19] "Zak was oddly a gifted rapper," Tim recalls. "I did most of the beats and music. It was just us up there, rapping over a crackly tape."[20] Bending the trappings of hip hop through a small-town white-boy prism, WCS was surprisingly listenable. The duo's inventive rhymes and catchy melodies lifted them above mere parody, even if their willful self-assurance belied a cavalier sort of cultural appropriation. Still, WCS was a joyful kind of oddity—fun, unique, and remarkable for its gestation in a small midwestern town.

Peoria likely has no greater claim to oddball bands than any other city its size, but it often felt like it did. As self-described purveyors of "geek rock," the members of Ham not only looked like kids but broadcast their awkwardness in triumphant fashion—tossing Nirvana, Devo, and Weezer into a blender, with matching orange uniforms and choreographed dance moves to boot. Never the "cool kids," the Ham bandmates were eventually rewarded for their tenacity, having become a much better group in the process.

Likewise, Pootinanny was a true Peoria original in both name and spirit. The irreverent, shambolic "soul trash" duo featured Mike Rugg (Pootinanny stage name: Jalopy Johnson) and Jesse Martin (aka "Sufferin' Josiah") trading off drums and guitar, their chaotic shows doubling as noisy performance art. Martin experimented with prepared guitar and studied the cosmic jazz of Sun Ra; many of his peers considered him a musical genius. But he tended to struggle in a traditional band setting.

"As we got more structured, it actually made things more difficult for [him]," Rugg says. "He got more uncomfortable with it."[21] This restless dynamic eventually led to the band's dissolution and Martin's long-term withdrawal from the Peoria music scene—a reclusiveness that lent him the aura of a Syd Barrett figure: unseen but beloved and not forgotten.

*　　*　　*

"Outsider music"—primitive and uncommercial, created by untrained artists, and often distinguished by a childlike naïveté—was on the rise in the mid-nineties. Ham frontman Tyson Markley took his obsession with the genre to another level, attempting to reach his favorite artists by telephone. "I remember calling the parents of Gene and Dean Ween, for instance," he laughs. "I had a knack for being really annoying to the point where they'd talk to me."[22] Having somehow managed to track down Wesley Willis's number, and after a series of "out-of-this-world" phone conversations, Tyson coaxed the Chicago-based artist/musician down to Peoria to play a show.

Wesley Willis, a 300-pound schizophrenic African American homeless man, was an "outsider" by almost any definition. Former Dead Kennedys singer Jello Biafra later called him "one of the most unique songwriters and entertainment personalities in history" and "the most courageous person" he had known, noting his "unrelenting drive to succeed and overcome his horrifically poor background, child abuse, racism, chronic schizophrenia, and obesity, among other things."[23]

He attracted no small measure of cult notoriety, first as a visual artist selling his ink-pen drawings on the streets of Chicago, then for his eccentric songwriting—strange and humorous crudities spoken-sung over his keyboard's hopelessly bland auto-accompaniment feature. Wesley wrote hundreds of songs describing the many bands he saw in concert and was known for his arsenal of customizable catchphrases: "[*Insert band name here*] really whips a llama's ass," for example. Nearly every Wesley Willis song ended with his trademark sign-off, "Rock over London, rock on Chicago," followed by a one-line commercial for an unrelated consumer product. He was also renowned for greeting everyone he met with an affectionate headbutt; his forehead was permanently bruised as a result.

Wesley's unlikely 1997 Peoria show was held at an equally unlikely venue, as the Madison Theater had essentially cut off the local punk scene after the Factory singer's disastrous stage dive two years earlier. In addition, the show took place not in the grand theater itself but in its lobby, which was better suited for the audience of a couple hundred. The cover was just three dollars and the domed-ceiling lobby was packed, with half the crowd peering down from the second-floor rotunda. "It was like playing on the *Titanic*," suggests Brody Maag, whose Rugg City joined Ham on the bill.[24] "Wesley Willis was at the height of his popularity," adds Mike Rugg. "It was a wild night. . . . Everybody was totally into him."[25]

"The rock show whipped a camel's ass," in Wesley-speak. But it was Wesley's larger-than-life character, Tyson explains, which made a longer-lasting impression: "I remember driving him from the train station and giving him a tour of Peoria. He was like a big, friendly child . . . with occasional paranoid outbursts. From time to time, he'd mutter to himself in this scary voice, 'I'm on a demon hell-ride.' I was never afraid of him, just scared for him. I worried someone would think he was on drugs or something and call the cops."[26]

He may have been the consummate outsider, but Wesley Willis was very much a real artist, Tyson insists. "In between fits of paranoid delusions, he would throw wisdom down. He wasn't just a savant pushing buttons on a keyboard."[27] Amid the perennial debate over outsider music, however, it was often difficult to reconcile the differences between fandom and exploitation. Wesley's time in Peoria was not without the latter—"and it really bummed me out," Tyson says: "He would basically say yes to anything. I think somebody [in Peoria] bought one of his keyboards for significantly less than it was worth—and also bought his paintings for less than they were worth. I know people wound up with his stuff, basically for free. I think that people at the time were also very young and didn't realize they were being manipulative or mean."[28]

"He was very obviously being taken advantage of as some kind of obscene circus novelty act by people who did not actually care about him," adds Suit and Tie Guy, who sat with Wesley after the show at Lums, a popular late-night Peoria restaurant where youth could commandeer a table for hours with the purchase of a single, bottomless cup of coffee. "Fortunately, later in life someone saw the same thing I did and . . . [made] his tour care a pet project. From what I hear, this was a very good thing for his well-being. Unfortunately, it didn't keep him from dying of leukemia."[29]

Neither Ham nor Rugg City would experience the honor of having a Wesley Willis song written about it (unlike Kevin Dixon's old band, Mustard Plug). The Peoria show was a mere footnote in Wesley's unlikely career, but he undoubtedly made his mark on the Whiskey City. "We remained friendly and stayed in touch," Tyson adds. A few years later, Wesley invited the Amazing Kill-O-Watts (the band Ham morphed into) to open for him in Columbus, Ohio. "He was much better then. He had a friend/manager with him and he had sorted his meds out. He was still out of this world."[30]

*   *   *

Among the region's oddballs and outsiders, one curly-haired, bespectacled, and (sometimes) behatted Chillicothe native stood out in the crowd. Though he's worn a coat and tie since grade school, James Eric Williamson claims he never really wore a suit. "I always wear pants. That's the joke, right? I'm not really 'Suit and Tie Guy.'"[31] In the mid-nineties, he began carving out a singular place in Peoria's all-ages punk scene, despite his own ambivalence toward much of its music. While he possessed a prickly individualism that sometimes rubbed people the wrong way, his stalwart resolve and undeniable passion allowed him to extend his brand far beyond Peoria.

Like Bloody Mess years earlier, Williamson assumed a name, created an identity, and grew into an underground icon of sorts; his own silhouette serves as the logo for STG Soundlabs, his renowned analog synth company. But the enigmatic Suit and Tie Guy ("Suit" or "STG") was no punk rocker—even if, in some ways, he was as "punk" as it gets.

"My wife went to high school with him," says Tyson Markley. "She says he wore the outfit and carried a briefcase when everyone else had backpacks. And

every day, he was berated. He just took it in and went about his business. . . .
Now he's making modular synth parts for deadmau5 and Skrillex!"[32]

While discussing the origins of his distinctive style, Suit muses about growing up in the eighties and watching a lot of golden-age TV. "I just wanted to dress
like a fucking adult, I guess," he chuckles sardonically. The STG moniker came
via a pair of drunk guys one night at Lums: "They were making fun of everyone
who walked in . . . just talking shit to each other. 'Look at this fucking suit-and-
tie guy.' I wound up getting a job at Key Industries in East Peoria, and those guys
worked [there] on the floor. They came up to me at work one day and said, 'Hey
Suit and Tie Guy, we're your fan club.' I became Suit and Tie Guy that day."[33]

From his early love for Huey Lewis and "Weird Al" Yankovic, Suit was turned
on to classical/synthesizer albums and organ music in junior high. In high
school, he took music theory classes and started making electronic music on
his computer. Emerson, Lake and Palmer and *Dr. Who* were game-changers,
and "discovering Robert Fripp's solo stuff made me want to make music live,"
he recalls. In the fall of 1996, Suit bought a PA and started putting on shows. "I
wanted to get a bunch of people together so I could play in front of them. The
best way to do that is to throw a party and make it cheap so everyone can come
to it."[34]

Soon after booking his first show in Creve Coeur (not far from the hall GG
Allin once stalked), Suit and Tie Guy became a regular promoter in the Peoria
area. If he wasn't on the bill proper, whether solo or with a band, he'd play between acts, his ambient synthesizer music enveloping an often bewildered or
indifferent audience. Soon he was lending his PA to other promoters as well.
"He'd provide sound in exchange for being able to perform on the side," affirms
Mike Rugg. "He was always trying to work that deal into the equation, so he
could get a little bit of exposure with his music."[35]

One night Rugg and Jesse Martin turned the tables on Suit, setting up outside
one of his shows and sneaking in a quick Pootinanny set during band change-
over. "Jesse and I used to give him hell," Rugg chuckles. "But we also hung out.
As much shit as we gave him, we kind of realized he was doing his thing, just
like everybody else."[36]

Suit had a knack for finding unusual and out-of-the-way venues—spaces
that had never witnessed an all-ages punk show. Some of his earliest productions took place at Midway Lanes in East Peoria, a deliberate nod to a specific
Chicago venue. "I saw the MIBs at the Fireside Bowl, and that was kind of a

Figure 19. Eric "Suit and Tie Guy" Williamson excelled at finding unusual venues. Here, he is performing at Squeaky Clean Laundromat in Peoria, April 2003. Courtesy of Eric Williamson.

religious experience," Suit recalls. "I was like, you can put on shows in a bowling alley?! I went to every fucking bowling alley in the [Peoria] area—that was the only one that would play ball."[37]

Suit booked shows regularly for a couple of years, though they became more sporadic over time. "My ability to book a show that people would actually come to no longer existed at a certain point," he laughs. "Eventually I became totally focused on *creating* music, as opposed to booking." He also started recording bands, referring to the laptop in his briefcase as the STG Fidelity Soundlab. "Then when I got into building hardware, I just shortened it to STG Soundlabs."[38]

Today, Suit and Tie Guy's outsider persona is celebrated worldwide by a dedicated cohort of followers. In addition to his work at STG Soundlabs, he's the founder of Knobcon, billed as "the world's only synthesizer convention."[39] And when Suit ventures out to play live—whether at a local coin laundry (seriously!) or in the planetarium at the Peoria Riverfront Museum—his immersive, 360-degree modular synth setup is a glorious sight to behold.

* * *

As 1996 drew to a close, so did another chapter of Peoria's punk scene. With the departure of Josh Shane, Dollface once again reconfigured itself as a trio, while the demise of Crackpot Records forced the band to self-release its follow-up to *Corvette Summer*—the brilliant, psychedelic *Dollface Lights the Pilot!!!* The nation's flirtation with alternative music had crested and would soon fade, while fate appeared to be conspiring against the band. "Crackpot was totally done," explains Matt Shane. "We did some gigs without a CD—Milwaukee, Chicago, Minneapolis, and Peoria . . . record-release shows with *no record*. Then Scott [Ligon] quit right before we got *Pilot*, so we had no drummer."[40]

A new incarnation of Dollface, with Joe Camarillo of Chicago's Hushdrops filling in on drums, played a few shows, but this lineup was short-lived. The band played its final show (at the time) on December 21—a Suit and Tie Guy production at Midway Lanes.

Seeking to regroup and find a new drummer, Dollface's Matt Shane and Jeff Gregory soon moved to Los Angeles—and they weren't alone. A mass exodus of Peoria creativity ensued as various members of Three Boyfriends, Fast Food Revolution, the Bugs, and Solar Wimp Trio, along with a wider circle of family and friends, joined them in heading west. Although Matt and Jeff recorded a sizable batch of new demos in LA, they were unable to bring Dollface back to life.

The familiar cliché of "musical differences" had taken its toll. While Matt and Jeff were firmly rooted in the punk scene, Scott Ligon and Josh Shane preferred the classic R&B and soul sounds of their other band, Peoria's beloved River City Soul Revue. After leaving Dollface, they next formed the Heatersons, whose retro mix of country, rock, jazz, and rockabilly was likened to a "teenage version of NRBQ"—which happened to be Scott's lifelong favorite band.[41] By 2011, Scott Ligon not only was a veteran of the Chicago music scene but had actually become an integral member of NRBQ itself.[42]

Despite attracting major-label attention at the height of the nineties alternative boom, Dollface never gained the stardom that seemed its for the taking. Very few bands did, however—and "getting signed" could be a curse of its own. In 1993, famed Chicago recording engineer Steve Albini penned a widely shared exposé of the corporate music industry. Breaking down the costs associated with recording and touring for a band making the jump to a major label, he showed how even sales of 250,000 albums (a massive success for an underground act and a gross of $3 million) would pocket each band member as little as $4,000. "Some of your friends are probably already this fucked," Albini concluded.[43] This was true all over the country. Chronicling the San Diego scene during this period, Ryan Moore paints a bleak picture of those who thought they had "made it": "The hype about the 'next Seattle' never translated into any real commercial breakthroughs. Within a few years all of the San Diego bands who had signed with major labels were dropped from their contracts. Two of those bands endured lengthy legal disputes with their record companies, who owned the music they recorded but refused to release it on the grounds that it had limited commercial appeal."[44]

For better or worse, Dollface did not get quite that far. Yet its legacy remains intact many years later—not only in the 2014 vinyl reissue of its two classic records but in the wave of Peoria bands it inspired. Tyson Markley reflects on the larger shift in popular music culture, which more or less paralleled the rise and fall of Dollface. "The weird indie band explosion that was 1991 to 1995—the optimism, the anyone-can-be-the-next-Nirvana type of feeling—was gone," he explains. "It was a big snowball effect. I was lucky to catch the height of it, and it was a bit of shellshock how fast it died."[45]

PART IV

Tolling of the Digital Bell: 1997–2007

By the late 1990s, punk rock had more or less returned underground. But unlike earlier periods, the scene no longer depended solely on word of mouth, reviews in *Maximum RocknRoll*, or the occasional record store gamble to find new bands. In the wake of Nirvana and Green Day, the ever-expanding internet soon spread music as quickly as it spread pornography.

The Peoria area already boasted punk-friendly recording studios, including Joel Madigan's Lisa Falzone Recording, Tom Hopwood's Stinky Pete Studios, and several others. Increasingly affordable CD burners and computer recording software further democratized music production, allowing bands to produce and record themselves without labels or studios—and on the cheap. MP3 players then made CDs obsolete as well, ironically ushering in a resurgence of vinyl. With the internet, connections were easier to make; self-marketing became the expected norm.

In Peoria's DIY underground, the digital age materialized amid the union of dozens of musical trends. Some bands drew clear influence from grunge, pop-punk, and adjacent "alternative" acts of the 1990s, from Weezer to Radiohead to Nine Inch Nails. Others offered throwbacks to early punk bands like the Dead Kennedys or built on the various iterations of hardcore that followed Minor Threat. Still others incorporated influences from popular threads of heavy music, including bands like Led Zeppelin, Motörhead, and Metallica. Emo and post-hardcore bands took inspiration from Rites of Spring, Fugazi, Jawbreaker, and Sunny Day Real Estate. There were ska bands, death metal bands, rockabilly bands . . . and Christian versions of each.

When they could find venues, so many Peoria-area bands were playing shows (and releasing their own CDs) that they did not all know one another. Multiple scenes operated independently and occasionally overlapped, a new development for the Peoria scene. While this explosion of creativity was notable for a city its size, it was not isolated. Across the nation, a constant flow of touring acts were longing to play anywhere—including Peoria.

Peoria musicians, too, hit the road in significant numbers, and some had national and even international success. While peak-nineties levels of punk-rock stardom were no longer really attainable, a broader music scene allowed more bands to find their own niches—and achieve their own modest slice of notoriety.

CHAPTER 15

Hidden by Cornfields

It was way off the beaten path, and the room was nothing more than a Boy Scout lodge. The sound was always terrible in there . . . weird vibes out in those woods.

—Adam Widener (of 52 Blue Candy Hearts, the Jet Set, Adam and the Cola Kids, and others)

The concrete floors did make for a sound nightmare for shows that were sparsely attended, and on nights when the place was packed, the floor would be as slippery as an ice rink. When all went well, though, it felt like the space belonged to all who were in attendance. And no one could fuck with us in our space.

—Chris Bennett (of Headstrong, Fairmont, Subsist, Blue Skies Lie, Minsk, Lark's Tongue, and others)

Even as one generation of Peoria punks set off for greener pastures, another was waiting in the wings. In 1997, two new venue options emerged for this new era of Peoria shows: the Optimist Club in the suburban woods of nearby Morton, and Tiamat Records near Bradley University in the heart of Peoria. Their aesthetics could hardly have been less alike, but they shared one important attribute: both locations were removed enough from residential and commercial interests that they generally could host live music without drawing noise complaints or police intervention. This quasi-independence allowed Peoria's punk scene to build its community and develop its politics—with messy and often contradictory results.

The year also saw the emergence of two bands that would become central to the Peoria punk mythos. Both embodied the personal/emotional traits of the mid-nineties emo/hardcore zeitgeist, and both found their roots in the DIY punk scene. Later, after cutting their teeth in the Midwest, key members of Subsist would find global success via the post-metal psychedelic world of Minsk, while Planes Mistaken for Stars would become one of the most influential post-hardcore acts of the new millennium.

*   *   *

Headquartered in St. Louis, Missouri, Optimist International is a service organization with nearly 3,000 clubs in more than twenty countries. The Optimist Creed, adopted in 1922, asks its members to pledge

> to be so strong that nothing can disturb your peace of mind.
> To talk health, happiness and prosperity to every person you meet.
> To make all your friends feel that there is something in them.
> To look at the sunny side of everything and make your optimism come true.[1]

Besides promoting the "sunny side" of life, the Optimists have served young people worldwide for more than a century: battling childhood cancer, combating high-school dropout rates, and facilitating other youth-centered projects. Morton's chapter was founded in 1931, hosting youth shooting contests and coordinating Little League baseball in its early years. In 1947, the Morton Optimists celebrated their high school football players with a keynote dinner featuring Olympic champion Jim Thorpe, then considered "the greatest athlete of all time."[2] In this upper-middle-class bedroom community—touted as the "Pumpkin Capital of the World" for the pumpkin cannery situated at its center— the Morton Optimist Club was a pillar of patriotism and community service.

The club's cabin was also available to rent for banquets, private parties, and community events, and in the late 1990s that roster of activities expanded to include DIY punk shows. All-ages shows were, to a degree, in line with the club's mission to provide recreational opportunities for youth, while the punks, for their part, helped further the organization's charity work with show rental fees. Inadvertently the punks and the Optimists formed a symbiotic, if awkward, partnership.

The building itself was, quite literally, a cabin in the woods. Located on the rural outskirts of Morton, a twenty-minute drive from downtown Peoria, it was somewhat isolated and not easy to find. Flyers for Optimist Club shows, by necessity, almost always included a detailed map. Through its large sliding-glass doors, showgoers regularly saw their friends drive by and miss the venue entirely, only to turn around and return minutes later. It "felt like it was just totally hidden by cornfields, because it kinda was," says Josh Haller of the Psychodelics. "But kids would flock out there for some of the most hardcore shows I've seen."[3]

The small brick cabin—described by Tom "Atomic" Satterfield as a "sound fiasco"—encompassed a pair of small bathrooms, a kitchen, and a meeting room centered around a large fireplace; a few picnic tables were scattered outside.[4] "It . . . looked like a Wes Anderson set," notes Steve Byrne, who booked shows there under the name Quagmire 9.[5] Like most halls, converting the space into a temporary rock club required bands, promoters, and their willing friends to arrive early to break down chairs and folding tables—and stay late to sweep, empty the trash, and return it to a more respectable form.

The first DIY punk shows at the Optimist Club appear to have been those set up by Jon Wright in the spring of 1997. They marked his return as a promoter, this time under the name Desperate Acts, having left the Naked Bums name behind. All three shows paired touring bands at the top of their game: Rainer Maria (from Madison, Wisconsin) and the Hal Al Shedad (Atlanta); the Promise Ring (Milwaukee) and Joan of Arc (Chicago); and Giants Chair (Kansas City, Missouri) and Castor (Champaign-Urbana). And crucially for the promoter, none of them lost money.

These shows were also personally gratifying, Wright explains. "When the Promise Ring and Joan of Arc set up next to each other and played [the Promise Ring's] 'A Picture Postcard' together, as if they were a single band, it was particularly transcendent." Nevertheless, aside from a house party in June featuring Iceburn (returning from Salt Lake City) and the Fully Celebrated Orchestra (Boston), they were also Wright's last shows as a regular promoter. "It was time to move on," he explains, "and let the 'next generation' have a shot."[6]

Others had stepped up in Wright's absence, and a congregation of new faces were being introduced to the local punk scene—often at the Morton Optimist Club. Sam McIntyre was Steve Byrne's partner in Quagmire 9, which got its start as an online zine in the early days of the internet. Their first show together, in January 1998, brought a then-unknown emocore act from Omaha, Nebraska, to the Optimist Club. "It was Cursive kind of before they were *Cursive*," McIntyre explains. "It was a magical night and I will never forget the energy . . . and the elation at having pulled something off that I had never tried before."[7]

As it turns out, the punks and the Optimists were perhaps closer than anyone suspected. The DIY spirit and the Optimist Creed were well intertwined—alive, if hidden, among the cornfields of central Illinois.

* * *

In June 1997, a fledgling hardcore band played one of its earliest shows at the Morton Optimist Club. Over the next three years, Subsist would become one of Peoria's most popular and influential acts—and one of the few (at the time) to tour outside of central Illinois. Subsist's members were open about their Christianity and devotion to a straight-edge lifestyle yet continually questioned the stereotypes of both. This inquiring mindset ultimately pushed them beyond the assurance of their faith-based origins into more expansive philosophical explorations.

While punk rock's connection to Christianity might seem strange or tenuous to some, it was not at all uncommon in the Midwest, as Jared Grabb explains: "My first exposure to punk rock, metal and everything indie came through the church I was attending. Mike Gilbert, a friend of mine from Sunday school, had been invited to a show at 'Crazy's' by a slightly older church youth, Devin Kreider, who played in [Fast Food Revolution]. Lucky for me, it turned out that several older youth who attended my church were musicians, and I would come to share in their love of music in years to come."[8]

Growing up in a strict churchgoing family in rural western Illinois, Subsist guitarist Chris Bennett found a lifelong refuge in music. As a kid, he "would soak up anything resembling metal and punk." But in those pre-internet days, finding new music outside of the mainstream took real work. The discovery of heavy bands like Mortification, Tourniquet, and Living Sacrifice—"who had a certain degree of respect in the metal world, even though they were considered 'Christian'"—was particularly impactful. "Being able to buy that in a Christian bookstore was huge, because you didn't have to worry about your parents over-analyzing it."[9] For Bennett, music was a ticket out of the small-town conservatism that defined his childhood: "When you're young . . . trying to reconcile this faith-based upbringing and find your place in the world, mixing that with more extreme music . . . seemed like a pretty freeing path to me—which would lead to eventually figuring out more ways to shed that baggage."[10]

When Bennett left home for Olivet Nazarene University, an evangelical school south of Chicago, he met Brian Guerin and Joel Madigan, both from the

Peoria area. It was a transformative encounter for all three aspiring musicians, who were on parallel spiritual journeys and soon put together a band. Their early partnership evolved into Headstrong, heavily influenced by post-hardcore acts like Helmet and Quicksand, the Soundgarden side of Seattle grunge, Christian indie/punk on the Tooth & Nail label, and a slew of metal and hardcore groups.

After his first year at Olivet, Bennett left school, moved to Peoria, and dedicated himself to playing music—a mission that would span decades and countless overlapping projects. (Even as Headstrong was making its name in Peoria, for example, he and Joel Madigan started a second band, Fairmont, whose soft/loud "screamo" dynamics were well in line with the mid-nineties emo boom.) By the time Subsist arose from the ashes of Headstrong, Bennett and Guerin had found their calling in the metal-infused direction taken by hardcore. The band described its sound in an early interview: "a huge pit mine truck running over a city, over and over again."[11]

Amid several early lineup shifts, Tim Mead came on board as Subsist's vocalist. The son of a Nazarene minister, he, too, had grown up in a devout religious family and also attended Olivet—the pairing was a natural fit. Joel Madigan, though not in the original Subsist lineup, was tapped on multiple occasions to play both drums and guitar[12]—one of ten different members of the group at various points in time. While not shying away from their faith, the Subsist bandmates collectively rejected preaching for a broader personal introspection and rebuffed any attempts to typecast them. In similar fashion, they spurned the rigid trappings of hardcore, as reflected in the liner notes to their *Lessons in Brokenness* EP: "We will not take part in the separation of the hardcore movement based on differences such as spiritual beliefs, lifestyle choices or anything else that divides us. . . . Hardcore isn't about straight edge, or veganism, or Christianity, or Krishna. . . . It's about being able to express your dedication to any of these ideals, even if no one in the world agrees with you."[13]

For the most part, the rise of a Christian-specific hardcore scene mirrored its larger counterpart, with the added dimension of faith. In the Midwest especially, this dynamic was amplified by the Cornerstone Music Festival. From 1991 to 2012, the yearly gathering brought dozens of faith-minded punk, hardcore, metal, and rock bands—along with some 20,000 annual attendees—to the small farm town of Bushnell, Illinois, sixty miles southwest of Peoria. The festival was organized by Jesus People USA, one of the more successful spiritual communities born of the post-hippie 1970s Jesus movement.[14]

During its heyday, Cornerstone served as an entry point to the counterculture for many midwestern youth—a chance to watch bands with international acclaim, connect with a larger community, and broaden one's worldview. Its Christian affiliation was key, allowing many of these kids to travel and attend unsupervised, often for the first time. "This was of huge importance," Bennett explains. "I give [Cornerstone] credit for showing me a wider world. The fact that Mortification—a band from Australia who was on Nuclear Blast [Records]— was playing about an hour from my small town was kind of a crazy thing for a sixteen-year-old kid who at that point had only dreamed of seeing a real metal show. I could have cared less that I was seeing bands talking about a monotheistic god. I just wanted every kind of aggressive music experience I could get."[15]

Cornerstone was perhaps *the* critical ingredient in positioning the Midwest as a hub for Christian hardcore. But that world could also be limiting. While Headstrong played an impromptu set at the festival one year, Subsist opted to pursue other avenues. "There were lots of Cornerstone-type bands that were content to just operate within the Christian world," Bennett explains. "We had some conscious idea that we wanted to *not* just do that."[16]

Instead, Subsist was passionate about playing anywhere and everywhere, whether for 500 kids or 5. By fostering its connections and networking on the early (chat room and instant messaging–focused) internet, the band built a loyal following throughout the Midwest. When they played in the Peoria area, carloads of fans came from all over Illinois—and even neighboring states—to take part in the fellowship. Between songs, vocalist Tim Mead would thank them for their travels, acknowledging an almost comically long list of the cities and towns represented. "This made a huge impression on me," he explains. "Here we were—just kids from nowhere—and yet there were people who would come from far away. . . . I just remember feeling so pumped, so overwhelmed that what we were doing actually mattered."[17]

"It really was amazing to see friends from all over the Midwest . . . driving for hours to attend a show at some out-of-the-way space on the outskirts of a small city like Peoria," Bennett adds, reflecting on those experiences: "It was just something that you did—you didn't think twice about driving long distances to see a band that only a tiny coterie of people cared about. I think it says so much about the human spirit, and our desire and capabilities for connection. . . . To establish a foundation where the ethics of doing things our own way, on our own terms, in the best way we saw fit, was so crucial to myself and to everyone involved."[18]

*   *   *

At the Morton Optimist Club, a whole generation of youth was experiencing punk rock for the first time. "I was maybe sixteen . . . and caught wind of a local hardcore band named Subsist," recalls Jon Beattie, who later played drums for Angeltread and RyeFieldCrane, among other bands. When he and some friends made the forty-minute drive from Chillicothe to Morton, they had no idea what to expect. "I walk in and there are all these . . . punks with tattoos, crazy hair, cool clothes. It was completely different from what I was used to. What struck me the most was how NICE these 'freaks' were, and the camaraderie. Scary-looking dudes with tattoos smiling and hugging one another . . . I knew right away it was something I wanted to be a part of."[19]

"The Morton Optimist Club shows were rad," notes Sam McIntyre. "We always got good feedback from bands visiting because it was such a chill atmosphere. There weren't a lot of distractions—you went for the show and that was it. The place wasn't too large and had an intimate feel to it. Plus, it was loud as hell."[20]

"I think the out-of-town bands who played there always had a great time," adds Chris Bennett. "Being able to bring Song of Zarathustra [Sioux City] to town sticks out in my mind, as they were a force to be reckoned with. . . . I remember Incision from St. Louis being amazed at the passionate response they received, and the way everyone gave their utmost attention to every band who played. For myself personally, being able to see Giants Chair at the Optimist Club was one of the highlights of my show-going career. . . . I will also never forget how Elliott [Louisville] would captivate the crowd a few years later."[21]

Other prominent touring acts that played the Morton Optimist Club—alongside nearly every Peoria band of the era—included American Football (Champaign-Urbana), Not Waving but Drowning (St. Louis), Fall Silent (Reno), Racebannon (Bloomington), Ten Grand (formerly the Vidablue; Iowa City), Burn It Down (Indianapolis), Kill Your Idols (Long Island), and Pave the Rocket (St. Louis).

In March 2000, Ed Gein Productions (aka promoters Dan Dirst and Amy Michael) organized a two-day hardcore/punk/metal festival at the Optimist Club, featuring a mix of bands from neighboring states and a host of locals. The event, which doubled as a fundraiser for TAPS, a no-kill animal shelter in nearby Pekin, was a labor of love and "became nearly a full-time second job for me," Dirst recalls. "I'm guessing I spent thirty hours a week between phone calls, flyering [and] getting the schedule to work for over twenty-five bands." This was still long before cell phones and social media—"flyering was the only way to get the word out. We put out the Ed Gein zine as a flyer of sorts, with all of the info about the fest . . . including directions, updated band info, and all sorts of gory pictures."[22]

For two months, Dirst came home from work to find his answering machine full of messages—one of his monthly phone bills, after fielding so many calls, added up to $600. "All of that money came out of pocket, since we wanted to donate the most we could to TAPS," he explains. "After paying the bands and space rental, we ended up with $1,600. When we took that out to TAPS, they were almost in tears. They said it would help keep them open for two to three months and . . . they are still open to this day. I would like to think that the Peoria punk/hardcore scene had something to do with that."[23]

* * *

Later that year, Subsist released a farewell album, *The Rhythm Method*, and played one final, highly emotional show at the Optimist Club. "It was oppressively hot that night," remembers Chris Bennett, which added to the strange tension of celebration and sorrow over the group's end. "We had poured ourselves

Figure 20. Subsist at the Morton Optimist Club, ca. 1998. Courtesy of Jimmy Singleton.

into that band for a solid four years, which is a large chunk of life [during] your late teens and early twenties."[24] Nearly two decades later, all the passion and fury of Subsist remain palpable in old photographs: guitars pointed to the sky, youthful voices captured mid-scream, feet in mid-leap, all baggy jeans and baseball caps, audience and band intertwined as one.

From the beginning, the Subsist bandmates had set their sights on the world beyond the cornfields of central Illinois—but their wanderlust was often thwarted by events beyond their control. The worst Illinois snowstorm in decades, for example, combined with a van breakdown on the way to Cleveland, blew up their plans for an extensive East Coast tour. "It kind of took the wind out of our sails," Bennett admits. Despite sharing stages with some of hardcore's biggest names—including Converge, Coalesce, the Dillinger Escape Plan, Zao, and Cave In—"we never actually fulfilled the mission of getting out of the Midwest."[25]

In hindsight, Subsist was merely a proving ground for what came next. Amid the band's pending dissolution, Bennett and Tim Mead discussed their desire to continue playing music together—and to take things to the next level. On the drive home to Peoria after playing a festival in Minneapolis—Subsist's next-to-last show—"we kind of laid out the plan for what Minsk would become," Bennett remembers. "We had a similar vision. . . . Tim and I were of a mind, considering our upbringing and desire to know more about the world—about spirituality, philosophy, esotericism, all those things. . . . Nothing was ruled out for us at that point. We just wanted to explore everything."[26]

Minsk would be a vehicle for those explorations. In the years to come, the two bandmates would stay together and tour the world. In addition, one of Subsist's former drummers, Mike Pareskuwicz, went on to play in an early incarnation of Fall Out Boy, who rose to pop-punk stardom in the new millennium, while one-time bassist Matthew Hartman played in Dead to Fall, an acclaimed metalcore band on Chicago's Victory Records.

But even as the members of Subsist looked outward, the Morton Optimist Club turned inward. For several years the venue had avoided noise and loitering complaints by virtue of its remote setting, but it lost this advantage over time as the village of Morton slowly sprawled toward it. Sometime around the turn of the twenty-first century, the Optimists closed their doors to the punk scene, ending their unusual but fruitful alliance. Years later, the local organization disaffiliated from Optimist International and changed its name to the Morton *Opportunity* Club—but not without noting that "the Optimist cabin still exists and all other club functions remain the same as they have been since 1931."[27] Almost the same, that is.

* * *

For some in the Peoria scene, the very concept of Christian hardcore felt like a contradiction in terms. "Rock and roll, punk rock, metal . . . and Christianity? It just doesn't mix," laughs Planes Mistaken for Stars frontman Gared O'Donnell. "Spirituality, sure. Philosophy, sure. But *Christianity*? It seemed counterintuitive. I was sort of snarky about that back then. It didn't make sense to me."[28]

In this light, Subsist's insistence on not being stereotyped as a "Christian band" is understandable. The formation of Planes Mistaken for Stars, whiskey-fueled and rough around the edges, in the fall of 1997 might seem to have provided a polar opposite to the straight-edge and relatively clean-cut Subsist—a perennial divide in the punk community going back to the days of Bloody Mess and the Stepes. But in this case, as then, it was a vast oversimplification that exaggerated the differences between the two groups.

The members of Planes were never really the miscreants that some (often themselves) suggested they were. At the same time, Subsist never fully bought into any orthodoxy: Christian, straight-edge, or otherwise. While the two bands briefly represented distinct factions within Peoria's punk community, they were far more connected by their love for music and aversion to mainstream culture than riven by contrasts of theology. (The debatable dichotomy was further muddled by the rise of Blue Skies Lie in 1998, another band of Bennett's that existed concurrently with Subsist and included members of both "factions.")

In any case, as Minsk developed out of Subsist—ditching the psychic baggage of Christianity altogether—and the vision for Planes matured, whatever differences that once might have existed seemed to vanish entirely. In the end, both bands landed in similar places. But in 1997, they were still discovering themselves—and just beginning to explore the world outside of Peoria.

Planes Mistaken for Stars, in its initial form, brought together former members of Dismiss (Gared O'Donnell and Matt Bellinger, guitar and vocals) and Keepsake (bassist Aaron Wise and drummer Mike Ricketts), a pair of emo-tinged punk bands with pop sensibilities. "'The Past Two,' one of Planes' first songs, was originally the last Dismiss song," Gared notes. "And when Dismiss broke up, I felt like Keepsake kind of filled that void."[29]

With Matt living in Arizona that summer, Gared started jamming with Aaron and Mike—and the chemistry was immediately evident. "It was like, 'Holy shit—*this works!*'" Gared recalls. "When Matt came back [to Peoria] in the fall, we had a set within a couple practices."[30]

The musical proposition of Planes Mistaken for Stars was much heavier and grittier than any of their previous bands. They were serious about touring, recording, and taking the world by storm. After gestating in central Illinois, the band left for Denver in early 1999. Gared recalls Planes' final Peoria show, at Tiamat Records, before the big cross-country move: "It felt like an actual spiritual event. That's where we came together with the 'Christian rock' thing: we weren't Christian, *but we had the spirit*. I felt like we were at church, but there was no flock, we were all god. We were all little gods . . ."[31]

CHAPTER 16

Our CBGB

Concrete floor. Concrete walls. Record store. Pool table. Support posts. Crust punks. Zines. Indie kids. Emos. Ska kids. Mods. SHARPs. Metal dudes. Feminists. Anarchists. Drug addicts. Pretty awesome.
—Tom "Atomic" Satterfield (of Ham, the Amazing Kill-O-Watts, Scouts Honor, Tina Sparkle, and others)

I strapped my memories to my back. I'm leaving. I'm already gone / And I was on a train somewhere wishing sweet stings to you / To make you never forget the poetry in wanting.
—Planes Mistaken for Stars, "Standing Still Fast"

Some people saw Peoria as little more than a dull, backwater farm town: a place to get a factory job, raise a family, and precious little else. But for those who were coming of age and bursting to leave their own even smaller towns, Peoria was the big city—and punk shows got them out of the cornfields. Marsha Satterfield (of Ham and the Amazing Kill-o-Watts) says that compared to the "very, very small town" she grew up in, the Peoria punk scene felt diverse, progressive, and welcoming. "I've always been out as gay, and the music scene gave me the confidence just to be me. It built me up."[1]

Paralleling the Morton Optimist Club's peak punk years, Tiamat Records hosted punk, hardcore, and metal shows from 1997 to 1999. Located near Bradley University on West Main Street in Peoria—across the street from Co-Op Records at Campustown and a couple of blocks from One World Coffee—Tiamat was right in the heart of the city. It was a record store by day, but at night, with the record bins pushed to the walls, it was the closest thing to an actual punk club that Peoria ever had.

Unlike a rented hall, Tiamat was consistent in hosting shows nearly every weekend. People could almost always drop by and catch live music, even if they hadn't seen a specific flyer. Where the Optimists took their money and (mostly) left the punks alone, Tiamat's owner was just as likely to be on-site, catering directly to them. A few dozen people could fill the place; a hundred people—all sweaty and crammed together—made for an exciting mess. "It felt like everyone knew everyone," says Josh Haller of the Psychodelics. "The scene felt very nurturing. Bands would come through Peoria and play there and just be freaking out, saying 'Man, you guys have a really awesome scene here. . . . You don't know how good you have it.'"[2]

Echoing that sentiment, Frankie Sturm of Aphrodite's Locket describes Tiamat shows as having "an energy and an intimacy that I never experienced anywhere else."[3] Writing the venue's obituary in 1999, David Moll of the *Peoria Journal Star* accurately called it a place "where there's practically no separation between the musicians and the crowd—where if you stand right up front you might accidentally get spat on."[4] The spitting could also be intentional, an unknowing nod to Bloody Mess and the local punk scene of a dozen years earlier.

When the Morton Optimist Club or various VFW and American Legion halls weren't being used for punk shows, they hosted bingo nights, barbecues, pancake breakfasts, public meetings, and other community events. Aside from the lingering stench of stale cigarette smoke, they were respectable enough for retirees and Boy Scout troops alike. In contrast, Tiamat very much embodied the raw essence of punk rock. Inside of what was essentially a concrete box, bands had to set up and play around inconveniently situated metal support beams. The walls were covered with tacked-up flyers, stickers, and colorful graffiti, and one Tiamat regular recalls "a hole in the brick wall where we could feed and watch mice during shows."[5] As owner Leanna Sweetland confirms, "I do remember a show where a huge rat—maybe a foot and a half—came stumbling out of the bathroom."[6]

Mike Malin says Tiamat "was the first 'punk' venue I'd ever been to, and it took me out of my comfort zone as a fifteen-year-old. . . . It made me feel out of place [to be] surrounded by crusty kids and adults who seemed way cooler than me. I saw a few of my favorite bands there, though, and grew to love it."[7]

In one sense, Tiamat offered an atmosphere of controlled danger for Peoria's youth; more than a few confess to telling their parents they were going elsewhere when they were really sneaking off to shows. To be fair, those parents' concerns were not entirely unfounded. Josh Haller recalls an especially memorable performance by 10–96 from Kenosha, Wisconsin—old-school punks and friends of Bloody Mess who'd been playing Peoria since the mid-eighties:

> Somebody in the crowd threw a beer bottle on "stage," and it broke. [Vocalist] Dean Dirt (RIP) took a shard of the glass and carved violently at his forehead and naturally began bleeding like crazy. My buddy Dan was videotaping the whole thing and Dean came over and spit blood all over Dan's camera—and all over Dan. He wasn't really cool with it . . . but he let it go.
>
> Later, I exchanged contact info with Ken, the bass player, and Dean . . . [, who] was still bleeding from his self-inflicted forehead injury, thusly dripped a few drops of blood on the paper I was to keep for contacting them with. I still have that paper with his blood in my *No Retreat* LP. Those guys were hardcore.[8]

Tiamat was no ordinary business; its part-time staff could more aptly be described as faithful volunteers. "We put in work there because we believed in the business . . . not for money," explains James Strevels. "I think there was a hope that Tiamat would have done well enough to where it would've became a paying part-time job. . . . [But] there were plenty of perks for helping at Tiamat with Leanna."[9]

Friendship, camaraderie, and a shared sense of mission compelled an unusually strong devotion. Tiamat existed solely for the purpose of music—specifically,

Figure 21. Tiamat Records storefront at 1113 West Main Street in Peoria, 1998. Photograph by Jonathan Wright.

underground music—and the local punk scene had an emotional stake in it. Like Airwaves several years earlier, it "was the first place a lot of us actually felt like was 'our' venue," explains Jared Madigan of Laura's Agent, Blue Skies Lie, and RyeFieldCrane. "It wasn't a Legion hall [where] we had to pay $150 to a World War II vet while they yelled at us to turn down all night. Leanna was one of us."[10]

"I was pretty idealistic at the time—and felt that social and political change needed to happen in smaller communities," Leanna affirms. "I was traveling to other places to see the bands I wanted to see, and always felt that Peoria would be a good place for bands to stop, since it was halfway between Chicago and St. Louis."[11] When the opportunity to purchase the record store (previously known as Rock of Ages) presented itself, she put together a business plan, sought out a bank loan, and made it happen.

Through Tiamat, Leanna proudly offered others the autonomy to book shows and gave bands a welcoming place to play. "Underground venues were often the first exposure that kids had to non-mainstream music and ideas at the time, being that the internet was in its earlier stages," she notes. "It was a place where people could have a sense of belonging. . . . That was the simple goal."[12]

Adam Widener, a veteran of bands in Peoria, Milwaukee, and San Francisco, describes Tiamat as the Peoria equivalent of New York City's CBGB or Berkeley, California's 924 Gilman Street, ragged but legendary punk venues that encapsulated the grimy essence of their time and place. It "was a good representation of what Peoria was capable of—that we could have this great DIY space," he explains. "It wasn't until years later, when I started touring and playing other towns, that I realized Tiamat was really a special thing. I was amazed to see that many towns didn't have anything like it."[13]

Dozens of local bands, across many subgenres of punk, hardcore, metal, emo, and indie rock, found a home at Tiamat. "I don't think of Peoria having a specific 'Peoria sound,' but I felt that the bands we did have [were] unique," says Widener. "Whirlybird [with former members of Nora Hate] had a very distinct sound. Pootinanny didn't quite sound like anyone else. The Electric Pants were their own thing. Ham/Kill-O-Watts, with their super-slick new wave/power-pop sound, had something new to offer."[14]

Josh Haller's band was a Tiamat staple, in part because he helped book many of the shows there. The Psychodelics (later known as Systematic Attribution) offered equal parts fun and obnoxiousness as they worked through their adolescent punk politics—sometimes with a cringeworthy political incorrectness. (Fittingly, the band recorded their first demos with former Bloody cohort Gabby

Skab, some of which later appeared on a split 7" with Bloody Mess and the Vaynes.) Drummer Kyle Waters recalls a show at some rural hall where they performed their own version of "Sweet Home Alabama," rewritten with anti-racist lyrics and a chorus of "*Fuck you, Alabama!*" The opening riff "got some of the yokels' attention," and the chorus "pissed [them] off quite a bit," he remembers. "That was a really fun part about playing in that band as teenager—seeing for the first time someone use their platform to speak their mind . . . and cause a little trouble."[15] That anyone in central Illinois connected so strongly with Lynyrd Skynyrd's version of Alabama is telling in itself.

Tiamat, for its part, was no neutral entity. It embodied an anarchist and feminist politics that made it considerably more radical than other venues, especially in conservative Peoria. In 1999 the shop participated in the National Day of Art to Stop the Execution of Mumia Abu-Jamal, hosting an art show that drew attention to the political prisoner's plight and the larger campaign to abolish the death penalty. More generally, Tiamat served as a distribution site for political literature, zines, and flyers. Molly Miller Rice describes the store as "DIY and very empowering"—a place where "women were seen as equals."[16]

Figure 22. Matt Beneventi, Jeremy Loberg, and Josh Haller (*left to right*) of the Psychodelics at Tiamat Records, ca. 1998. Courtesy of Jared Madigan.

And the ties of progressive politics it engendered were strong enough to outlast the store itself.

In 2001, a couple of years after Tiamat closed, Geoff Frost (of died at birth, another Tiamat "house band") joined with several other Tiamat-affiliated punks in planning a protest of white supremacist leader Matt Hale and his World Church of the Creator followers, who were preparing to hold a forum at Peoria's downtown library. The hundred or so protesters—mostly from Peoria, but including anti-racist activists from Chicago—confronted Hale and outnumbered his supporters; the meeting ended in "insults, flying chairs and a punch or two . . . before [Hale] could even utter two sentences," according to the *Peoria Journal Star*.[17] Not for the first time, Peoria's punk scene was at the forefront of the resistance.

"That protest . . . was definitely a continuation of the Tiamat community in my mind," notes Frost, whose picture featured prominently in the newspaper account. "After that played out in the local media, the administrators from Bradley [University], where I was going to college at the time, called me in . . . to tell me they were worried about my safety since I had been something of a spokesperson in the media. At the time I kind of laughed it off, but in hindsight, I probably should've taken the threat a bit more seriously."[18]

Perhaps so. Just a year and a half later, Matt Hale was arrested for soliciting the murder of a federal judge who had ruled against him. The East Peoria native, who was expelled from Bradley University, is currently serving a forty-year federal prison sentence, projected for release in 2037.

*   *   *

After playing their first show at Tiamat Records, Planes Mistaken for Stars took flight quickly. Their eight-song, twenty-four-minute debut came together within months, and its initial run of hand-packaged CDs was as DIY as it gets. The pre-digital cover photo, captured on Kodak film by Jon Wright, depicted the band in fiery performance at Tiamat. And with Wright's Desperate Acts logo stamped on the back, it was indisputably a product of Peoria—even if the label had already flamed out for good.

Taking cues from mid-nineties emo/punk stalwarts like Hot Water Music, Lifetime, and Christie Front Drive, Planes' initial dispatch was of the moment, yet its quality was undeniable. "I wrote [punk/hardcore distros] Very Distribution and Ebullition and sent them all free copies, thinking it would be cool if we even got a review," recalls Planes frontman Gared O'Donnell. "And all these distro companies started writing back, saying they could use more."[19]

In 1999 their debut was reissued by Deep Elm Records, a New York imprint that was building its name on a series of compilations known as *The Emo Diaries*. Between the label's somewhat "soft" reputation and the band's incredibly emo-sounding name, Planes Mistaken for Stars was initially overlooked as just another brooding, heart-on-sleeve nineties band. But they had already evolved beyond their early influences, embracing classic rock and metal while growing hairier (in both sound and style) with each release. It would take a while for the world to catch up.

In the meantime, the bandmates established themselves as an aggressive touring machine, fulfilling their original romantic intent—"to seek adventure and explore the world outside of the Peoria area," according to drummer Mike Ricketts. "You and your closest friends driving across the country in a van, playing music that you made and loved to anybody that would listen, spreading a message of catharsis and love and acceptance and unity . . . it was irresistible! And for the most part, everything we expected it to be."[20]

Prior to joining Planes, Mike says he "never thought touring outside of our area was a possibility without help from a record label or manager. But meeting Gared and Matt [Bellinger] made me realize it *was* possible": "They had done it before when [Dismiss] went with Braid on a mini-tour to Florida and back, and it basically consisted of calling phone numbers listed in the back of zines. So when we started playing music together in the summer of 1997, our goal was to write some songs, record them, and book a west-coast tour for the following summer. This first tour experience was what fueled our lust to escape Peoria and explore the world. So we did!"[21]

In January 1999, Planes Mistaken for Stars played a farewell show at Tiamat before relocating to Denver, Colorado, with a dozen or so close friends. Situated a mile high and tucked against the Rocky Mountains, Denver represented the "promised land" of sorts—a fresh setting, free of cornfields, where the band could build their identity anew. Gared swears that moving across the country with a houseful of people "didn't seem so grandiose at the time" but was a logical next step for the entire crew. "I never felt like Planes was just the four of us," he explains. "It was a rolling circus. . . . We were like the Goonies."[22]

The move, combined with the band's devotion to the open road, landed like a bombshell on the Peoria punk scene. Bands and musicians had moved away before—there had even been mass exoduses of a similar scale—but Planes' departure was different. From their new headquarters in Denver, they would achieve success on a level no other Peoria band had yet found. And in leaving, they inspired a wave of local bands to tour and seek their own new opportunities elsewhere. But the move drew bitterness and jealousy from some, who saw it perhaps as a slight, whether to themselves personally or to Peoria more broadly. Gared still doesn't understand that reaction. "We didn't mince words about how suffocating Peoria could be, but we also said we were proud to be from here," he explains. "I guess in your early twenties . . . Peoria was a great place to be from, but it wasn't a great place to stay."[23]

In both their music and rhetoric, Planes members seemed to embody a love/hate relationship with their hometown—a contradiction many Peorians identified with. "This city always had a tendency to eat bands up," Gared notes. "There were so many great bands from Peoria. I was so proud of Dollface and Nora Hate . . . but it bugged the shit out of me that outside of Peoria, nobody knew who they were."[24] Planes Mistaken for Stars were determined to chart a different course—and the hunger with which the bandmates reached for their goals was contagious.

"Tiamat was rocking that night," says Jared Madigan of the band's farewell show. "Everybody was moving as one unit. It was definitely one of the most fun shows I've ever been to."[25] Gared remembers it for another reason as well—he chipped his tooth on the microphone, forcing him to develop "a mic technique to keep from getting my teeth knocked out. . . . That show was bananas. It was galvanizing and heartwarming. . . . It felt like we were doing the right thing by leaving, because it turned out there were people who were proud of us, who got it. . . . I felt like the kids a few years younger than us were really rooting for us. . . . They saw that if we could do it, they could, too. Anybody could."[26]

In the years to come, a host of Peoria bands would follow Planes Mistaken for Stars' lead onto the road. Meanwhile, the great Planes bombshell was not limited to Peoria; the Denver punk scene was equally shaken by their arrival. "When Planes got to town they put us all on notice—they were for fucking real, and we all had some catching up to do," recalls Chuck Coffey, a friend and veteran of countless Denver punk bands. "I mean that in a really fun way. . . . I think Planes helped many bands want to rock harder."[27]

*   *   *

In utilizing Tiamat as a venue, Leanna Sweetland wanted to link Peoria to "the network that runs across genres in the independent, DIY, underground music scene." In this aim, she was undoubtedly successful. Besides incubating a host of Peoria bands, the space presented an eclectic mix of touring acts from all over the country and even the world: from long-running death metal act Defiled (Tokyo, Japan) to a sparsely attended performance by a little-known emo-folk act called Bright Eyes (Omaha, Nebraska), and many, many others.[28]

When the New Bomb Turks (Columbus, Ohio) came through Peoria, the *Journal Star*'s David Moll called their set of raucous garage-punk "one of the livelier things I've ever seen"—crediting, in part at least, the forced intimacy at Tiamat. "There's something about musicians and a crowd being packed onto the same concrete floor together that creates a kind of energy you can't find at, say, a Madison Theater show, no matter how good the band is."[29]

Clearly, the Madison Theater would never have hosted the likes of CrimethInc. labelmates Catharsis and Zegota, who tore the proverbial house down at Tiamat in the summer of 1999. As significant as their music was the message the North Carolina bands preached, the same anarchist/anti-capitalist politics that would shut down the World Trade Organization summit in Seattle later that year. CrimethInc. artists, and Catharsis in particular, advocated a worldview that prized personal autonomy and self-determination above all else—of living life on one's own terms, free from the hand of government, market, or ideology. Their tours were as much about disseminating those values as they were about playing music.[30]

"The things he [singer Brian Dingledine] would say in between songs . . . were very challenging to people," explains Chris Bennett, whose Blue Skies Lie also played Tiamat that night. "I felt very happy that that was happening in Peoria."[31]

At the end of its set, Catharsis's fiery cocktail of hardcore morphed into a drum circle/parade which ultimately marched out the back of the venue, audience members in tow, while a spontaneous fire performance paired kaleidoscopic visuals with the onslaught of tribal percussion. "They had friends who put together these rags on chains and did a fire-eating and fire-swinging show in the alley," recalls Molly Miller Rice.[32] For her and several dozen witnesses, the display had the feel of an ancient ritual, a primal act that transcended its urban backdrop with otherworldly abandon. It was as if authority figures did not exist, Bennett adds, and could hardly have been more powerful. "To have this celebratory carnival atmosphere . . . *'Let's march through the fucking streets.'* . . . It was a little glimpse into what that kind of a world could be like, even if it was just for a few moments. That's something really special—and it had a huge impact on people. I know it did on me."[33]

To add fuel to the fire, none other than Planes Mistaken for Stars were slotted on the six-band bill, alongside their old friends in Blue Skies Lie, Nemo-Non, and died at birth. With Planes returning to Peoria for the first time since moving to Denver, the show was an emotional homecoming. And with Catharsis's pyrotechnic display, it was a fantastic mix of surrealism and familiarity that could not have occurred anywhere in Peoria but at Tiamat.

But all good things must come to an end. Tiamat's next-door neighbor was a Jimmy John's sandwich shop, and in the fall of 1999, the franchise owner purchased the adjacent property and evicted both the record store and Leanna, who lived upstairs. He then had the building torn down, ostensibly to create additional parking for Jimmy John's patrons. As more parking spaces hardly seemed necessary, many suspected the move was intended to drive away the unwanted contingent of loitering punks (who, admittedly, frequented the shop for free cups of water).

While Leanna concedes it may simply have been a business decision, other motives may have played a role as well: Tiamat punks widely suspected the franchise owner of right-wing political leanings. "At the time, it did feel like the owner of Jimmy John's bought his way out of a perceived problem," she says. "We had been there for almost two and a half years with no complaints from the community."[34]

Little could be done to stop the eviction. Nevertheless, a handful of Tiamat regulars engaged in a multiday protest to express their disapproval, echoing the Peoria punks of an earlier generation who once staged a "sit-in" at Owens Center. Geoff Frost recalls "standing on the sidewalk outside Jimmy John's at evening rush hour with signs to the passing cars."[35] But their intentions carried little weight, and the topic remains a sore subject for many. "To this day, I do not ever eat at Jimmy John's," notes Josh Haller, a common sentiment among Peoria punks even two decades later.[36]

Prior to closing its doors for good, Tiamat hosted one last marathon show—a bittersweet occasion that James Strevels likens to a family reunion. "All of the bands were made up of friends, and lots of proverbial family pictures exist from that night," he explains. "I think very fondly back to the honor of getting booked to close the show out."[37]

Strevels's band, the Fucked Ups, ended Tiamat's punk rock reign in style: with fake blood splattered everywhere and friends and comrades beating percussive rhythms on overturned metal trashcans. Despite the show's somber overtones, it was one last exciting mess—"a fitting end to an awesome venue," suggests Ryan Martin of the Paper Dolls.[38] "We were all writing goodbye messages on the walls," remembers Bryan Polk of 1209towanda. "I saw folks I hadn't seen at shows for years—there to say goodbye and pay their respects."[39]

Two decades on from the wrecking ball, Leanna Sweetland reflects on the significance of what she created at Tiamat. For all the memories of great bands and the music they made, "the most important thing was the relationships," she stresses. "Friendships were rekindled and new (now old) friends were made."[40]

Like CBGB on the Bowery, the spirit of Tiamat still lives on Peoria's West Main Street—even if Jimmy John's was the business left standing. Facing new challenges in a new century, that spirit breathes and evolves even today. "I think it's important not to live in the past too much," Leanna adds. "I know too many folks who seem to live in their perceived notion of 'old school' or cling to the days where they felt punk was still relevant. Now more than ever, it's important to keep living our lives in the way *we* want to—not the way the corporate system depends on us to."[41]

CHAPTER 17

Peoria Heights . . . and Lows

Getting drunk and rowdy, and breaking beer bottles on the ground . . .
these antics were not too dissimilar from the fratty bullshit we had
been trying to avoid by playing all-ages/non-bar shows.
—Drew McDowell (of Laura's Agent, the retaliation project,
RyeFieldCrane, Minsk, and others)

The last time I saw Ryan [Rhodes], he was just wasted,
in bad shape. . . . I think we all knew the writing was
on the wall—we just didn't want to read it.
—Gared O'Donnell (of Planes Mistaken for Stars)

With a few notable exceptions, Peoria's all-ages punk shows in the late 1990s
and into the next decade were organized by the musicians themselves, who
rented venues, paid friends with mics and PA speakers to run sound, and invited out-of-town acts to play with their bands. To prevent booking conflicts in
these early days of the internet, Tom Lane, known online as "Melvin Malone,"
launched the "Peoria Shows" page.

"I'd been playing around with HTML, which was more mysterious in the
nineties than it is now," he recalls. "I was getting annoyed that there'd be conflicting local shows on one night during a weekend, and nothing the other night.
It happened a lot where there'd be two or three shows on Friday and nothing on
Saturday, for example." As for his use of a pseudonym, "I didn't trust the internet
and still don't. Melvin was the name of my barber when I was a kid, and Tom
Malone [of the Blues Brothers band] was one of my favorite trombone players."[1]

For several years, Lane's crude website was an indispensable hub for Peoria's punk community. Besides listing upcoming shows, it included links to band pages and discussion boards, as well as contact information for area promoters, recording studios, and sound engineers. "The most frustrating thing was constantly updating it," he notes. "This was before smartphones and social media, so I had to go in and add shows in the code from my home PC or the ICC computer lab every time I got an email or a flyer."[2]

With its iconic if inelegant "hot rod" flame design, it was "an excellent example of how not to design a webpage," as fellow showgoer Josh Finnell later reflected. But as the internet began to redraw the economic realities of a world transitioning from industry to automation, Finnell adds, "The youth of a rusted city used the Peoria Shows page to gather in American Legions and church basements to insulate themselves and recapture, even for a brief moment, power in a powerless city."[3] If nothing else, it helped Peoria punks coordinate their calendars and keep up with an expanding roster of venues.

With Tiamat shuttered and the more distant Morton Optimist Club generally relegated to a backup plan, finding venues became a competition of sorts. DIY promoters scoured the area for undiscovered options, which came to encompass an American Legion hall in nearby Metamora, the VFW Post 2602 in Peoria Heights, a gym at Superstar Sports Center in north Peoria, various spaces at Bradley University, a house near Bradley's campus at 1620 W. Ayres, and the short-lived Bicycle Bus, among others—essentially anywhere with electricity and an obliging proprietor. Though perhaps less selective than in the Naked Bums era, and suddenly less stable without Tiamat Records, Peoria's changing music scene offered new opportunities.

*　　*　　*

Having felt excluded from the "cool club" a year or two earlier, Ham (soon to be known as the Amazing Kill-O-Watts) had since become one of the most established—and recognizable—bands in town. With members' matching uniforms and unrepentant geekiness, as well as "matching guitar straps with lightning bolts and occasionally goggles," according to drummer Tom "Atomic" Satterfield, the band sought to play anywhere that would have it.[4] As frontman Tyson Markley recalls, "We played the Madison [Theater], all of the Legion halls, the riverfront, a nursing home, a couple of movie theaters, a bunch of bars, house parties, a garage sale, some yards, carnivals, stores. . . . We just played everything that came our way."[5]

Among the most unconventional was a series of shows at the Willow Knolls 14 movie theater. "[Those] gigs were spectacular," Tyson says. "They were doing this 'Midnight Madness' thing a couple times a month where they'd run old . . . cult classics. From 11:15 up until the movie started, they'd have a band play in front of the screen on this raised platform."[6]

During this time, DIY promoters also leaned more heavily on existing venue options, like the Peoria Pizza Works in Peoria Heights. In the 1970s, the Pizza Works had hosted live music in its adjoining lounge, then known as the Other Side; the great Peoria bluesman Luther Allison even recorded a live album there in 1979. Under different ownership, the family-owned restaurant later experimented with karaoke nights and other entertainment before establishing open mic nights sometime in the early nineties. By 1997, Eric "Suit and Tie Guy" Williamson, among others, had begun renting space in various back rooms from manager Gary Besler.

Tyson Markley gives Besler and the Pizza Works a lot of credit for their willingness to host punk shows. "Most of the venues, as I recall, balked at doing shows, or required a massive security deposit, or liability insurance," he explains. "Gary took on a lot of risk and allowed local shows at his place—and all-ages ones at that."[7]

Unlike most rented spaces, the Pizza Works was more insulated than the average garage—some of its rooms were even carpeted. It also sold food, featured a patio and some pool tables, and existed in a reasonably central location. Nearly every local band of the period played there at some point, alongside touring acts like Boilermaker (Leucadia, California), Jejune (Boston), Pave the Rocket (St. Louis), and Ghost Buffalo (with former members of Planes Mistaken for Stars, from Denver). A wild performance by the Subsonics (Atlanta) in 1998 made an especially strong impression on Adam Widener: "The singer, Rockin' Clay Reed, was wearing this one-piece, velvet, skintight body suit thing and had pancake makeup all over his face. He slobbered and drooled as he sang. At one point as he pulled his face away from the microphone, he carried this long string of snot that dangled like a tightrope from his lips to the mic. I'll never forget that."[8]

Occasional bouts of drool notwithstanding, most people in Peoria's punk scene were not too far afield of the Pizza Works' late-night bar and pool hall clientele. Others, at times, clashed with the eatery's more conventional dinner-hour customers. Josh Haller recalls some of these less-than-family-friendly audience members: a new crew of skinheads who were "sick of all the 'PC assholes'":

> They would show up at shows . . . and go breaking tables and chairs. I'd yell at these guys for busting up crap at a place that was cool enough to let us have these crazy-ass shows, and they'd get mad at me for trying to defend the place and its property. Next thing you know, I start getting word that if I am at *that* show—that *I* was putting on [for the Murderers, a punk band from Minnesota]—there was going to be a whole crew of people from the "Chi-Town Mafia" coming down to kick my ass.[9]

Young punks were continually searching for freedom from adult supervision, but that autonomy left them on their own to deal with dangerous situations. Haller had reason to be concerned: the Chi-Town Mafia Skinheads were in fact one of Chicago's most violent street gangs. Despite claiming to be anti-racist, they were notorious for vicious assaults on strangers, reportedly even setting homeless people on fire. The group's founder, John Haley, was well-known to Chicago's punk community as someone to steer clear of. But he also spent time wreaking havoc in Peoria, as a disturbing article in the *Peoria Journal Star* revealed in 2003:

> A 22-year-old man faces criminal charges after a 15-year-old Metamora girl was repeatedly tattooed during a bizarre party involving alcohol and drugs. . . .
> The owner of the house . . . told police he had met the girl only once before. . . . Both times she was accompanied by an acquaintance of his, 23-year-old John Haley of Chicago.[10]

The tattooist, a resident of Peoria Heights, was booked on charges of tattooing the body of a minor. Haley, though uncharged in this incident, went to prison years later on a manslaughter conviction.

According to scattered accounts on the internet, when the Chi-Town Mafia was driven out of Chicago by other punk/skinhead groups, its members migrated to various other Illinois cities, including Peoria—where they could be found "hanging out in the parking lots of punk shows to beat up teenagers."[11] Fortunately for Josh Haller and the Pizza Works, the potential for confrontation at this particular show was brought to a peaceful resolution. As Haller recounts, "I took money at the door, and there actually was a decent-sized crew of skinheads lurking in the parking lot. This big fella . . . [got] up in my face, trying to act as though I wouldn't let his 'crew' in. I asked him if he was going to break shit or start shit. . . . He said, 'No.' I said, 'Five bucks.' He paid and . . . seemed to have fun at that show, and he didn't hurt anything."[12]

Not every show was so fraught with potential danger or harbored such fringe characters. Sometimes the bands themselves tested the limits of the venue's tolerance for punks, no skinheads needed. "We all sort of came of age at the Pizza Works," notes Tyson Markley of Ham. "I never drank until sometime in my early twenties, and when I finally did, I wasn't so good at gauging my intake." At one show, after some friends bought him a series of shots, his intake came out. "In the middle of a rotten cover of Buddy Holly's 'Rave On,' I puked, and kept puking, and kept playing like nothing happened. It was like that scene in *The Exorcist*. . . . I remember the crowd cheering like it was part of the show, but mostly I remember [bandmates] Tom and Marsha [Satterfield]'s mom cleaning it up while we were still trying to play. . . . I was so embarrassed . . . but of course, it was 'punk as fuck' to the kids."[13]

"If anything was 'punk rock' about Ham, that would have been one of them," agrees Marsha Satterfield. "I can still remember the smell. . . . Maybe that's why I never liked Jägermeister." As for their mom cleaning up the mess, it was just another example of their parents' above-and-beyond support for her and her brother's musical endeavors. As DIY as the Peoria scene was, supportive parents— including those of the Stepe and Shane siblings, as well as the Satterfields—were consistent, if unheralded, contributors. Marsha explains:

> When Ham was putting out our first couple of albums, I was still very underage. We played a handful of shows . . . [where] my mom had to be there, or I wouldn't be allowed in the bar. She and I would just hang out, we'd play our set, and then I'd hang out with her at the bar. . . . We'd get home at 4:00 in the morning on a school night.
>
> Tom and I were really lucky, having our parents support us the way they do. . . . A lot of the kids who were going to shows ended up being really good friends with our parents. I feel really happy about that, because there were a lot people who had shitty parents. . . . It became kind of a big family, I guess. . . . We still treat it that way.[14]

Perhaps hoping to distance the punks from their other patrons, the Pizza Works periodically reconfigured the rooms it offered for rental. On December 19, 1999, hundreds of young people packed into the restaurant's large back room—a two-story loft at the time—where they surrounded the bands on both floors and lined the staircase in between. Jon Beattie believes it may have been the best Peoria show he ever attended. "Lots of talent in that room," he notes. "Lots of camaraderie as well."[15]

Planes Mistaken for Stars were the headlining act, returning from Denver again for the holidays, on the cusp of the release of their second record, *Knife in the Marathon*. It was also the finale for Blue Skies Lie, whose guitarist Ryan Rhodes had passed away a few months earlier.

*   *   *

Paralleling the dynamics of Peoria's early punk scene, Blue Skies Lie straddled various social groups, skateboarding crews, and lifestyle choices. Merging hardcore and metal influences, several of its members came from a straight-edge (or at least straight-edge adjacent) group of friends, including vocalist Jared Madigan, guitarist Chris Bennett, and drummer Joel Madigan. Ryan Rhodes ran in different social circles, and his challenges with alcohol and other self-medications were no secret. Perhaps in part because of these contradictions, the band cycled through a dozen members in a relatively short period of time while building a sizable following around Peoria.

Prior to Blue Skies Lie, Ryan had played bass for Erebus, whose ferocious metal-hardcore fusion forged an influential blueprint for numerous Peoria bands to come. "Ryan and I formed Erebus after Superego broke up," says drummer Mike Theobald, tracing the band's lineage from its origins as a post-hardcore instrumental three-piece.

> We played a show with Dismiss [which by then included ex-Superego guitarist Matt Bellinger]. . . . That's where [vocalist] Zed [Smith] saw us, and that's where he comes in. We all wanted to do something different—something metal. . . .
>
> Ryan heard of this guy James [Logsdon] from East Peoria who was a really good metal guitarist. . . . [We] took him to a graveyard and told him he was in. Things were going good . . . and then drugs and alcohol took its toll. We parted ways with Ryan and just filled the bass slot with James's buddy Adam Brooks, and thus, Nemo-Non.[16]

Nemo-Non was essentially Erebus with a new bass player, while Ryan switched over to guitar when he joined Blue Skies Lie. Both bands were crushingly heavy, and they played together often, including the seminal Catharsis/Zegota show

180

Figure 23. Ryan Rhodes of Blue Skies Lie at the Morton Optimist Club, June 1999. Courtesy of Jared Madigan.

at Tiamat in June 1999 (Ryan's final performance) as well as the Pizza Works show that December with Planes Mistaken for Stars (with a new guitarist taking Ryan's slot in Blue Skies Lie).

For his friends and bandmates, Ryan Rhodes's death left a hole in the Peoria punk scene—an absence that still lingers. For all his demons, Ryan had a lot to offer, both as a person and as a musician. In spite of their differences, Jared Madigan says he initially started talking to Ryan about forming a band because he was so drawn to his style: "He played his bass like it was a guitar."[17]

"He had a natural gift," offers Gared O'Donnell of Planes, who included a picture of Ryan in the liner notes to *Knife in the Marathon*. "Matt [Bellinger, Planes guitarist] and Ryan were so very close, and I had been friends with Ryan since junior high. I sold him my first bass, and that was *his* first bass. That's how deep the history goes."[18]

Earlier that summer, Planes had even tried to convince Ryan to join the caravan and move to Denver. "I begged him to come with us," Gared remembers. "The last time I saw him, I said, 'You are still welcome to hop in the van today and come to Denver with us. You need to get your shit together.'" Just days later, he was dead—only twenty-two years old. "Everybody was gutted. Matt was despondent."[19]

Amid an especially affecting set at the Pizza Works that December, Gared told the crowd, "This is a bit overwhelming. . . . Everybody I care about on earth is here. Everybody we all care about—"

"Except for one person, who means a lot to us," Matt noted, interrupting. "And this whole show, for me, is dedicated to him."

"Love you, Ryan," Gared finished. And the band played on.[20]

More than two decades later, Ryan's life and death remain the same cautionary tale—no less heartbreaking for the years that have passed. "It shocks me how fucking young he was," Gared muses. "All of us have our own demons. His were just next-level. . . . It wasn't just addiction; it was severe depression." He continues:

> It breaks my heart, but I don't want people to forget that everybody tried to help that guy. *Everybody*. I loved him like a brother, but towards the end, he was really not a nice guy. . . . That's what addiction and mental illness will do. . . . At his best, the guy was fucking hysterical. At his worst, he was mean as a rattlesnake. . . .
>
> I wish I would have tried harder. I wish I would have tried *a lot* harder. . . . In your early twenties, you don't realize how quickly shit can go off the rails. If there's a lesson, it's to pay attention when people are headed in that direction. He needed some serious help.[21]

After relocating from Peoria to Denver, Planes Mistaken for Stars came into their own. They toured all over the world for the next several years, across the United States, Europe, and Japan. They played legendary punk clubs—including 924 Gilman Street in Berkeley and CBGB in Manhattan—and issued records on numerous independent labels: Deep Elm, No Idea, Deathwish, and Steve Aoki's Dim Mak Records. They shared bills with the likes of Cursive, Against Me!, Propagandhi, Hot Water Music, Botch, City of Caterpillar, Avail, Thursday, the Dillinger Escape Plan, and Mastodon, among countless others. In effect, Planes lived out their band ethos—as screamed on their 2001 *Fuck with Fire* LP—that this is "your last dance . . . so fuck your standing still." In other words, you only live once, so you had better get moving. "We worked hard," Gared affirms. "We hit the road. We chased the dragon. . . . We just went for it."[22]

Ryan Rhodes stayed behind and his demons caught up with him, leaving his Blue Skies Lie bandmates to finish recording their only album without him.

"You are either defeated by the environment or you mold it to your own, and unfortunately, Peoria caved in on a lot of people," Jared Madigan says. "Some of them saw it happening and left before it completely collapsed. Others died because of it. The ones who are still there . . . were strong enough to not let it affect them."[23]

The Peoria Pizza Works—one person's "dirty and dark . . . loud and packed," and another's "clean, inviting and perfect size"—was a coveted space for local bands and promoters, but it was not always dependably available.[24] Manager Gary Besler had a love/hate relationship with the punk scene and periodically chose to discontinue rentals (and not without good reason), including a de facto hiatus from late 2000 to 2005. But by once again hosting shows mid-decade and beyond, the Pizza Works is unique in Peoria punk lore. It transcended a specific moment in time, spanning multiple generations of show-going punks.

*   *   *

In the meantime, however, with the Pizza Works out of the running, the search for new venues produced mixed results. The Navy-Marine Club, also located in Peoria Heights, was among the yield. Yet another small, members-only veterans bar, its walls, like those at the Morton Optimist Club, were adorned with American flags, commemorative plaques, and patriotic decor. Unlike Tiamat or the Pizza Works, the Navy-Marine Club evoked a Fourth of July picnic or a Boy Scouts meeting, a faded image of what previous generations had wanted "All-American" Peoria to be. It was respectable, and with a dozen or so fold-up tables and chairs stacked in its tiny back room, punk shows straddled the line between wonderfully intimate and uncomfortably cramped.

The first shows at the Navy-Marine Club were set up by the band Laura's Agent in 1998, and several promoters rented the space over the next few years. "I really liked the Navy-Marine Club," says Kevin Dixon, who booked numerous shows there. "It had a really low-key vibe. It wasn't big, so if you had a small turnout it wasn't bad. . . . Thirty to forty people felt like a packed room."[25] Given such close quarters, frustrating interactions between the aging vets up front and the punks in the back were unsurprisingly common. As Drew McDowell (of Laura's Agent, the retaliation project, and others) recalls, the bartender-manager often failed to respect the show's decorum by choosing to collect the rent money mid-song, for example, rather than between performances or at the end of the night. Says Drew,

[Laura's Agent] would . . . turn off all the overhead fluorescent lights and turn on a couple of dim, red lights we had brought—or sometimes a strobe light. One night we were playing a song called "pitchblackandfireflies." It's an intentionally monotonous and eerie song until the loud screamer of a chorus bursts in out of nowhere. Unfortunately, [the bartender-manager] beat me to the punch.

He barged into the back room, flicked on all the lights, and shouted my first and last name. I was certain that someone had called to say my mom had been killed in a car accident or something. I mean, Jesus Christ, masked gunmen announce they're conducting a stick-up more subtly![26]

Similar confrontations erupted around the club's single-occupancy restrooms, which divided the front and back rooms and were shared by the retired sailors and teenage punks accordingly. One time Drew says he asked his girlfriend to stand guard, as "there was no lock on the door, and it opened to a full view of, and from, the bar." Within moments, he heard "an angry, gravelly voice" seeking entrance: "'It's a two-man.'" But it was *really* a one-man. "True, there was a urinal and a stool side by side," Drew continues, "but there was no divider, and I was not about to . . . allow this old drunk to urinate a foot away from my face." As the sailor barged past his girlfriend, muttering "It's a two-man," Drew raced to finish his business. "I got the hell out of there. Our set was angrier than usual that night."[27]

For all its shortcomings, the Navy-Marine Club was one of the only games in town at the time. With few other venue options, punk rock beggars could not be choosers. And it wasn't all bad bathrooms—at its best, the space was about musical transcendence. Kevin Dixon recalls a performance by the notoriously spastic Ten Grand (formerly known as the Vida Blue, who frequently visited Peoria from Iowa City) as "fucking bonkers. Dude jumped off his amp and trashed his hand. It was just insane. He played with blood on his hands—just played right through it—it didn't even matter."[28]

Though generally tame compared to some of the shows of earlier eras, several people recall shows at the Navy-Marine Club as being especially prone to drunken behavior. While underage drinking was frowned upon by most promoters (who wanted to reclaim their deposits and continue using the space at hand), not everyone shared the same philosophy—on alcohol, or even on having rules at all. Adam Widener recalls one close call with the authorities: "Blue-Haired Jeni [Goertzen] was booking a show at the Navy-Marine Club. . . . All of a sudden she busted in and told everyone to ditch their drinks because the police were outside. Suddenly, about twenty kids threw their beer cups in the trash. It was kind of funny because it felt like the whole room tipped to one side with everyone rushing to the garbage can."[29]

"A couple of suspicious cops came in," Widener continues. "We thought at any second they were gonna shut the show down and start searching people." But they were apparently satisfied simply to make their presence known. "I think they gave a little speech about receiving some complaints and that we should all go home. But I don't think anyone did. The show continued with no problems after that."[30]

Like other past Peoria venues, the Navy-Marine Club became a public arena for one of punk rock's oldest debates: essentially, GG Allin or Ian MacKaye? Was punk nihilistic and antisocial—rebellion simply for its own sake? Or was it constructive and communal—a force for positive change? Could it, in fact, be both? Where was the line between the two, and who should decide? Peoria's punk scene encompassed a range of opinions, but the decisions of a handful to get drunk, destroy venue property, or attempt to get into shows without paying the modest cover had negative repercussions for everyone.

Drew McDowell admits he "felt a little territorial" about the Navy-Marine Club, since he had "found" it and built a relationship, albeit a rocky one, with the management.[31] He was not impressed by how some other promoters and punks treated the establishment, and neither were its neighbors. When the club opted to stop booking shows—canceling all previously booked engagements—Drew pleaded with management to make an exception. "'There's never been a problem at one of our shows,' I said. 'The people that come to our shows don't drink,' I said, without getting into a lengthy explanation of straight-edge culture. But they couldn't be swayed."[32]

By 2001, the Navy-Marine Club, like the Peoria Pizza Works, was off-limits to punks, and the self-destructive tendencies of some of their own were at least partially to blame. "It was back to the Yellow Pages," Drew explains, and the search for new venues continued in seeming perpetuity.[33]

CHAPTER 18

For God and Country (Alternate Take)

> The Vineyard [Café] had its charm. Considering it was in a
> church basement and there was no alcohol, it could really
> weed out the people who were not there for the music.
>
> —Jon Beattie (of Angeltread, RyeFieldCrane, and others)

> We were kids just trying to busy ourselves in a small town
> with cornfields on all sides. Central Illinois at the end of the
> last millennium claimed the mild musical successes of Hum
> and Planes Mistaken for Stars. For some of us, this was all
> we needed for an invitation into the world of DIY touring.
>
> —*Ten Years of Thinker Thought*
> (anniversary compilation CD), liner notes

For several years beginning in the late 1990s, the Agape Java Hut in Bloom-ington-Normal hosted all-ages shows in the basement of a church. Numerous Peoria bands played the venue alongside national touring acts like the Promise Ring, Jets to Brazil, Alkaline Trio, Pedro the Lion, and Ted Leo, and Peorians frequently made the forty-mile drive to see shows—as previous generations had done before them. With Peoria's own pizza joints, clubs, and banquet halls effec-tively tapped out, a new cohort of DIY promoters brought this model back home.

Having come of age in the local punk scene, Jeremiah Lambert and Jared Grabb were among Peoria's busiest promoters in the early 2000s. The two Wash-ington, Illinois, natives—friends, classmates, and sometime bandmates—ini-tially bonded over visual art as well as music; in high school they briefly copub-lished a zine (*Persona of a Geek*), combining their mutual passions via original comics and music reviews. Both came from a Christian background, so the use of church basements for shows seemed sensible in light of the lack of venues. And by cutting alcohol out of the mix, a number of other problems were solved as well—for a while, at least.

Some punks were uncomfortable with this direction, viewing organized religion as an extension of the mainstream culture they sought to oppose. But Christian bands had long been involved in the Peoria scene (even at Tiamat), while youth-friendly churches were politically comparable to (if not marginally more progressive than) the halls punks had rented for years. As usual, they worked with what was available to them.

From roughly 1999 to 2002, Jeremiah Lambert ran the Vineyard Café in the basement of his family's home church, the Vineyard Christian Fellowship Church in East Peoria. The space—a youth activity room repurposed into a drug- and alcohol-free venue—was able to accommodate a few hundred people, and it often did. Despite the wooden planks and flattened cardboard boxes leading showgoers inside from the parking lot, they often dragged mud through the backdoor entrance and across the basement's concrete floor. Summer shows, in particular, were sticky and muddy affairs.

The Vineyard afforded Lambert the freedom to book shows as he wished, so long as he cleaned up afterward. Equally important: it had an in-house sound system and a stage and didn't charge a rental fee—a DIY promoter's nirvana. "It was pretty smooth sailing at first," he recalls. "They just let me do what I wanted."[1]

Although he brought a mix of bands to the Vineyard, "almost every show I did had at least one Christian band," Lambert notes.[2] This was both a nod of respect to the venue and a reflection of his personal tastes at the time. Heavily influenced by Subsist, his band nimbus similarly straddled the spiritual and secular, incorporating the soft side of nineties emo with dashes of screamo hardcore, and was a regular at the Vineyard. In the summer, Lambert would piggyback off the enormous Cornerstone Music Festival outside of Bushnell, enticing renowned Christian metal and hardcore bands like Living Sacrifice (from Little Rock) and Zao (Parkersburg, West Virginia) to come to Peoria.[3]

But as Lambert's Vineyard shows grew increasingly larger, so did the challenge of maintaining good faith with the church elders. In early 2001, Planes Mistaken for Stars—returning from Denver again to record their pivotal *Fuck with Fire* record—attracted a full house to the church basement. "It was so packed, and it was kind of a different crowd . . . a little crustier," Lambert recalls.[4] Over time, the accumulation of cigarette butts and litter, complaints from the neighbors, the etching of profanities onto a church picnic table, and other concerns eroded the partnership, and Lambert decided to move his booking efforts elsewhere. "There was no ultimatum," he adds. "But I was feeling pressure and just didn't want to deal with it anymore."[5]

With some overlap, from about 2001 to 2003, Jared Grabb booked shows in another church basement across the river: at Peoria's Church of the Brethren. Like the Vineyard Café, the Meeting House was drug- and alcohol-free, and its stark-white walls provided an additionally sobering backdrop. The venue may well have been the aesthetic and spiritual opposite of Tiamat Records, but it would still "get really wet and sweaty down there during hardcore shows," recalls Guthrie Moore of Burning Love Letters and the Serpent Son.[6] The space was dubbed the "Meeting House" by his mother, Grabb explains: "'Meeting Houses' were what the small Brethren churches used to be called. I had been running house shows near Bradley University . . . before the Meeting House took shape. It was probably my mother's idea to start the venue upon me talking to her about what [promoter] Jenny Tsiakals was achieving in Normal with Agape Java Hut."[7]

In just those few years, Grabb paired Peoria bands with an impressive lineup of touring bands and artists, including Against Me! (Gainesville, Florida), Minus the Bear (Seattle), the Velvet Teen (Sonoma County, California), Hey Mercedes (Milwaukee), Kind of Like Spitting (Portland, Oregon), William Elliott Whitmore (Iowa), Fifth Hour Hero (Montreal), and Owen (Chicago). He was also a prolific songwriter and performer in his own right, launching Thinker Thought Records to release a CD of his band Cherry Lane in 2001. Over the next decade, Thinker Thought grew to become the Peoria area's longest-running and most successful independent record label. Inspired by his predecessors in the DIY punk scene, Jared Grabb was now writing its next chapter.

Besides making music, releasing records, and running a venue, Grabb took his acts on tour, spreading Peoria-sourced music across the United States and even Europe. "Watching Planes Mistaken for Stars hit the road was a big inspiration," he explains, "and *Book Your Own Fucking Life* (BYOFL.org)"—*Maximum RocknRoll*'s punk rock touring guide—"was the door." He worked hard to create opportunities, and "persistence was the key," he adds. "I probably contacted twenty promoters for each tour show I managed to book in the early days. The internet wasn't what it is now, so you really had to get out on the road if anyone was going to hear your music."[8]

In addition to Jared Grabb's own bands (Scouts Honor, the Forecast, and Cherry Lane) and solo work, Thinker Thought issued albums by bands from the Peoria area (the Amazing Kill-O-Watts, Tina Sparkle, Dripping Slits) and beyond, from North Carolina to Colorado to Montana. In 2004, the label released *If It Plays . . .,* an unofficial sequel to Naked Bums' *Now Playing in Peoria* compilation CD of nine years earlier, featuring a diverse mix of bands with ties to Peoria and Thinker Thought.

While the Meeting House was later revived by different promoters, Grabb stopped hosting shows there in 2003. "I wanted to book more bands that were irreverent or in opposition to organized religion," he explains. "This led me to do as many others did and rent out the East Peoria American Legion hall."[9] His friend Jeremiah Lambert had already done the same, moving his shows from the Vineyard Café to the American Legion hall a mile down the road.

*   *   *

East Peoria—as full of contradictions as its sister city—had been home of the Stepe brothers as well as the notorious white supremacist Matt Hale. It claimed a Co-Op Records location and had hosted punk shows—in a community college gym and, more recently, in the basement of a church. Visible from I-74 and situated next to a Wendy's fast-food franchise, the city's American Legion Post 983 had hosted all-ages shows only sporadically, including a late-eighties Bloody Mess production and a 1996 Naked Bums effort featuring the Chicago art/noise band U.S. Maple. For whatever reason, the punk scene hadn't used it in years.

Then, from roughly 2001 to 2006, East Peoria's American Legion hall became the gravitational center of the punk scene, booked by a rotating cast that included Grabb and Lambert as well as Dustin Addis (the Forecast), Drew McDowell (RyeFieldCrane), Adam Widener (the Jet Set), Nate Lucas (RyeFieldCrane), and Kent Wagenschutz (Scouts Honor), among others—and visited by hundreds of bands from all over the country.

The Legionnaires' preferred decor of American flags, white Christmas lights, and a stage backdrop of musical notes and cowboy boots paired well with the hall's regular gig: "live country music and dancing." But it was often comically

189

incongruous with punk rock—if somewhat emblematic of the Peoria scene. Jarrod Briggs remembers the East Peoria Legion as "a dump . . . and not in a charming way."[10] Tom Satterfield describes the space in slightly more positive terms: "grungy" but with "a bathroom you could poop in."[11] Charming or not, "this place was my youth," claims Guthrie Moore. "Every show happened [there]—massive touring acts, random guys in vans from across the country. You name it, they played here."[12]

Despite being a rented hall, the Legion offered similar advantages to previous mainstays like Tiamat and the Pizza Works. It was accessible, dependably available, and relatively self-contained, aside from the Wendy's next door. "[It] was so commonly used that it established a familiar audience," Jared Grabb explains. "The shows were all-ages, but there was [also] a bar for older fans in attendance to have beers."[13]

Alcohol-fueled problems had plagued previous venues; in a sense, sober spaces like the Meeting House and the Vineyard Café had all but saved the scene. But this combination of all-ages access and available beer performed the vital function of keeping the scene's veterans involved while inviting in a new wave of teenage punks.

A new wave of Peoria bands popped up as well, reflecting the growing popularity of metal-influenced hardcore ("metalcore") at the opening of the new millennium. They included Jeremiah Lambert's post-nimbus act Angeltread, as well as Metal Warriors, Declaim, RyeFieldCrane, and Nonetheless, which soon changed its name to Burning Love Letters and later morphed into the Serpent Son. Featuring twin brothers Galen and Guthrie Moore on guitar and Ryan Thomas (later of Minsk) on drums, Burning Love Letters/the Serpent Son attracted a dedicated following of local headbangers, offering a visceral ferocity that was as much death metal as hardcore. They, along with Scouts Honor and the Forecast, were Peoria's biggest acts for the remainder of the decade. Each represented a distinct pillar of the larger scene, explains Lambert (who joined Burning Love Letters in 2004 and was also a member of Scouts Honor), and they played together often.

> Some of the biggest shows were [the] Forecast shows with Scouts Honor and the Serpent Son or Burning Love Letters. . . . And there were two buddies of ours in the metal scene, Devil's Pie and Black the Sky, and we'd all kind of mix up. Those were always the hugest shows—several hundred [people] every time. . . . All the Forecast kids would come out for the Forecast, all the metal kids would

come out for us, and all the indie rock kids would come out for Scouts Honor. And then they all mixed together, too, in little ways.[14]

The effort to connect various factions of a fractured music scene was in part a practical concern (maximizing turnout), Lambert acknowledges, but it also made for better shows. "I liked all that music and wanted to bring it together," he explains. "There was some unity in the early [to mid-]'00s . . . of rock bands and metal bands and hardcore bands and folk bands and emo bands together on one show—and having bigger shows for it. . . . We worked to make the scene bigger and better, and have hundreds and hundreds of people at these shows."[15]

The East Peoria Legion hall was the predominant backdrop for this new generation of showgoers and remained so for half a decade—an eternity in the life of an all-ages music scene. But as with so many other past venues, problems accumulated with time. Litter and loitering were minor transgressions; small acts of vandalism (both accidental and intentional) were more serious. When more than one mosh pit got out of hand—a broken nose here, a sliced-up finger there—the limits of unbridled exuberance were put to the test. "My brother Galen broke his back at the Legion during [the performance of Quad Cities hardcore band] Bled for Days," recalls Guthrie Moore. "He was spin-kicking and Bill Wingfield ran into him. A stretcher came in—it was an ordeal. My mom almost had a heart attack from that one."[16]

Whether it was this or another ambulance visit or the time "some Chi-Town Mafia dudes [threw] a brick through Suit & Tie Guy's van window [for] no real reason,"[17] such incidents understandably challenged the Legionnaires' willingness to rent their space. Random acts of immaturity or stupidity or plain bad luck might not have fazed a more traditional music venue, but in Peoria there was no such thing. The punk scene had always relied on the good graces of others—a consistent and prevailing obstacle in the long run.

The East Peoria Legion hall, too, closed its doors to all-ages shows, but its legacy as a venue was lasting, if only in the memories of bygone youth. Still visible from the interstate, few passersby are aware of the sprawling lineup of bands this building once hosted, from Peoria and across the country: These Arms Are Snakes (Seattle), Minus the Bear, the Velvet Teen, Gaza Strippers (Chicago), the Makers (Spokane), the Eyeliners (Albuquerque), Trial by Fire (Washington, DC), the Great Redneck Hope (Colorado Springs), Terror (Los Angeles), Chargers Street Gang (Cleveland), Daryl (Houston), the Hoods (Sacramento), Haste the Day (Carmel, Indiana), the Stivs (Portland, Oregon), He

Who Corrupts (Chicago), the Sutek Conspiracy (Indianapolis), Bear vs. Shark (Highland, Michigan), Dispensing of False Halos (Des Moines), Dead Like Dallas (with former members of Laura's Agent and the Psychodelics, from Portland, Oregon)—and of course, Planes Mistaken for Stars.

*　　*　　*

During the late 1990s and into the next decade—with the success of bands like Jimmy Eat World, At the Drive-In, Fall Out Boy, and Dashboard Confessional—the punk underground once again made brief inroads into popular music. While nowhere near the cultural impact of the mid-nineties alternative explosion, the turn of the millennium marked the last gasp of corporate retailers before the internet took over the industry for good. After effectively abandoning music altogether, MTV briefly delved back into music videos with MTV2. The Vans-sponsored Warped Tour took festival-scale punk rock on the road, while Hot Topic and even Best Buy partnered with major label distributors to sell independent-label CDs. Commercial potential, it seemed, was again tantalizingly within reach.

The former Peorians in Planes Mistaken for Stars were reaching the peak of their popularity—appearing at festivals and on magazine covers; touring the United States, Europe, and Japan with acts ranging from Converge to the Ataris; opening for High on Fire and even Motörhead. Having muscled through emo genericisms, the band had matured into "a totally fuzzed-out, heavy-as-shit rock-and-fucking-roll band."[18] They garnered respect for their work ethic and epic live shows and were regularly cited for their seminal influence. Hot on their heels, a number of Peoria bands were also reaching new levels of achievement.

After issuing their early recordings on Jared Grabb's Thinker Thought label, the Forecast signed with Chicago's Victory Records in 2005. Having recently achieved mainstream success with emo-pop acts such as Thursday, Taking Back Sunday, and Hawthorne Heights, the venerable hardcore label saw similar potential in the Forecast. A vehicle for Dustin Addis's songwriting, the band (whose early membership at various times included Grabb, Marsha Satterfield of the Amazing Kill-O-Watts, and Jenni Black from the Velouria Beat) developed a significant following with their unique brand of midwestern pop, rooted in Planes-like emo/hardcore and dusted with an occasional alt-country twang. They also took cues from Planes' love/hate bond with Peoria—inspired by "the blue-collar lives in their hometown" while painting a decisively bleak portrayal of that town as "dying by degrees"[19]—conveying pride of place in tandem with a desperate longing for escape.

"We come from a town that is pretty easy to get discouraged in," Addis said, "and witnessing some of [our friends and family] give up their dreams for factory jobs or worse helped form some of our songs."[20] The Forecast's success was a testament not only to their memorable songs and vocal interplay (with bassist Shannon Burns and guitarist Matt Webb joining Addis for two- and three-part harmonies) but also to their extensive touring and Addis's savvy approach to music promotion.

"Dustin was the first person in our scene who was really running his band and his shows like a business," suggests Tyson Markley. "By the time he started the Forecast, he took [everything] he learned from when he was in a punk band, Citizen 66, basically built a Peoria supergroup, and then saw . . . [that in order to succeed, you had to] get the fuck away from here." In other words: "[Peoria] is your home, but play everywhere else *but* here."[21]

All of that touring ultimately paid off for the Forecast, which released two stellar albums on Victory in 2005 and 2006, complete with music videos that nodded to their small-town flyover roots. But for all their achievements, the band never earned the stardom their fans felt they deserved. "It's genuinely befuddling that the Forecast aren't absolutely huge," raved *Alternative Press* magazine several years later.[22]

Just as the Forecast was receiving national attention, Scouts Honor (then comprising Jared Grabb, Tom Satterfield, and Chris Mackey) released *I Am the Dust* on Florida's No Idea Records in 2006. The band had formed four years earlier as an extension of Grabb's solo project, "playing 'heavy' country/blues/folk songs on acoustic guitars"[23] with the Forecast's Dustin Addis. After going electric, the group assumed various incarnations—as a duo, trio, and quartet (including at times both Addis and Jeremiah Lambert in its revolving membership)—while spanning punk, indie rock, and Americana influences. No Idea Records described Scouts Honor as perhaps "the only band that has been compared to both Against Me! and the Melvins."[24] Playing well over 400 shows across forty-five states and Europe in its seven-year existence, the band was accurately described by *Razorcake* zine as a "touring machine."[25]

In 2007, another band with Peoria roots was on the cusp of wider acclaim. Signing with Relapse Records, perhaps the world's foremost purveyor of underground metal, Minsk released its sophomore album, *The Ritual Fires of*

Abandonment, to rave reviews: "nothing short of epic, a one-hour journey that's alternately gripping, haunting, mesmerizing and intimidating." Its music was layered, exploratory, and complex, informed by a deep-seated mysticism and personal ties stretching back to the mid-nineties Peoria scene. It was a beast "both ugly and beautiful,"[26] just as its founders intended.

Built around former Subsist members Chris Bennett and Tim Mead, Minsk had been playing and touring since 2002 before hitting its stride, shuffling through a who's who of Peoria scene veterans (Brian Barth, Anthony Couri, Jared Madigan, Drew McDowell, Jeff Hyde, Dustin Addis, Ryan Thomas, Aaron Austin, and Zac Livingston) as well as engaging Sanford Parker, the renowned Chicago recording engineer. With Bennett and Mead as constants, Minsk would prove to be a durable institution, successfully returning from periodic hiatuses and lineup shifts to renew its creative vision. Like Planes Mistaken for Stars, the band's extensive touring and routine visits to Europe helped ensure Peoria's representation on the global stage.

At times, Peoria's underground music scene, slowly on the rise since the early nineties, seemed on the verge of achieving larger recognition. It was never going to be the "next Seattle"—a cash cow for the music industry—but other scenes in smaller cities had built viable models of tight-knit communities around bands and independent labels: No Idea Records in Gainesville, Florida, for example, or Omaha, Nebraska's Saddle Creek Records and related bands. Despite sporadic bouts of success, however, the Peoria scene never quite achieved this distinction of its own.

Following in the footsteps of Jon Ginoli, Bloody Mess, and the Planes Mistaken for Stars crew, many Peoria punks sought out their own versions of the "next Seattle," populating scenes and starting bands in Chicago, St. Louis, Milwaukee, Portland, San Francisco, and other cities across the country. What played in Peoria, in many cases, really could play anywhere.

* * *

After the East Peoria American Legion hall stopped hosting shows, the VFW Post 8662 on Peoria's south side briefly served as an even grungier and less charming alternative. In its 1940s and 1950s heyday, the VFW had sponsored Peoria's air show ("America's topmost names in air show history in one great three-hour entertainment event!").[27] A half century later, the clubhouse—described by one showgoer as "grimy, cheap, small, sweaty and unsafe"—hosted touring punk bands and locals alike, as well as an alarming amount of violence that had nothing to do with music.[28]

Rocky Maple, who started going to shows there at age thirteen, recalls the time "a guy broke a bottle and stabbed another guy with it" and another occasion when "a woman started punching a guy who was drinking a 40-ounce and he hit her over the head" with it.[29] Jared Grabb lends some credence to these stories, noting, "Kids going to shows [there] got robbed on more than one occasion."[30] A relic of Peoria's past, the VFW painted a grim picture of the city's historical trajectory. With few redeeming qualities outside of its roof and four walls, the space did not last long.

For more than a decade—from the mid-nineties Naked Bums productions to shows at the Optimist Club, Tiamat, the Pizza Works, and finally a pair of church basements and veterans halls—Peoria was a regular midwestern stop for touring bands of note, large and small. But the VFW Post 8662 seemed to bring an end to that period, as well as to the broader era of hall shows—and on a fairly sour note.

All-ages shows then migrated to a range of other venues: Johnny's Coffee House in Metamora, the Bean Coffeehouse in East Peoria, the Freudian Sip in Washington, the Peoria Pizza Works (again), the Meeting House (again), One World Coffee (again), Bradley University (where a student group called "Think for Yourself" promoted shows), Planet X Rollerworld (where Darkest Hour from Washington, DC, played in 2005) and Calvary Baptist Church in Pekin (which hosted a two-day hardcore festival called "Bonesaw Fest" in 2004), the Warp Zone and No Fun House (house parties), Broken Tree and thirty-thirty (more coffee shops), and undoubtedly many others. At the same time, local bars like the Plank Road Pub, Brass Rail, and Red Barn began hosting regular twenty-one-and-over punk shows. This inevitable migration of the Peoria scene's older contingent away from all-ages shows effectively severed ties between the more established musicians and younger generations.

Even as the scene continued to fragment both geographically and demographically, it was also fracturing musically, despite various efforts over the years to maintain some semblance of that old punk rock ideal, "scene unity." Reflecting broader cultural trends, this dynamic was recognized at least as early as 2000, when Joe Martin of the Paper Dolls lamented to the *Peoria Journal Star*, "There's a certain contingent—the indie and pop-punk contingent—they'll all put on shows with each other. Then there's the punk and hardcore contingents, and they'll put on shows with each other. There's certain crowds that go to both, but the crowds rarely intermingle."[31]

In one sense, Peoria's punk scene was a victim of its own success; its very growth made splintering unavoidable. That fragmentation, however, often came at the expense of the scene's historical quirkiness and genre diversity. For years prior, wildly different bands had been forced to share bills—and the need for critical mass at shows necessitated outreach throughout the area. This was Peoria's hidden strength, as Frankie Sturm reflects:

> Punk, ska, hardcore, metal, indie rock, pop rock . . . all of these found a home in Peoria. Devout Christians shared mic time with atheists, while straight-edge devotees frequented the same haunts at potheads. In fact, sometimes the same band had a mixture of all such personalities. And why not? The prevailing mindset was not one of orthodoxy, but of sincerity.
>
> To see that individuals of such divergent tastes and convictions could create a common cause is to believe that democracy has a future. I didn't know it at the time, but we were honing the skills that make societies decent and communities vibrant. Whether we stayed in Peoria or moved away with the passing of the years, those are talents that will outlive any band.[32]

In some ways the slicing and dicing of the Peoria scene, driven by technology and ever-narrower micro-genres (among many factors), seemed to bring an end to the unusual alliances that spawned such an interesting counterculture. Perhaps the rise of the internet undercut the need for face-to-face outreach, which had exposed wave after wave of young people to the DIY punk scene. In its ruthless effectiveness, the internet was certainly less personal than discovering a flyer at Co-Op Records. As the algorithms of social media facilitated echo chambers, virtual communities, often unknowingly, turned inward.

Or maybe we just don't know the "real" story. Regardless, our version ends here. Without judgment of what followed in later years, we leave it to someone else to pick up those threads—to fill in the gaps we missed and write the next chapters. Maybe the period of time covered in this book was just a prelude to an impending golden age of Peoria counterculture. Perhaps its best years are still to come—we certainly hope so.

But, if not, to paraphrase the famous Peoria bumper sticker, could the last person to leave the scene please turn out the lights?

Conclusion

As strange, fascinating, frustrating, and inspiring as the people and places in this book were, they probably were not unique to Peoria, Illinois. Rather than staking a claim to Peoria exceptionalism, this could easily be the story of a dozen or more Rust Belt cities, whether Des Moines, Iowa; Sioux Falls, South Dakota; or Kenosha, Wisconsin. During the same time period, youth in thousands of other places around the world, from Brazil to Indonesia to Iran, scraped together similar communities and music scenes in cities that did not want them.[1]

If Peoria was in fact "Anywhere, USA," however, its story deserves telling as much as any other. It may even reveal something about why the world is the way it is, something missing from parallel histories of New York, Los Angeles, or Chicago. While neither groundbreaking nor extraordinary, the Peoria scene was more than a weak carbon copy of the more celebrated arts communities of those large urban centers.

The backdrop to Peoria punk rock—the decline of the industrial Midwest—was among the most significant political and economic implosions in US history. Yet even as they made use of the city's fading historic buildings, the young people in this book seemed largely unaware they were living through a crisis. Many had family members impacted by layoffs and strikes, but they themselves had never known anything else. For them, the cultural backlash of the period—attempts to cling to an imagined past or to find someone to blame—was just how things had always been.

Much about Peoria was characteristic of a small town—one that often felt smaller and more stifling than it actually was. For many of its youth, the DIY punk scene was a life-affirming outlet that helped cure a persistent sensation of cultural claustrophobia. But it was no nirvana, much as they might have wished it to be. The most rewarding part about running the Peoria Shows website, Tom Lane explains, "was living the illusion that all the . . . bands and their fans in the area came together and got along in a utopian paradise. It turns out in reality that wasn't always the case."[2] The Peoria scene's most beautiful quality was always its potential, and living up to its ideals was a constant struggle.

To some, Peoria "represented everything backward and prejudiced and racist" about the midwestern United States, and its countervailing punk scene was not always a clear *counter*culture.[3] It reflected many of the same political and social dynamics of its conservative hometown, and young people creating their own world did so with many of the same assumptions that had driven them away from "straight" society.

To their credit, at times, Peoria punks acted on anti-racist principles: by staging an anti-apartheid benefit in 1986, for example; confronting Matt Hale at the public library in 2001; and clashing with neo-Nazis periodically in between. Tiamat Records probably reflected these politics most brazenly, but even then, the scene never came close to reflecting the city's racial diversity. People of color did participate in the scene, but the punks were predominantly white kids.

That white supremacists were routinely drawn to shows (in Peoria and elsewhere) exposes the reality that the punk rock underground was, for the most part, a visibly white space. Further, even within punk, countering white supremacy explicitly was considered "political." Some people within the Peoria scene insisted that music should be independent of politics, but the world around them was anything but neutral. By one estimate, in 2019, the city had the most racially segregated public school system in the entire country.[4]

Race—whiteness, rather—also bridged the otherwise immense cultural and generational divides between the scene and the gatekeepers of the Peoria area's VFW and American Legion halls. As quickly as the punks burned those bridges, it is hard to imagine the initial opportunity being extended so readily to youth of color.[5]

The scene was also too often a boys' club, macho and prone to various forms of subtle and open sexism. Marsha Satterfield, for example, says that even after playing in bands for twenty years, she still gets backhanded compliments that she's "really good"—"like, even as good as one of the guys!" At this point, she explains, "I'm just so used to that. I just roll my eyes."[6]

But the sexist assumption that "guys" are the default belies the reality that women were always active musicians in Peoria's punk scene: from Becky Slane and Kate Dusenbery, to Dallas Maag and Jen Boniger Dixon, to Jenni Black, Nathalie Haurberg, and many others. Women—including Kami Tripp LaVallier, Amee Snyder Suydam, Jeni Goertzen, Dana Anderson, and Amy Michael—also organized and promoted shows, while Leanna Sweetland owned Tiamat, perhaps the city's most significant punk venue. Women additionally supported the scene as friends, such as Caustic Defiance's inner circle—the original "cornchips." Their contributions of moral and financial support are often invisible in histories like this one, but they were no less vital to the scene's success and survival.

Generally speaking, the Peoria punk scene was queer-friendly in a city and a historical moment that was not. More than one Peoria punk recalls the ubiquity of homophobic slurs in the area (sometimes shouted at them from a passing car), while numerous area musicians were LGBTQ and out. Accounts of hanging out at Fulton Plaza in the 1980s present the punk/cornchip scene as relatively inclusive, if not always sophisticated. While the punk scene could certainly be homophobic—misguided attempts at irony come to mind—it was generally a community of people targeted by anti-gay epithets, not hurling them.

Punk-scholar Zack Furness argues that at its best, punk rock is fun. It builds friendships and creates "non-commercial spaces for free expression and the staking out of positions . . . pushing people toward a participatory, 'bottom up' view of culture." In short, punk can offer an empowering and invigorating take on democracy and community. At its worst, Furness adds, "punk can be . . . a fashion show . . . and a constellation of practices that perpetuate varying degrees of machismo, sexism, homophobia, white privilege, classism, hyper-individualism, anti-intellectualism, [and] passive conformity."[7] In Peoria's case, the punk scene showed signs of all the above.

At times, it was insular and unwelcoming. There were cliques, and there were fights. There were unchecked egos. Great musicians could also be fuck-ups, and close friends could behave like jerks. The Peoria scene was far from perfect, and its members often fell short of their aspirations. Most of the people in this book were in their teens or early twenties during the periods in question, coming of age and trying to figure out who they would become. Many of the small differences that divided them seem petty in retrospect.

In any case, for decades, Peoria punk provided a home for hundreds of central Illinois's oddballs and weirdos, from Bloody Mess to Suit and Tie Guy and beyond. Despite its flaws, it was a home they needed and could not find elsewhere. As George Hurchalla concludes from his examination of the US scene in the 1980s, even if punk rock was not the "groundbreaking, revolutionary culture" that some hoped it might be, it was still "a supportive community for those who felt alienated by society and a place to hear great, high-octane music with thoughtful messages."[8] Peoria punk shows, if nothing else, provided companionship to the disaffected for a few hours at a time.

Sadly, because it drew in part from a pool of desperate youth, Peoria's counterculture seemed to suffer a high number of casualties—from overdoses, suicides, domestic violence, and auto accidents. In 2017, our good friend Matt Bellinger (formerly of PND, Superego, Dismiss, Planes Mistaken for Stars, Ghost Buffalo, and Il Cattivo) joined that long, tragic list. His passing cast an undeniable shadow over the later stages of writing this book. In 2018, Jeremy Loberg, once the charismatic young singer of the Psychodelics, and Eric Simkins, who played bass in Telepathy in Green, passed as well.

*   *   *

The story of the Peoria music scene affirms the central premise of DIY punk rock: that music is for everyone, and that anyone can (and should) create meaningful art. The music industry—the major record labels, the corporate media, the Grammys—can create and reward pop stars, but commercial success is often unrelated to talent, originality, or passion. Over the course of the roughly twenty-five years presented in this book, Peoria was home to a couple hundred good-to-great punk, emo, hardcore, ska, and metal bands—far more than made it onto these pages. Many other cities can make similar claims. That's one reason punk rock is so powerful.

In Peoria, it allowed young people who felt they had nowhere else to turn to connect with one another and with touring musicians from around the country. Epic performances became legend, if only to a few hundred people. Simple acts of generosity by bands passing through—7 Seconds, Hum, and Fugazi, for

Figure 24. Gared O'Donnell, Mike Ricketts, Matt Bellinger, and Jamie Drier (*left to right*) of Planes Mistaken for Stars at New York's famed CBGB, 2002. Photograph by C. French.

example—became lifelong lessons in ethics and kindness. And Peoria punks sent their own onto the road to provide the same service to others.

Peoria-grown bands and musicians toured throughout the United States, Europe, and beyond, in some cases. They shared stages with formative heroes, signed with prominent record labels, and achieved varying degrees of renown and influence. If Peoria felt culturally isolated, Bloody Mess, Dollface, Planes Mistaken for Stars, Minsk, and many others ensured that its music scene was in fact just a degree or two of separation from nearly every band in the world.

"At the end of the day, the real magical thing that I took away from my time in the Peoria punk scene was the joy of creating your own artistic path," notes Adam Widener. "I've always felt that my friends and I were an island—and if we ever wanted to accomplish anything, we had to go out and do it ourselves. Being in an isolated place like Peoria really instills that attitude in oneself."[9]

Today, former Peoria punks are scattered across the country, engaged with the world in a variety of ways. They are veterinarians and lawyers, artists and craftspersons, schoolteachers and tattooists, engineers, pastors, professors, and more. Some still play in bands; most keep in touch with their old friends from Peoria. And while this book must come to a conclusion, punk rock in the Whiskey City need not do the same.

Rather, the story continues via the many longtime scene vets who stuck around playing music into middle age, and it renews with the passing of the torch to bands like Ghost Key, whose relentless DIY ethic was shaped in the cornfields of central Illinois. "Growing up, we had a lot of sick bands to look up to," declares vocalist Austin O'Brien. "When we started [in 2011] . . . our only goal was to be another cool Peoria band that people looked up to—like we did to all of the bands we loved."[10]

In 2007, Drew McDowell—an alum of the Peoria punk scene then working at the *Peoria Journal Star*—interviewed Gared O'Donnell just before Planes Mistaken for Stars played Peoria on their initial farewell tour. "What are you most proud of about Planes?" Drew asked. "We managed to stay a band for a long time and stay vital," Gared responded. "Every record was better than the one before it. There's kids in Germany with our lyrics tattooed on their arms. *We've meant something to people.* . . . Maybe we've made some people feel a little less alone."[11]

Despite their breakup, Planes' fan base continued to grow unabated. Just a few years later, the band returned to action, the first of numerous periodic reunions. A brand-new album, *Prey*, even arrived in 2016, their first in a decade, prefaced by a series of videos from members of Converge, Mastodon, and other notable acts testifying to Planes' influence. At the same time, vinyl reissues of Dollface, Caustic Defiance, and Hate in the second decade of the new millennium confirm the enduring impact of Peoria punk rock—and that is a story worth celebrating.

In an interview with *Indie HQ*, Jared Grabb explored the meaning behind the Scouts Honor song "Prison Bars." It concludes with a line of resigned content, of stark midwestern poetry: "Cornstalk prison bars have served me well." As Jared explains, "This song sums up most of my life and a lot of the lives of people I know and/or meet on the road. It basically talks about hating your hometown for its limitations and at the same time appreciating that it is home. Everywhere we go on tour, kids complain about their hometowns. Nowhere is perfect."[12]

Figure 25. Scouts Honor at the Peoria Pizza Works performing a surprise reunion show to celebrate ten years of Jared Grabb's Thinker Thought Records, 2011. Photograph by Skyler Edwards.

Peoria punks were often harshly critical of their hometown (living there "sure will bore ya . . ."), but they weren't actually the ones who wrote its elegy. The "Would the last person to leave Peoria please turn out the lights?" bumper stickers of the 1980s announced the city's demise in near-apocalyptic terms. It was a dismal inheritance for the young people of that period, but the punks built their communities in the figurative ashes nonetheless. In this, there is a lesson about resilience and rebirth for postindustrial cities like Peoria, and perhaps for humanity more broadly. *We can always create something new together.*

For some young people, DIY punk culture offered a roadmap out of their city's limitations, converting obstacles overcome into points of pride. At its best, it modeled an ethical way to live and think outside of the quintessentially mainstream. To do it yourself was to care that much more. These were lessons many Peorians carry with them forever.

"The main thing that Peoria instilled in me is the ability to make something from nothing," suggests Kate Dusenbery. "To see potential where there is very little, to understand that if you love something, if you want to create and make something happen, if you can get just a few people to believe it and help you do it, you can make it happen. That is love, and that is art, and that is music."[13]

Notes

Introduction

1. "Peoria City, Illinois," United States Census Bureau, accessed June 10, 2019, www.census.gov.

2. Mark Jurkowitz, "How Scranton Became the New Peoria," *Real Clear Politics*, August 27, 2008, www.realclearpolitics.com.

3. Dave McClelland, "Weldon Evangelist in Run-In," *Bloomington Pantagraph*, September 1, 1973; "Jesus People Leaving City," *Decatur Daily Review*, August 27, 1973; "Gov. Wallace Wows 'Em at Peoria, Ill," *Mt. Vernon Register-News*, March 12, 1976.

4. Particularly since documentation was so sparse, we are exceedingly grateful to the many Peoria punks who spoke to us about their experiences and shared their flyer collections and photographs.

5. "Illinois Results," *New York Times*, November 8, 2016, www.nytimes.com.

6. Scott Hilyard, "Fake-Naked President Trump Stirs Anger at West Peoria Parade," *Peoria Journal Star*, July 5, 2017, www.pjstar.com.

7. Matt Miller, "*The Daily Show* Cracks How a Twitter Parody Account Won This Guy $125,000," *Esquire,* October 16, 2015, www.esquire.com; Anna Spoerre, "Youth Black Lives Matter Rally Preaches Conversation over Confrontation," *Peoria Journal Star*, July 22, 2016, www.pjstar.com.

8. Mark Clark organized Peoria's Black Panther Party chapter and its children's breakfast program before moving to Chicago, where he was murdered by police alongside Illinois party chairman Fred Hampton. Haas, *Assassination of Fred Hampton*. On

Manson, see Phil Luciano, "Charles Manson Had a Police Record in Peoria," *Peoria Journal Star*, November 20, 2017, www.pjstar.com.

9. *Rock Island Daily Argus*, April 21, 1885; Brian Fox Ellis, "Peoria's Whiskey Barons," *Peoria Magazines*, November/December 2009, www.peoriamagazines.com.

10. Saul, *Becoming Richard Pryor*.

11. For example, "Peoria, Coopers' Strike," *Chicago Tribune*, July 27, 1877; "Strikers Talk of Shooting," *Rock Island Daily Argus*, August 22, 1891; "Strike of the Mine Managers," *Rock Island Argus*, April 24, 1900; "Shots Fired in Peoria Strike," *Rock Island Argus*, August 13, 1919.

12. Haynes Johnson, "The View From Peoria: It's Not Playing Well," *Washington Post*, June 30, 1974, on the website Richard Pryor's Peoria, www.becomingrichardpryor .com.

13. Kozlowski, "Will Globalization Play in Peoria?," 24, 27, 33, 36, 52, 105. As Scott Saul notes, in 1940, some 40 percent of Black Peorians were unemployed, while two-thirds reported police brutality—a condemnation of Peoria at large, undercutting the myth of Caterpillar's paternalistic role. Saul, *Becoming Richard Pryor*, 24.

14. Hilton Als, "A Pryor Love," *New Yorker*, September 13, 1999; Victoria Berkow, "Long Awaited Richard Pryor Statue Unveiled in Peoria," *Peoria Journal Star*, May 3, 2015. See also Saul, *Becoming Richard Pryor*.

15. "Paul Robeson Defies Peoria Ban: Dodges Police, Vows to Return for Court Test," *Chicago Defender*, April 26, 1947, on the website Richard Pryor's Peoria, www .becomingrichardpryor.com; Bill Knight, "Paul Robeson Defied Racism in Peoria," *Community Word*, October 31, 2018, www.thecommunityword.com.

16. David K. Berninghausen, "Film Censorship," *ALA Bulletin* 44, no. 11 (December 1950): 447–48.

17. George Cloos and Philip Cummins, "Economic Upheaval in the Midwest," *Economic Perspectives,* January 1984, 3–4; Whitford, *New Old Economy*, 9.

18. Many punk and rock and roll histories revolve around specific venues at specific moments: New York's CBGB, San Francisco's Mabuhay Gardens, and Chicago's Cubby Bear, for example. Peoria's story is one of dozens of short-lived venues, most of them never intended to host live music. In *Underground*, Daniel Makagon outlines similar dynamics elsewhere, including small-town punk shows at bingo parlors, fire stations, and picnic pavilions. Makagon, *Underground*, 23–26.

19. "Entering a War Zone," *Peoria Journal Star*, February 25, 1993; Matt Buedel, "Caterpillar Official Names Deerfield Its Headquarters," *Peoria Journal Star*, January 8, 2018, www.pjstar.com.

20. Wahl and Bobbitt, *It Didn't Play in Peoria*, back cover.

21. Hurchalla, *Going Underground*, 390.

Part I. The Rise of Peoria Punk Rock: 1956–1986

1. Among many others, see Patton, *Punk Crisis*, 107–13; Hurchalla, *Going Underground*; Blush, *American Hardcore*; and Azerrad, *Our Band Could Be Your Life*, 13–60, 119–57.

2. Peter W. Colby and Paul M. Green, "Election 1980: Downstaters Decide," *Illinois Issues*, September 1981, 6–9; Lenore Sobota, "Reagan's 'Quintessential' Story Began at Eureka College," *Peoria Journal Star*, July 9, 2018, www.pjstar.com.

Chapter 1. Heebie Mesolithic Eon Drizzle

Epigraph: Sisson, Zacher, and Cayton, *American Midwest*, xxii; Johnson, "Thunder-pussy: Documents of Captivity," in Knight, *Rick Johnson Reader*, 53.

1. "Professional Presleyans Put On Peoria Premiere," *Peoria Journal Star*, February 7, 1957.

2. "Bill Reardon Presents Teen-Age Frolics," *Peoria Journal Star*, February 1, 1957.

3. Eugene Gilbert, "Rock n' Roll: Is It a Menace or Harmless Teen-Age Fun?," *Peoria Journal Star*, August 12, 1956.

4. Billy Miller, "Rockin' R's," Rockabilly Hall of Fame, May 2005, www.rockabillyhall.com.

5. Bill Knight, "Freddie Tieken Made SCENES," *Bill Knight Blog*, November 15, 2012, www.billknightcolumn.blogspot.com.

6. Hinman, *The Kinks*, 58.

7. Nick Vlahos, "Nick in the AM: Remembering When the Clock Got Busted in East Peoria," *Peoria Journal Star*, September 14, 2016, www.pjstar.com.

8. Phil Luciano, "Can You Believe the Doors Played in Canton?," *Peoria Journal Star*, May 26, 2013.

9. Craig Moore, Facebook post, March 12, 2018, www.facebook.com.

10. One audience member's memory of Black Sabbath in Peoria was that the band was "totally wasted," prompting him to leave the concert midway through the set.

11. See John Parker, "Peoria's African-American History," *PeoriaStory* (blog), March 7, 2009, peoriastory.typepad.com, among other accounts.

12. "Peoria, Ill. Fans Riot When Teen Star Fails to Show," *Jet*, January 17, 1963, 58.

13. Bill Hudnall, online comment, "Memories of Peoria" Facebook group, March 7, 2018, www.facebook.com.

14. Jay Goldberg e-mail to Jonathan Wright, November 8, 2017.

15. Mike Kramer, "Former Pekin Man Working on Book about Local Recording Studio," *Chillicothe Times-Bulletin*, July 2, 2017, www.chillicothetimesbulletin.com.

16. Graham Walker interview by Jonathan Wright, October 9, 2017.

17. Walker interview.

18. Douglas McCombs e-mail to Jonathan Wright, October 28, 2017.

19. Jon Ginoli interview by Jonathan Wright, May 12, 2017.

20. Ginoli interview.

21. Ginoli interview; Nault, *Queercore*, 74–86.

22. Ginoli interview.

23. Ginoli interview; Ginoli, *Deflowered*, 1–10.

24. Friedan, *Second Stage*, 6.

25. Dudley, *End of the Line*, xxii–xxiii.

Chapter 2. Creating the Peoria Scene

Epigraphs: Electric Cool-Aid, "Livin' in Peoria," ChopperStepe.com, 1984, www.chopperstepe.com; Bloody Mess interview by Jonathan Wright, May 17, 2017.

1. Losurdo and Tillman, *You Weren't There*.

2. Bob Gordon interview by Jonathan Wright, July 24, 2015.

3. Barry Stepe online interview by Jonathan Wright and Dawson Barrett, August 21, 2015.

4. Joe Losurdo, "Out of Stepe," *Roctober* 33 (Summer 2002).

5. Reckless Records, "Negative Element, Shouts of Rebellion: 1982–1983," Reckless Records, accessed October 9, 2019, www.reckless.com.

6. B. Stepe interview.

7. B. Stepe interview.

8. Todd "Chopper" Stepe, "Negative Element," ChopperStepe.com, accessed December 19, 2019, www.chopperstepe.com.

9. Daniel Kreps, "Foo Fighters Rock Chicago in 'Sonic Highways' Premiere," *Rolling Stone*, October 18, 2014, www.rollingstone.com.

10. B. Stepe interview.

11. B. Stepe interview.

12. Steve Albini, record review, photocopied zine, date unknown. Though perhaps best known for recording Nirvana's 1993 *In Utero* album, Albini was already established for recording bands like the Jesus Lizard, Pixies, and Tar, as well as performing in his own, including Big Black and Shellac.

13. B. Stepe interview.

14. "Caustic Defiance/Negative Element CD" review, The Punk Vault, August 28, 2009, www.punkvinyl.com.

15. Jeff Gregory interview by Jonathan Wright, May 8, 2018.

16. T. Stepe, "Your One Stop Chop Shop," ChopperStepe.com, accessed December 19, 2019, www.chopperstepe.com.

17. B. Stepe interview.

18. Gordon interview.

19. Gordon interview.

20. B. Stepe interview.

21. Known primarily for skull imagery, Brian Schroeder (aka Pushead) has designed album covers, T-shirts, skateboards, and posters for numerous underground and mainstream acts.

22. B. Stepe interview.

23. T. Stepe, "Your One Stop Chop Shop."

24. Anonymous quote.

25. Bloody Mess interview by Jonathan Wright, May 17, 2017.

26. Bloody Mess interview.

27. Gordon interview.

28. Bloody Mess interview.

Chapter 3. Punks Live on Straight Edge

Epigraphs: Bill Knight, "Punks Live on 'Straight Edge,'" *Peoria Journal Star,* July 30, 1985; Barry Stepe, response to "Shot of the Week: Skateboarding Stepe Brothers," *Skate and Annoy* (blog), January 19, 2010, www.skateandannoy.com.

1. Bob Gordon interview by Jonathan Wright, July 24, 2015.

2. "Supreme Court Report: Narcotics . . . Drug Related Equipment," *American Bar Association Journal* 68 (April 1982): 480.

3. Gordon interview.

4. Brent Schlosser interview by Jonathan Wright, March 17, 2018.

5. Bloody Mess interview by Jonathan Wright, May 17, 2017.

6. See Lahickey, *All Ages*; and Blush, *American Hardcore*, 26–29.

7. Barry Stepe online interview by Jonathan Wright and Dawson Barrett, August 21, 2015.

8. Mike "C. P." O'Russa e-mail to Jonathan Wright, December 12, 2015.

9. B. Stepe interview.

10. O'Russa e-mail.

11. Brad Krohn e-mail to Jonathan Wright, October 21, 2017.

12. B. Stepe interview.

13. B. Stepe interview.

14. O'Russa e-mail.

15. *Skate and Spurs* zine, date unknown.

16. Bloody Mess interview.

17. Todd "Chopper" Stepe, "Caustic Defiance," ChopperStepe.com, accessed December 19, 2019, www.chopperstepe.com.

18. B. Stepe interview.

19. O'Russa e-mail.

20. Joe Borsberry interview by Jonathan Wright, June 25, 2015.

21. Borsberry interview.

22. B. Stepe interview.

23. B. Stepe interview.

24. T. Stepe, "Caustic Defiance."

25. B. Stepe interview.

26. Andersen and Jenkins, *Dance of Days*, 180, 182, 188, 191–92.

27. Jim Moran interview by Jonathan Wright, April 8, 2015.

28. B. Stepe interview.

29. David "Flea" Wagner, online comment, "I Was a Mutant Cornchip and YOU WEREN'T!!!" Facebook group, February 5, 2009, www.facebook.com.

30. Krohn e-mail.

31. Borsberry interview.

32. B. Stepe interview.

Chapter 4. The Underground Goes Aboveground

Epigraph: Various artists, *Livin' in Peoria*, self-released cassette tape, liner notes, 1986.

1. GG Allin, "America's Favorite Son," unreleased autobiography.
2. Bloody Mess interview by Jonathan Wright, May 17, 2017.
3. Mike "C. P." O'Russa e-mail to Jonathan Wright, December 12, 2015.
4. Bloody Mess interview.
5. Bloody Mess interview.
6. Jim Moran interview by Jonathan Wright, April 8, 2015.
7. Bloody Mess interview.
8. Bloody Mess interview.
9. Bloody Mess interview.
10. Brad Krohn e-mail to Jonathan Wright, October 21, 2017.
11. Todd "Chopper" Stepe, "E.C.A. (Electric Cool Aid) aka Chip's Patrol [*sic*] aka Hate," ChopperStepe.com, accessed December 19, 2019, www.chopperstepe.com.
12. Bob Gordon, "Sh*t Happened! GG Allin's Notorious 1985 VFW Show in Creve Coeur," *Meanwhile, Back in Peoria…* (blog), January 19, 2013, www.meanwhilebackin peoria.com.
13. Bloody Mess interview.
14. Bloody Mess e-mail to Jonathan Wright, July 30, 2019. The Bloody Mess and Hate 7", complete with inserts and three bonus tracks, finally saw official release on vinyl in 2019. Says Bloody, "I admit it's not a record I would stand behind or be proud of if it was current.... [It] was made when I was a completely nihilistic punk rocker and historically I have left it exactly as it was back then.... If you are easily offended or extremely politically correct, this record is not for you, I guarantee it."
15. O'Russa e-mail.
16. Youth Brigade, *Sound and Fury* LP (BYO Records, 1982).
17. Barry Stepe online interview by Jonathan Wright and Dawson Barrett, August 21, 2015.
18. B. Stepe interview.
19. Quoted in Lahickey, *All Ages*, 159.
20. Krohn e-mail.
21. O'Russa e-mail.
22. Doug Love e-mail to Jonathan Wright, August 23, 2015.
23. B. Stepe interview.
24. Bloody Mess interview.
25. Gordon interview.
26. Gordon interview.
27. Bloody Mess, online comment on Facebook, October 2018, www.facebook.com.
28. Mike Bailey, "Language, Spitting Close Concert Early," *Peoria Journal Star*, March 4, 1986.
29. Bloody Mess and Hate, "Spit on My Face."

Chapter 5. I Was a Mutant Cornchip . . .

Epigraph: Teresa Ozuna, online comment, "I Was a Mutant Cornchip and YOU WEREN'T!!!" Facebook group, October 10, 2008, www.facebook.com.

1. Moira McCormick, "Midwestern Chain Rebuilds Despite Depressed Economy," *Billboard*, December 21, 1985.

2. Bob Herington interview by Jonathan Wright, April 23, 2017.

3. Bob Gordon interview by Jonathan Wright, July 24, 2015.

4. Jim Moran interview by Jonathan Wright, April 8, 2015.

5. Mike "C. P." O'Russa e-mail to Jonathan Wright, December 12, 2015.

6. Herington interview.

7. Bloody Mess interview by Jonathan Wright, May 17, 2017.

8. Matt Shane interview by Jonathan Wright, March 22, 2017.

9. Herington interview.

10. Herington interview.

11. Bruce Swigart, online comment, "I Was a Mutant Cornchip and YOU WEREN'T!!!" Facebook group, October 21, 2011, www.facebook.com.

12. Gordon interview.

13. Stacey Donovan e-mail to Jonathan Wright, April 12, 2017.

14. Tracey Bettermann Wetzstein, online comment, "I Was a Mutant Cornchip and YOU WEREN'T!!!" Facebook group, October 10, 2008, www.facebook.com.

15. Jeff Gregory interview by Jonathan Wright, May 8, 2018.

16. Kate Dusenbery e-mail to Jonathan Wright, September 19, 2017.

17. Eric Kingsbury interview by Jonathan Wright, July 14, 2017.

18. Kimberly "Sparky" Luft e-mail to Jonathan Wright, September 22, 2017.

19. Joel Hess, online comment "I Was a Mutant Cornchip and YOU WEREN'T!!!" Facebook group, October 16, 2008, www.facebook.com.

20. Donovan e-mail.

21. Jerry Klein, "New Kandy Kane—Night Club Haven for Teen-Age, Hip-Swinging Twisters," *Peoria Journal Star*, September 19, 1962.

22. Pam Adams, "I Went to Teen-Age Nightclubs," *Peoria Journal Star*, February 21, 1986.

23. Julie Maag interview by Jonathan Wright, May 13, 2015.

24. Kingsbury interview.

25. Shane interview.

26. Shane interview.

27. Barry Stepe online interview by Jonathan Wright and Dawson Barrett, August 21, 2015.

28. Shane interview.

29. Both Facebook groups were invaluable sources of context and inspiration for this chapter.

Part II. Building the Scene: 1986–1992

1. Andersen and Jenkins, *Dance of Days*, 159–61; Martin Sprouse and Tim Yohannan, from "Interview: Anti-Racist Action," *Maximum RocknRoll*, no. 78 (November 1989), in Duncombe and Tremblay, *White Riot*, 146–51.

2. See Edge, *924 Gilman*.

Chapter 6. Great Loser Bands and Loosey-Goosey Backwash Gigs

Epigraphs: Jeff Wilson interview by Jonathan Wright, November 11, 2017; Ed Young interview by Jonathan Wright, November 27, 2017.

1. Barry Stepe online interview by Jonathan Wright and Dawson Barrett, August 21, 2015.

2. Todd "Chopper" Stepe, "The Outbreaks," ChopperStepe.com, accessed December 19, 2019, www.chopperstepe.com.

3. Jeff Wilson interview by Jonathan Wright, November 11, 2017.

4. Becky Slane interview by Jonathan Wright, June 22, 2017.

5. Wilson interview.

6. Joe Borsberry interview by Jonathan Wright, June 25, 2015.

7. Borsberry interview.

8. Mike "C. P." O'Russa e-mail to Jonathan Wright, December 12, 2015.

9. Ed Young interview by Jonathan Wright, November 27, 2017.

10. Jeff Warren interview by Jonathan Wright, December 9, 2017.

11. Warren interview.

12. Patrick Dwyer interview by Jonathan Wright, July 25, 2018.

13. Dwyer interview.

14. Mary Wroblewski, "Toxic Shock Band: Rock with a Sense of Humor," *Bloomington Pantagraph*, April 16, 1983.

15. Warren interview.

16. Warren interview.

17. Warren interview.

18. Young interview.

19. Young interview.

20. Bill Kemp, "Eddy Building among Lost Downtown Landmarks," *Bloomington Pantagraph*, March 12, 2017.

21. Wilson interview.

22. Young interview.

23. Steve Smedley, "A Whole Gallery for a Kup," *Bloomington Pantagraph*, January 9, 1988.

24. Young interview.

25. Wilson interview.

26. Young interview.

27. Young interview.

28. Young interview.

29. Young interview.

30. Jered Gummere e-mail to Jonathan Wright, June 27, 2018.

31. Brody Maag interview by Jonathan Wright, May 13, 2015.

32. Young interview.

33. Warren interview.

34. Wallace and Manitoba, *Official Punk Rock Book of Lists,* 285.

Chapter 7. What Played (and Didn't Play) in Peoria

Epigraphs: "Andy Kubiszewski of Stabbing Westward," *Entertainment Ave!,* November 21, 1996, www.entertainmentavenue.com; Doug Love e-mail to Jonathan Wright, August 23, 2015.

1. Doug Love e-mail to Jonathan Wright, August 23, 2015.

2. Love e-mail.

3. Love e-mail.

4. Todd "Chopper" Stepe, "Your One Stop Chop Shop," ChopperStepe.com, accessed December 19, 2019, www.chopperstepe.com.

5. Love e-mail.

6. Daed Kcis 1987 biography, provided to Jonathan Wright by Eric Kingsbury, July 1, 2017.

7. Eric Kingsbury interview by Jonathan Wright, July 14, 2017.

8. *Food for Thought* fanzine, 1988.

9. Kingsbury interview.

10. Matt Shane interview by Jonathan Wright, March 22, 2017.

11. Shane interview.

12. Bob Gordon interview by Jonathan Wright, July 24, 2015.

13. Love e-mail.

14. Jenny Shank, "Westward Ho," *Westword,* November 26, 1998, www.westword.com.

15. Love e-mail.

16. Love e-mail.

17. Love e-mail.

18. Dayglo Abortions, "Kill Johnny Stiff," *Here Today Guano Tomorrow* LP (Fringe Product, 1988).

19. As explored in Wahl and Bobbitt, *It Didn't Play in Peoria.*

20. T. J. O'Brien e-mail to Jonathan Wright, August 14, 2015; Painted Willie, *Live from Van Nuys* EP (SST Records, 1986).

21. Like many bands of the era, a new lineup of Black Flag with just one original member, guitarist Greg Ginn, has embarked on a series of "reunion" tours in recent years.

22. Love e-mail.

23. Joe Carroll, "Fame's First Daed Kcis," *Bradley Scout*, February 12, 1988.

24. Love e-mail.

25. Love e-mail.

26. Love e-mail.

27. Bloody Mess interview by Jonathan Wright, May 17, 2017.

28. Love e-mail.

29. Bloody Mess interview.

30. Bloody Mess interview.

31. Bob Herington interview by Jonathan Wright, April 23, 2017.

32. Bloody Mess interview.

33. Jim Moran interview by Jonathan Wright, April 8, 2015.

34. Bloody Mess interview.

35. Love e-mail.

36. Amee Snyder Suydam, online comment, "I Was a Mutant Cornchip and YOU WEREN'T!!!" Facebook group, September 26, 2011, www.facebook.com.

37. Kami Tripp LaVallier online interview by Jonathan Wright and Dawson Barrett, February 4, 2015.

38. Mike "C. P." O'Russa e-mail to Jonathan Wright, December 12, 2015.

39. WHOI Channel 19 broadcast, "Peoria's Underground," August 1987.

40. Kortland Bottger, online comment on Kimberly Gomi No On'nanoko's Facebook post, August 6, 2018, www.facebook.com.

41. Lynn Weber Cisco, online comment on Becky Slane's Facebook post, August 5, 2018, www.facebook.com.

42. Love e-mail.

Chapter 8. Public Enemy Number-One

Epigraphs: Matt Shane interview by Jonathan Wright, March 22, 2017; Michael Rowster, "Semicids Don't Do That," *Pig State Recon* (blog), March 4, 2010, www.mrowster. wordpress.com; Bob Gordon interview by Jonathan Wright, July 24, 2015.

1. Bloody Mess interview by Jonathan Wright, May 17, 2017. All quotes from Bloody in this chapter are from this interview.

2. Anonymous comment.

3. Mike "C. P." O'Russa e-mail to Jonathan Wright, December 12, 2015.

4. Jason Pellegrino interview by Jonathan Wright, July 5, 2017.

5. Another anonymous comment.

6. Bloody Mess, *Fanatic* zine, date unknown.

7. Jeff Gregory, *People of Peoria* magazine, date unknown.

8. Naturally, Peoria mirrored this national phenomenon. Just days before Halloween 1988, the *Peoria Journal Star* published a series of articles titled "Satan's Children: A Cult Rises in Central Illinois," detailing a monthlong investigation into reports of satanic activity including blood rituals, suicide pacts, slaughtered animals, cemetery desecra-

tions, and church burglaries. "Up to 500 [area] teenagers are believed to be involved in organized satanic cults," the paper reported on October 26. Relying exclusively on quotes from police officers, youth counselors, and unidentified former cult members, the articles offered no verifiable facts and seem only to have stoked baseless fears in the populace.

9. Matt Shane interview by Jonathan Wright, March 22, 2017.

10. William Ryberg, "Punk-Rock Band Burns Flag at Davenport Bar, Fires Up Protest," *Des Moines Register*, July 8, 1989.

11. Welch, *Flag Burning*, 4–9.

12. Ensminger, *Out of the Basement*, 78.

13. Jon Wiederhorn, "Drummer Paul Cook on the Sex Pistols' Legacy: 'We Were Public Enemy Number One,'" Yahoo Music, October 27, 2017, www.yahoo.com.

14. Under the leadership of Tipper Gore and Susan Baker, the Parents Music Resource Center testified before Congress in 1985 about the "growing trend in music toward lyrics that are sexually explicit, excessively violent, or glorify the use of drugs and alcohol" and pushed the music industry to adopt parental advisory warnings. Susan Baker and Tipper Gore, "The Parents Music Resource Center, Statement before Congress," in Cateforis, *Rock History Reader*, 243–49.

Chapter 9. Montage of Madness

Epigraphs: Kate Dusenbery e-mail to Jonathan Wright, September 19, 2017; John San Juan, liner notes to Dollface, *Corvette Summer* reissue LP (Bird Dialect, 2014).

1. Joe Carroll, "Fame's First Daed Kcis," *Bradley Scout*, February 12, 1988.

2. Eric Kingsbury interview by Jonathan Wright, July 14, 2017.

3. Kingsbury interview.

4. Daed Kcis 1990 bio, provided to Jonathan Wright by Eric Kingsbury, July 1, 2017.

5. Kingsbury interview.

6. Known in part for its members' elaborate makeup, Mudvayne won an MTV Music Video Award in 2001 and was nominated for a Grammy for Best Metal Performance in 2006.

7. Kate Dusenbery e-mail to Jonathan Wright, September 19, 2017.

8. Jason Pellegrino interview by Jonathan Wright, July 5, 2017.

9. Pellegrino interview.

10. Pellegrino interview.

11. Matt Shane interview by Jonathan Wright, March 22, 2017.

12. Jeff Gregory interview by Jonathan Wright, May 8, 2018.

13. Dusenbery e-mail.

14. Smoldering Remains interview, *Thrashcore* zine, 1989.

15. Pellegrino interview.

16. Scholars of social and political movements have long pointed to the importance of semi-autonomous spaces for building community, using a range of similar

terms to describe them, including "hubs," "free spaces," and "havens." Though more ephemeral for the punks than for their original tenants, the rented halls of the Peoria scene served similar purposes as noncommercial places to exchange ideas that were beyond the reach of authority (in this case, adults). Ramirez, *Native Hubs*; Evans and Boyte, *Free Spaces*; Hirsch, *Urban Revolt*.

17. Pellegrino interview.
18. Jim Moran interview by Jonathan Wright, April 8, 2015.
19. Pellegrino interview.
20. Bill Knight, "Peoria's Wild Things," *Peoria Journal Star*, December 14, 1989.
21. Dusenbery e-mail.
22. Dusenbery e-mail.
23. Sean Pope interview by Jonathan Wright, November 9, 2017.
24. Pope interview.
25. Shane interview.
26. Shane interview.
27. Shane interview.
28. Ben Ruddell interview by Jonathan Wright, January 15, 2018.
29. Shane interview.
30. Shane interview.
31. Ed Carper interview by Jonathan Wright, April 17, 2017.
32. Shane interview.
33. Pope interview.
34. Pope interview.
35. Dusenbery e-mail.

Chapter 10. Nazi Punks Fuck Off

Epigraphs: Though translations vary, the sentiment and quote are widely attributed to Marcel Proust's *In Search of Lost Time*; see, for example, Ed Yong, "Memory Lane Has a Three-Way Fork," *The Atlantic*, October 25, 2016, www.theatlantic.com; John Landis, dir., *The Blues Brothers* (Universal Pictures, 1980).

1. Jim Moran interview by Jonathan Wright, April 8, 2015.
2. Tim Meidroth, "Two Cited after Slam-Dancing Melee," *Peoria Journal Star*, July 24, 1991.
3. Bloody Mess interview by Jonathan Wright, May 17, 2017.
4. Matt Shane interview by Jonathan Wright, March 22, 2017.
5. Meidroth, "Two Cited after Slam-Dancing Melee."
6. Shane interview.
7. Tim Meidroth, "More Tickets Issued in Slam-Dancing Case," *Peoria Journal Star*, July 24, 1991.
8. Kate Dusenbery e-mail to Jonathan Wright, September 19, 2017.
9. Jeff Gregory interview by Jonathan Wright, May 8, 2018.

10. Shane interview.

11. Balleck, *Modern American Extremism and Domestic Terrorism*, 144–46; "From Matt Hale, a Wake Up Call," *Peoria Journal Star*, April 6, 1995.

12. Chris Hauk, *I Used to Be Disgusted*, zine #7, February 1990.

13. See J. Moore, *Skinheads Shaved for Battle*.

14. Tom Nieukirk interview by Jonathan Wright, July 17, 2018.

15. Ben Ruddell interview by Jonathan Wright, January 15, 2018.

16. Jason Teegarden-Downs e-mail interviews by Jonathan Wright, February 7 and 10, 2018.

17. Andrew Wisecarver, alt.music.ska Google group, September 23, 1997, www.groups.google.com.

18. Nieukirk interview.

19. Pam Adams, "Rap, Politics, Prejudice and Style," *Peoria Journal Star*, May 2, 1993.

20. Nick Lippert, Facebook post, December 1, 2017, www.facebook.com.

21. Gregory interview.

22. Gregory interview.

23. Bloody Mess interview.

24. Bloody Mess interview.

25. Bloody Mess interview.

26. Bloody Mess interview.

Part III. The Next Nirvana: 1992–1997

1. *Rolling Stone* cover, April 16, 1992.

2. Leor Galil, "The Definitive Oral History of Jawbreaker's *24 Hour Revenge Therapy*," *Pitchfork*, April 28, 2017, www.pitchfork.com.

Chapter 11. Teenage Airwaves

Epigraph: Ben Leitch online interview by Jonathan Wright and Dawson Barrett, February 6, 2015.

1. Unlike his opponent, George H. W. Bush, Clinton attempted to appeal to young voters by pledging to sign into law the "Motor Voter" bill, which had been promoted by the band R.E.M., among others. "Long Box," *99% Invisible*, July 22, 2014, www.99percentinvisible.org.

2. John Williams e-mail to Jonathan Wright, January 10, 2018.

3. Jeff Hyde, Facebook post, 2017, www.facebook.com.

4. Jeremy Kerner interview by Jonathan Wright, December 29, 2017.

5. "Local Band Hopes to Make It Big," *Tazewell News* (Tazewell County, IL), July 22, 1992.

6. Dave Moe e-mail to Jonathan Wright, February 10, 2018.

7. Gary Thomas interview by Jonathan Wright, July 6, 2015.

8. Thomas interview.

9. Thomas interview.

10. Williams e-mail.

11. Brody Maag interview by Jonathan Wright, May 13, 2015.

12. Julie Maag interview by Jonathan Wright, May 13, 2015.

13. Jeff Gregory interview by Jonathan Wright, May 8, 2018.

14. R. Moore, *Sells Like Teen Spirit*, 142–43; Ginia Bellafante, "Where's the Next Seattle?," *Time*, October 25, 1993; Paul Tough, "The Next Next Seattle," *New York Times*, December 19, 1993; Peter Kobel, "Chapel Hill, N.C.: The New Seattle?," *Entertainment Weekly*, January 8, 1993; *Rolling Stone* quoted in Holly Kruse, "Subcultural Identity in Alternative Music Culture," *Popular Music* 12, no. 1 (January 1993): 33.

15. Gina Arnold, "College Rock: 'Left of the Dial,'" in Cateforis, *Rock History Reader*, 215–20.

16. Makagon, *Underground*, 42–43.

17. Ben Ruddell interview by Jonathan Wright, January 15, 2018.

18. Matt Shane interview by Jonathan Wright, March 22, 2017.

19. Ben Leitch online interview by Jonathan Wright and Dawson Barrett, February 6, 2015.

20. Ruddell interview.

21. Ben Leitch, online comment on Facebook, 2018, www.facebook.com.

22. Thomas interview.

23. Leitch online interview.

24. Jason Teegarden-Downs e-mail to Jonathan Wright, February 10, 2018.

25. Sam Dantone, online comment on Facebook, February 6, 2018, www.facebook.com.

26. Thomas interview.

27. Jared Madigan online interview by Jonathan Wright and Dawson Barrett, March 1, 2015.

Chapter 12. For God and Country

Epigraphs: "The Jesus Lizard—Peoria Illinois—June 10, 1995," YouTube, www.youtube.com; Matt Diehl, "America, Welcome to the Jesus Lizard," *Rolling Stone*, August 10, 1995, www.rollingstone.com.

1. Ben Leitch online interview by Jonathan Wright and Dawson Barrett, February 6, 2015.

2. John Williams e-mail to Jonathan Wright, January 10, 2018.

3. Paul Gentile online interview by Jonathan Wright and Dawson Barrett, February 2, 2015.

4. Jonathan Wright online interview by Dawson Barrett, March 9, 2015.

5. Wright online interview.

6. Wright online interview.

7. Clarence Moore, "'Crowd Surfing' Overshadows Madison Show," *Peoria Journal Star*, April 2, 1995.

8. Later that year, Hum reached number one on Billboard's "Heat Seekers" album chart, its monitoring of new artists. The band performed on the Lollapalooza tour and was a musical guest on *Late Night with Conan O'Brien*. Its song "Stars" was later featured on MTV's *Beavis and Butthead* and in a Cadillac commercial. *Billboard*, August 12, 1995, 17.

9. Wright online interview.

10. Wright online interview.

11. Jesus Lizard, *Jesus Lizard Book*, 113.

12. Wright online interview.

13. Wright online interview.

14. Erin Page e-mail to Jonathan Wright and Dawson Barrett, February 8, 2015.

15. Wright online interview.

16. Wright online interview.

17. Matt Diehl, "America, Welcome to the Jesus Lizard," *Rolling Stone*, August 10, 1995, www.rollingstone.com.

18. Jerry Klein, "Freedom of Expression? Much of Today's Music Is More Like Raw Sewage," *Peoria Journal Star*, August 20, 1995; Jerry Klein, "New Kandy Kane—Night Club Haven for Teen-Age, Hip-Swinging Twisters," *Peoria Journal Star*, September 19, 1962.

19. Klein, "Freedom of Expression?"

20. Wright online interview.

21. Wright online interview.

Chapter 13. This Is Not a Fugazi Chapter

Epigraph: Fugazi, "Peoria, IL USA, 10/09/95," Dischord Records, www.dischord.com.

1. "Bartonville—Peoria State Hospital," Atlas Obscura, www.atlasobscura.com; "Illinois Asylum for the Incurable Insane Paranormal Tours," Ghosts and Stories, www.ghostsandstories.com.

2. Phil Luciano, "Extra: Area's Greatest Ghost Story Came from Peoria State Hospital Founder Dr. George Zeller," *Peoria Journal Star,* October 16, 2014, www.pjstar.com; Janine Crandell, "A Man ahead of His Time," www.peoriacountyillinois.info.

3. Brian White e-mail to Jonathan Wright, March 8, 2018.

4. Jared Grabb online interview by Jonathan Wright and Dawson Barrett, February 1, 2015.

5. White e-mail.

6. Ian MacKaye phone interview by Jonathan Wright, spring/summer 2004.

7. Mason Adams, "Why Fugazi's Politics Are as Frighteningly Relevant Today as They Were in 1988," Vice, March 7, 2015, www.noisey.vice.com.

8. Stan Wood interview by Jonathan Wright, June 3, 2018.

9. Fugazi, "Peoria, IL USA, 10/09/95," Dischord Records, www.dischord.com.

10. Jonathan Wright online interview by Dawson Barrett, March 9, 2015.

11. Wright online interview.

12. Natalie Gott, "Fugazi Singer Hates to See Show Ruined for Fans," *Peoria Journal Star*, October 19, 1995.

13. Julie Bozman e-mail to Jonathan Wright and Dawson Barrett, February 22, 2015.

14. Fugazi, "Peoria, IL USA, 10/09/95."

15. Wright online interview.

16. Gott, "Fugazi Singer Hates to See Show Ruined for Fans."

17. Mackaye phone interview.

18. Jen Boniger Dixon, online comment on Jonathan Wright's Facebook post, March 27, 2018, www.facebook.com.

19. Jeff Gregory, online comment on Jonathan Wright's Facebook post, March 27, 2018, www.facebook.com.

20. Wright online interview.

21. Ian MacKaye postcard to Jonathan Wright, October 19, 1995.

22. Ian MacKaye postcard to Jonathan Wright, January 10, 1996.

23. Wright online interview.

24. Allison Stewart, "Alternative Nation's Last Stand: Lollapalooza 1995, an Oral History," *Washington Post*, August 11, 2015, www.washingtonpost.com.

25. Tyson Markley e-mail to Dawson Barrett, August 31, 2017.

26. Sharon Berardino e-mail to Jonathan Wright, February 18, 2018.

27. Wright online interview.

28. Wright online interview.

29. Douglas McCombs e-mail to Jonathan Wright, October 28, 2017.

30. Greg Peters e-mail to Jonathan Wright, June 14, 2018.

31. Greenwald, *Nothing Feels Good*, 34.

32. Sharon Berardino, *Between the Covers* zine, 1994.

Chapter 14. Rock Over London, Rock On Peoria

Epigraphs: Tyson Markley e-mail to Dawson Barrett, August 31, 2017; Wesley Willis at Peoria's Madison Theater, January 17, 1997.

1. Brian White e-mail to Jonathan Wright, April 21, 2018.

2. White e-mail.

3. Tyson Markley e-mail to Dawson Barrett, August 31, 2017.

4. Tom "Atomic" Satterfield, "Nobody Liked Our Band," *atomicramblings* (blog), December 17, 2013, www.atomicramblings.wordpress.com.

5. Satterfield, "Nobody Liked Our Band."

6. Mike "Rugg" Perveiler interview by Jonathan Wright, March 11, 2018.

7. Nick Roseman, "@Tiamat December 17, 1997: SUBSONICS, SIN SONNETS, THE SKALLOPS, & THE DEFILERS," *Ear Scum!* (blog), July 7, 2015, http://earscum.blogspot.com.

8. Perveiler interview.

9. Eric "Suit and Tie Guy" Williamson interview by Jonathan Wright, April 18, 2018.

10. Satterfield, "Nobody Liked Our Band."

11. Markley e-mail.

12. Sharon Berardino e-mail to Jonathan Wright, February 18, 2018.

13. Sharon Berardino e-mail to Jonathan Wright, May 14, 2018.

14. Among other accolades, *Rolling Stone* lists the Walkmen's "The Rat" as the forty-ninth best song of the 2000s. "100 Best Songs of the 2000s," *Rolling Stone*, June 17, 2011.

15. Kevin Dixon interview by Jonathan Wright, May 13, 2018.

16. Dixon interview.

17. Dixon interview.

18. Tim Beck e-mail to Jonathan Wright, April 8, 2018.

19. Tim Beck e-mail to Jonathan Wright, April 7, 2018.

20. Beck e-mail, April 8, 2018.

21. Perveiler interview.

22. Markley e-mail.

23. Gil Kaufman, "Wesley Willis Dies: Street Musician was a Favorite of Indie Rockers," *Rolling Stone*, August 22, 2003.

24. Brody Maag interview by Jonathan Wright, May 13, 2015.

25. Perveiler interview.

26. Tyson Markley interview by Jonathan Wright, April 24, 2018.

27. Markley interview.

28. Markley interview.

29. Williamson interview.

30. Markley interview.

31. Williamson interview.

32. Markley interview.

33. Williamson interview.

34. Williamson interview.

35. Perveiler interview.

36. Perveiler interview.

37. Williamson interview.

38. Williamson interview.

39. "Knobcon—The World's Only Synthesizer Convention," Knobcon, accessed June 10, 2019, www.knobcon.com.

40. Matt Shane interview by Jonathan Wright, March 22, 2017.

41. Anne Ford, "The Opposite of Selling Out," *Chicago Reader*, September 27, 2007, www.chicagoreader.com.

42. Formed in Kentucky in 1965, the New Rhythm and Blues Quintet (later Quartet) has released more than thirty albums and cycled through a dozen members during its long career.

43. Steve Albini, "The Problem with Music," *The Baffler*, no. 5, 1993, www.thebaffler .com.

44. R. Moore, *Sells Like Teen Spirit*, 151.

45. Markley e-mail.

Chapter 15. Hidden by Cornfields

Epigraph: Adam Widener online interview by Jonathan Wright and Dawson Barrett, February 13, 2015; Chris Bennett e-mail to Dawson Barrett, October 26, 2015.

1. "The Optimist Creed," Optimist International, accessed June 20, 2019, www. optimist.org.

2. "Jim Thorpe to Speak at Football Banquet," *Bloomington Pantagraph*, December 5, 1947.

3. Josh Haller online interview by Jonathan Wright and Dawson Barrett, February 4, 2015.

4. Tom "Atomic" Satterfield online interview by Jonathan Wright and Dawson Barrett, February 1, 2015.

5. Steve Byrne online interview by Jonathan Wright and Dawson Barrett, February 1, 2015.

6. Jonathan Wright online interview by Dawson Barrett, March 9, 2015.

7. Sam McIntyre online interview by Jonathan Wright and Dawson Barrett, February 2, 2015.

8. Jared Grabb online interview by Jonathan Wright and Dawson Barrett, February 1, 2015.

9. Chris Bennett e-mail to Dawson Barrett, October 26, 2015; Chris Bennett interview by Jonathan Wright, April 13, 2018.

10. Chris Bennett interview by Jonathan Wright, August 30, 2018.

11. "Interview with Subsist," Friends Like You, accessed June 20, 2019, www.friends likeyou.tripod.com.

12. A longtime scene stalwart, Joel Madigan played multiple instruments in more than a dozen Peoria bands over the years and recorded many of them at his Lisa Falzone home studio.

13. Subsist, *Lessons in Brokenness* EP (Akeldama Records, 1998).

14. Cusic, *Encyclopedia of Contemporary Christian Music*, 176.

15. Bennett e-mail.

16. Bennett interview, April 13, 2018.

17. Tim Mead interview by Jonathan Wright, October 8, 2018.

18. Bennett e-mail.

19. Jon Beattie online interview by Jonathan Wright and Dawson Barrett, March 5, 2015.

20. McIntyre online interview.

21. Bennett e-mail.

22. Dan Dirst e-mail to Dawson Barrett, March 23, 2015. Bands that played the two-day fest included Usurp Synapse (Lafayette, IN), Maneurysm (Manitowoc, WI), John Q. Public (Lafayette), and a host of local acts, including Subsist, Systematic Attribution, Laura's Agent, Whirlybird, Lucigen, and Nemo-Non.

23. Dirst e-mail.

24. Bennett e-mail.

25. Bennett interview, August 30, 2018.

26. Bennett interview, August 30, 2018.

27. Morton Opportunity Club website, post of August 2, 2016, www.mortonclub.blogspot.com.

28. Gared O'Donnell interview by Jonathan Wright, August 29, 2018.

29. O'Donnell interview.

30. O'Donnell interview.

31. O'Donnell interview.

Chapter 16. Our CBGB

Epigraphs: Tom Satterfield online interview by Jonathan Wright and Dawson Barrett, February 1, 2015; Planes Mistaken for Stars, "Standing Still Fast," *Self-Titled* EP (Deep Elm Records, 1998).

1. Marsha Satterfield interview by Dawson Barrett, July 7, 2018.

2. Josh Haller online interview by Jonathan Wright and Dawson Barrett, February 4, 2015.

3. Frank Sturm online interview by Jonathan Wright and Dawson Barrett, February 8, 2015.

4. David Moll, "Tiamat Records Bids Farewell to Peoria Locale," *Peoria Journal Star*, September 9, 1999.

5. Molly Miller Rice online interview by Jonathan Wright and Dawson Barrett, February 2, 2015.

6. Leanna Sweetland e-mail to Dawson Barrett, July 29, 2017.

7. Mike Malin online interview by Jonathan Wright and Dawson Barrett, April 4, 2015.

8. Haller online interview.

9. James Strevels e-mail to Jonathan Wright, August 5, 2018.

10. Jared Madigan online interview by Jonathan Wright and Dawson Barrett, March 1, 2015.

11. Sweetland e-mail.

12. Sweetland e-mail.

13. Adam Widener online interview by Jonathan Wright and Dawson Barrett, February 13, 2015.

14. Widener online interview.

15. Kyle Waters e-mail to Dawson Barrett, July 29, 2017.

16. Rice online interview.

17. Angela Green, "Protesters, Hale Supporters Hurl Insults, Chairs in Brawl," *Peoria Journal Star*, March 25, 2001.

18. Geoff Frost e-mail to Dawson Barrett, April 22, 2018.

19. Gared O'Donnell interview by Jonathan Wright, August 29, 2018.

20. Mike Ricketts e-mail to Dawson Barrett, October 11, 2017.

21. Ricketts e-mail.

22. Gared O'Donnell interview by Dawson Barrett, July 15, 2017.

23. O'Donnell interview, July 15, 2017.

24. O'Donnell interview, July 15, 2017.

25. Jared Madigan online interview by Jonathan Wright and Dawson Barrett, March 1, 2015.

26. O'Donnell interview, July 15, 2017.

27. Chuck Coffey, Facebook post, May 11, 2018, www.facebook.com.

28. Other notable traveling acts who played at Tiamat included the Woggles (Athens, GA), Squad Five-O (Savannah, GA), Incantation (Johnstown, PA), Jungle Rot (Kenosha, WI), Dear Ephesus (Orlando), Sidekick Kato (Chicago), the Timmys (Springfield, IL), the Traitors (Chicago), the Jerk-Offs (South Bend, IN), My Lai (Chicago), the Gunga Dins (Springfield, IL), Urban DK (Waukegan, IL), Undying (Raleigh, NC), the Sutek Conspiracy (Indianapolis), and Intercede (Milwaukee).

29. Moll, "Tiamat Records Bids Farewell to Peoria Locale."

30. For example, from the CrimethInc. primer: "This is how the revolution begins: a few of us start chasing our dreams, breaking our old patterns, embracing what we love . . . daydreaming, questioning, acting outside the boundaries of routine and regularity." CrimethInc. Workers' Collective, *Days of War*, 275–76.

31. Chris Bennett interview by Jonathan Wright, April 13, 2018.

32. Rice online interview.

33. Chris Bennett interview by Jonathan Wright, August 30, 2018.

34. Sweetland e-mail.

35. Geoff Frost e-mail to Dawson Barrett, April 22, 2018.

36. Haller online interview. Haller was just one of several Peoria punks to offer up, unprovoked, their continued distaste for Jimmy John's.

37. Strevels e-mail.

38. Ryan Martin, "Re: Best Shows EVAR," OpeningBands.com, September 21, 2002, www.openingbands.com.

39. Bryan Polk online interview by Jonathan Wright and Dawson Barrett, February 4, 2015.

40. Sweetland e-mail.

41. Sweetland e-mail.

Chapter 17. Peoria Heights . . . and Lows

Epigraph: Drew McDowell e-mail to Dawson Barrett, August 22, 2017; Gared O'Donnell interview by Dawson Barrett, July 15, 2017.

1. Tom Lane e-mail to Dawson Barrett, September 25, 2018.

2. Lane e-mail.

3. Joshua Finnell, "It Played in Peoria," Medium.com, April 27, 2016, www.medium. com.

4. Tom Satterfield, "'Hipsters' and the Barnes and Nobel [*sic*] Music Department (1997ish–2000ish)," *atomicramblings* (blog), March 13, 2015, www.atomicramblings. wordpress.com.

5. Tyson Markley e-mail to Dawson Barrett, August 31, 2017.

6. Markley e-mail.

7. Markley e-mail.

8. Adam Widener online interview by Jonathan Wright and Dawson Barrett, February 13, 2015.

9. Josh Haller online interview by Jonathan Wright and Dawson Barrett, February 4, 2015.

10. Dave Haney, "Booze and Cocaine Party Leads to Tattooing of Teen," *Peoria Journal Star,* November 14, 2003.

11. "Elizabeth, Chicago, IL," comment, September 10, 2007, on "Harbor Drowning Detailed in Court," *Chicago Tribune*, September 6, 2007, Topix, www.topix.com.

12. Haller online interview.

13. Markley e-mail.

14. Marsha Satterfield interview by Dawson Barrett, July 7, 2018.

15. Jon Beattie online interview by Jonathan Wright and Dawson Barrett, March 5, 2015.

16. Mike Theobald e-mail to Jonathan Wright, August 28, 2018.

17. Jared Madigan interview by Dawson Barrett, July 15, 2017.

18. Gared O'Donnell interview by Dawson Barrett, July 15, 2017.

19. O'Donnell interview.

20. "Planes Mistaken for Stars—Peoria, IL @ Pizza Works 12/19/99," YouTube, www .youtube.com.

21. O'Donnell interview.

22. O'Donnell interview.

23. Jared Madigan online interview by Jonathan Wright and Dawson Barrett, March 1, 2015.

24. Jeff Eagan online interview by Jonathan Wright and Dawson Barrett, February 2, 2015; Bryan Polk online interview by Jonathan Wright and Dawson Barrett, February 4, 2015.

25. Kevin Dixon interview by Jonathan Wright, May 13, 2018.

26. Drew McDowell e-mail to Dawson Barrett, August 22, 2017.

27. McDowell e-mail.

28. Dixon interview. Among many other touring bands to play the Navy-Marine Club were Proudentall (Lawrence, KS); Haymarket Riot (Chicago); Pave the Rocket (St. Louis); RX Bandits (Orange County, CA); Ring, Cicada (St. Louis); Esteem (Naples, FL); Fed by Ravens (Minneapolis); Mara'akate (IN); Allister (Chicago); and Peralta (also of Chicago, featuring multiple Peoria punk expats and future members of Planes Mistaken for Stars).

29. Widener online interview.

30. Widener online interview.

31. McDowell e-mail.

32. McDowell e-mail.

33. McDowell e-mail.

Chapter 18. For God and Country (Alternate Take)

Epigraph: Jon Beattie online interview by Jonathan Wright and Dawson Barrett, March 5, 2015; *Ten Years of Thinker Thought* CD (Thinker Thought Records, 2011).

1. Jeremiah Lambert interview by Jonathan Wright, October 15, 2018.

2. Lambert interview.

3. Other prominent bands who played the Vineyard included Luti-Kriss (Douglasville, GA), Burn It Down (Indianapolis), Underoath (Tampa), Dead to Fall (Chicago), Ester Drang (Broken Arrow, OK), and Hopesfall (Charlotte, NC).

4. Lambert interview.

5. Lambert interview.

6. Guthrie Moore online interview by Jonathan Wright and Dawson Barrett, February 6, 2015.

7. Jared Grabb e-mail to Dawson Barrett, February 13, 2017.

8. Grabb e-mail; on BYOFL, see Makagon, *Underground*, 60–64.

9. Grabb e-mail.

10. Jarrod Briggs online interview by Jonathan Wright and Dawson Barrett, February 2, 2015.

11. Tom Satterfield online interview by Jonathan Wright and Dawson Barrett, February 1, 2015.

12. Moore online interview.

13. Jared Grabb online interview by Jonathan Wright and Dawson Barrett, February 1, 2015.

14. Lambert interview.

15. Lambert interview.

16. Moore online interview.

17. Adam Widener online interview by Jonathan Wright and Dawson Barrett, February 13, 2015.

18. "Planes Mistaken for Stars," *Exclaim!*, December 15, 2007, www.exclaim.ca.

19. "The Forecast" bio page, Victory Records, accessed August 19, 2019, https://victoryrecords.com/artist/the-forecast.

20. "The Forecast."

21. Tyson Markley interview by Jonathan Wright, April 24, 2018.

22. Annie Zaleski, "The Forecast—Everybody Left," *Alternative Press*, April 15, 2012, www.altpress.com.

23. "Scouts Honor" bio page, Thinker Thought Records, accessed August 19, 2019, www.thinkerthought.com.

24. Scouts Honor, *I Am the Dust*, No Idea, accessed August 19, 2019, www.noidearecords.com.

25. Review of Scouts Honor, *I Am the Dust*, *Razorcake*, July 13, 2006, www.razorcake.org.

26. Sergey Mesenov, "Minsk—The Ritual Fires of Abandonment," AllMusic.com, accessed August 19, 2019, www.allmusic.com.

27. "2nd Annual Peoria Air Fair," *Bloomington Pantagraph*, June 13, 1952.

28. Briggs Mushrush online interview by Jonathan Wright and Dawson Barrett, February 4, 2015. Touring bands that played there included Playing Enemy (Seattle), Sweet Cobra (Chicago), Intronaut (Los Angeles), Thee Fine Lines (Springfield, MO), and Believing in June and Dead Like Dallas (both Portland, OR).

29. Rocky Maple online interview by Jonathan Wright and Dawson Barrett, February 2, 2015.

30. Grabb online interview.

31. Gary Panetta, "The Underground Alternative—In Living Rooms, VFW Halls and Church Basements, There Is a Bona Fide Music Scene," *Peoria Journal Star*, August 3, 2000.

32. Frankie Sturm online interview by Jonathan Wright and Dawson Barrett, February 8, 2015.

Conclusion

1. For example, Duncombe and Tremblay, *White Riot*, 295–338; and Greene, *Brave Punk World*.

2. Tom Lane e-mail to Dawson Barrett, September 25, 2018.

3. Kate Dusenbery online interview by Jonathan Wright and Dawson Barrett, February 14, 2015.

4. Steve Tarter, "A City Divided: Report Says Peoria School System Most Segregated in Country," *Peoria Journal Star*, January 24, 2019, www.pjstar.com.

5. In a convincing damnation of punk as inherently radical or revolutionary, punk-scholar Mimi Nguyen argues that "whitestraightboy" hegemony dominates punk rock, determining access and parroting the flawed logic of "color-blind" racism. With a few notable exceptions, there is very little to suggest the Peoria scene harbored such illusions or even ambitions. Peoria punks likely did, however, have an inflated sense of the difference between what they organized and the mainstream society they purportedly opposed. Mimi Nguyen, "It's (Not) a White World: Looking for Race in Punk," in Duncombe and Tremblay, *White Riot,* 257–68.

6. Marsha Satterfield interview by Dawson Barrett, July 7, 2018.

7. Furness, *Punkademics*, 10–11.

8. Hurchalla, *Going Underground*, 387.

9. Adam Widener online interview by Jonathan Wright and Dawson Barrett, February 13, 2015.

10. "Interview with Austin O'Brien from Ghost Key," *Scobonixxx*, February 6, 2015, scobonixxx.blogspot.com.

11. Drew McDowell, "CUE & A—Reconnecting Flight—Planes Mistaken for Stars Touch Down in Hometown on Farewell Tour," *Peoria Journal Star*, November 29, 2007.

12. "Interview with Jared Grabb of Scouts Honor," *Indie HQ,* April 17, 2007, www.indiehq.com.

13. Dusenbery online interview.

Bibliography

Andersen, Mark, and Mark Jenkins. *Dance of Days: Two Decades of Punk in the Nation's Capital*. New York: Akashic Books, 2001.

Azerrad, Michael. *Our Band Could Be Your Life*. Boston: Little, Brown, 2001.

Balleck, Barry J. *Modern American Extremism and Domestic Terrorism: An Encyclopedia of Extremists and Extremist Groups*. Santa Barbara, CA: ABC-CLIO, 2018.

Blush, Steven. *American Hardcore: A Tribal History*. Los Angeles: Feral House, 2001.

Cateforis, Theo, ed. *The Rock History Reader*. New York: Routledge, 2019.

Cornfield, Daniel B., ed. *Workers, Managers, and Technological Change: Emerging Patterns of Labor*. New York: Plenum Press, 1987.

CrimethInc. Workers' Collective. *Days of War, Nights of Love: Crimethink for Beginners*. Atlanta: CrimethInc., 2002.

Cusic, Don. *Encyclopedia of Contemporary Christian Music: Pop, Rock, and Worship*. Santa Barbara, CA: ABC-CLIO, 2009.

Dudley, Kathryn Marie. *The End of the Line: Lost Jobs, New Lives in Postindustrial America*. Chicago: University of Chicago Press, 1994.

Duncombe, Stephen, and Maxwell Tremblay, eds. *White Riot: Punk Rock and the Politics of Race*. New York: Verso, 2011.

Edge, Brian, ed. *924 Gilman: The Story So Far . . .* San Francisco: Maximum RocknRoll, 2004.

Ensminger, David A. *Out of the Basement: From Cheap Trick to DIY Punk in Rockford, Illinois, 1973–2005*. Portland, OR: Microcosm Publishing, 2017.

Evans, Sara, and Harry Boyte. *Free Spaces: The Sources of Democratic Change in America*. Chicago: University of Chicago Press, 1986.

Friedan, Betty. *The Second Stage.* With a new introduction. Cambridge, MA: Harvard University Press, 1988.

Furness, Zack, ed. *Punkademics: The Basement Show in the Ivory Tower.* Brooklyn: Minor Compositions, 2012.

Ginoli, Jon. *Deflowered: My Life in Pansy Division.* Jersey City, NJ: Cleis Press, 2009.

Greene, James, Jr. *Brave Punk World: The International Rock Underground from Alerta Roza to Z-off.* Lanham, MD: Rowman and Littlefield, 2017.

Greenwald, Andy. *Nothing Feels Good: Punk Rock, Teenagers, and Emo.* New York: St. Martin's Griffin, 2003.

Haas, Jeffrey. *The Assassination of Fred Hampton: How the FBI and the Chicago Police Murdered a Black Panther.* Chicago: Chicago Review Press, 2011.

Hinman, Doug. *The Kinks: All Day and All of the Night: Day by Day Concerts, Recordings, and Broadcasts, 1961–1996.* San Francisco: Backbeat Books, 2004.

Hirsch, Eric. *Urban Revolt: Ethnic Politics in the Nineteenth-Century Chicago Labor Movement.* Berkeley: University of California Press, 1990.

Hurchalla, George. *Going Underground: American Punk, 1979–1989.* Oakland, CA: PM Press, 2016.

Jesus Lizard. *The Jesus Lizard Book.* New York: Akashic Books, 2013.

Knight, Bill, ed. *Rick Johnson Reader: Tin Cans, Squeems and Thudpies.* Elmwood, IL: Mayfly Productions, 2007.

Kozlowski, Jason. "Will Globalization Play in Peoria? Class, Race, and Nation in the Global Economy, 1948–2000." PhD diss., University of Illinois, 2011.

Lahickey, Beth. *All Ages: Reflections on Straight Edge.* Huntington Beach, CA: Revelation Records, 1997.

Losurdo, Joe, and Christina Tillman, dir. *You Weren't There: A History of Chicago Punk, 1977–1984.* Factory 25, 2009.

Makagon, Daniel. *Underground: The Subterranean Culture of DIY Punk Shows.* Portland, OR: Microcosm Publishing, 2015.

Moore, Jack B. *Skinheads Shaved for Battle: A Cultural History of American Skinheads.* Madison, WI: Popular Press, 1993.

Moore, Ryan. *Sells Like Teen Spirit: Music, Youth Culture, and Crisis.* New York: New York University Press, 2010.

Nault, Curran. *Queercore: Queer Punk Media Subculture.* New York: Routledge, 2018.

Patton, Raymond A. *Punk Crisis: The Global Punk Rock Revolution.* New York: Oxford University Press, 2018.

Proust, Marcel. *Swann's Way.* New York: Modern, 1913.

Ramirez, Renya. *Native Hubs: Culture, Community, and Belonging in Silicon Valley and Beyond.* Durham: Duke University Press, 2007.

Saul, Scott. *Becoming Richard Pryor.* New York: HarperCollins, 2014.

Sisson, Richard, Christian Zacher, and Andrew Cayton, eds. *The American Midwest: An Interpretive Encyclopedia.* Bloomington: University of Indiana Press, 2006.

Wahl, Gregory, and Charles Bobbitt. *It Didn't Play in Peoria: Missed Chances of a Middle American Town*. Charleston, SC: Arcadia Publishing, 2009.

Wallace, Amy, and Dick Manitoba. *The Official Punk Rock Book of Lists*. Milwaukee: Hal Leonard, 2007.

Welch, Michael. *Flag Burning: Moral Panic and the Criminalization of Protest*. Hawthorne, NY: Aldine De Gruyter, 2000.

Whitford, Josh. *The New Old Economy: Networks, Institutions, and the Organizational Transformation of American Manufacturing*. Oxford: Oxford University Press, 2005.

Index

JONATHAN WRIGHT is a writer, editor, musician, and longtime veteran of the Peoria music scene. He is editor in chief at Peoria Magazines.

DAWSON BARRETT is an associate professor of history at Del Mar College. His books include *The Defiant: Protest Movements in Post-Liberal America*.

MUSIC IN AMERICAN LIFE

"Maximum Clarity" and Other Writings on Music   *Ben Johnston,*
    edited by Bob Gilmore
Staging Tradition: John Lair and Sarah Gertrude Knott   *Michael Ann Williams*
Homegrown Music: Discovering Bluegrass   *Stephanie P. Ledgin*
Tales of a Theatrical Guru   *Danny Newman*
The Music of Bill Monroe   *Neil V. Rosenberg and Charles K. Wolfe*
Pressing On: The Roni Stoneman Story   *Roni Stoneman, as told to Ellen Wright*
Together Let Us Sweetly Live   *Jonathan C. David,*
    with photographs by Richard Holloway
Live Fast, Love Hard: The Faron Young Story   *Diane Diekman*
Air Castle of the South: WSM Radio and the Making of Music City   *Craig P. Havighurst*
Traveling Home: Sacred Harp Singing and American Pluralism   *Kiri Miller*
Where Did Our Love Go? The Rise and Fall of the Motown Sound   *Nelson George*
Lonesome Cowgirls and Honky-Tonk Angels: The Women of Barn Dance
    Radio   *Kristine M. McCusker*
California Polyphony: Ethnic Voices, Musical Crossroads   *Mina Yang*
The Never-Ending Revival: Rounder Records and the Folk Alliance   *Michael F. Scully*
Sing It Pretty: A Memoir   *Bess Lomax Hawes*
Working Girl Blues: The Life and Music of Hazel Dickens   *Hazel Dickens*
    and Bill C. Malone
Charles Ives Reconsidered   *Gayle Sherwood Magee*
The Hayloft Gang: The Story of the National Barn Dance   *Edited by Chad Berry*
Country Music Humorists and Comedians   *Loyal Jones*
Record Makers and Breakers: Voices of the Independent Rock 'n' Roll Pioneers
    John Broven
Music of the First Nations: Tradition and Innovation in Native North America
    Edited by Tara Browner
Cafe Society: The Wrong Place for the Right People   *Barney Josephson,*
    with Terry Trilling-Josephson
George Gershwin: An Intimate Portrait   *Walter Rimler*
Life Flows On in Endless Song: Folk Songs and American History   *Robert V. Wells*
I Feel a Song Coming On: The Life of Jimmy McHugh   *Alyn Shipton*
King of the Queen City: The Story of King Records   *Jon Hartley Fox*
Long Lost Blues: Popular Blues in America, 1850–1920   *Peter C. Muir*
Hard Luck Blues: Roots Music Photographs from the Great Depression
    Rich Remsberg
Restless Giant: The Life and Times of Jean Aberbach and Hill and Range Songs
    Bar Biszick-Lockwood
Champagne Charlie and Pretty Jemima: Variety Theater in the Nineteenth
    Century   *Gillian M. Rodger*
Sacred Steel: Inside an African American Steel Guitar Tradition   *Robert L. Stone*
Gone to the Country: The New Lost City Ramblers and the Folk Music Revival
    Ray Allen

The University of Illinois Press
is a founding member of the
Association of University Presses.

———————————————

University of Illinois Press
1325 South Oak Street
Champaign, IL 61820-6903
www.press.uillinois.edu